WITH
STYLE

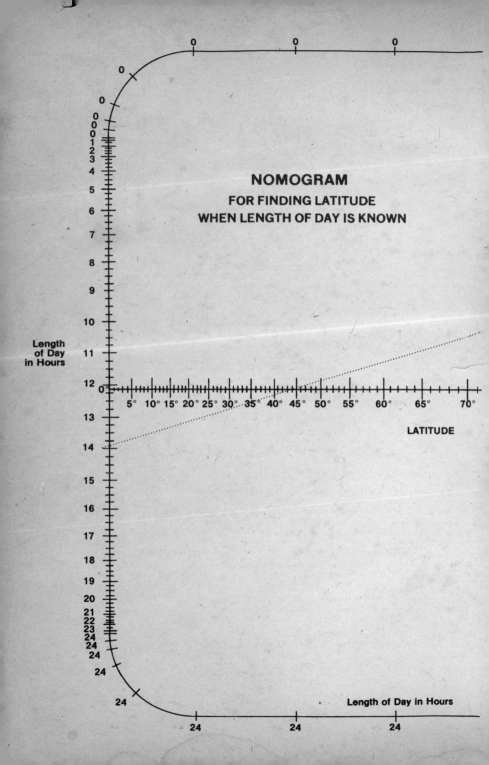

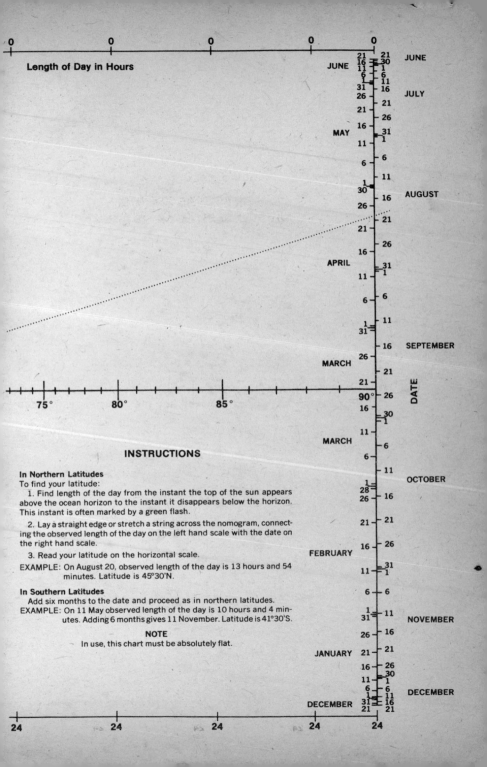

Length of Day in Hours

75°   80°   85°   90°

DATE

JUNE
JULY
AUGUST
SEPTEMBER
OCTOBER
NOVEMBER
DECEMBER

JUNE
MAY
APRIL
MARCH
MARCH
FEBRUARY
JANUARY
DECEMBER

INSTRUCTIONS

In Northern Latitudes
To find your latitude:
   1. Find length of the day from the instant the top of the sun appears
above the ocean horizon to the instant it disappears below the horizon.
This instant is often marked by a green flash.
   2. Lay a straight edge or stretch a string across the nomogram, connecting the observed length of the day on the left hand scale with the date on
the right hand scale.
   3. Read your latitude on the horizontal scale.
EXAMPLE: On August 20, observed length of the day is 13 hours and 54
        minutes. Latitude is 45°30′N.

In Southern Latitudes
   Add six months to the date and proceed as in northern latitudes.
EXAMPLE: On 11 May observed length of the day is 10 hours and 4 min-
      utes. Adding 6 months gives 11 November. Latitude is 41°30′S.

NOTE
In use, this chart must be absolutely flat.

24   24   24   24   24

SURVIVAL WITH STYLE

in trouble or in fun... how to keep body
and soul together in the wilderness

BRADFORD ANGIER

ILLUSTRATIONS BY ARTHUR ANDERSON

VINTAGE BOOKS
A Division of Random House
New York

For Claire and Joe Barkley and the
other sourdough neighbors who live
near our log cabin in Hudson Hope,
British Columbia, Canada, where
this book was written.

VINTAGE BOOKS EDITION March 1974

Copyright © 1972 by Bradford Angier

All rights reserved under International and Pan-American Copyright
Conventions. Published in the United States by Random House, Inc.,
New York, and simultaneously in Canada by Random House of
Canada Limited, Toronto. Originally published by Stackpole Books,
in 1972.

Book design by Bowie Graphic Art Services, Inc.

Library of Congress Cataloging in Publication Data

Angier, Bradford.
    Survival with style.
    Reprint of the ed. published by Stackpole Books,
Harrisburg, Pa.
    1. Wilderness survival.   I. Title.
[SK606.A54   1974]   613.6′9   73–14691
ISBN 0–394–71982–4

Manufactured in the United States of America

CONTENTS

Living Off The Land 1

Anybody at any moment can find himself thrown upon his own resources for survival. It takes very little time, effort, and even less money to be ready for an emergency. But if you are not prepared, one may take your life.

You might stray, or perhaps become stranded by flood or by the crippling of a companion. Thousands among this continent's fifty million licensed hunters and fishermen do annually, all too often with fatal results. Then there are the millions of casual picnickers and vacationers who each year visit the national parks, forests, and monuments. Many are exposed to what, only because of their inability to handle them, often become deadly wilderness hazards.

Yet as this book details, nearly always, where far too many individuals suffer — terrified — and frequently die, wild food is free for the picking, shelter for the constructing, direction for the finding, clothes for the creating, and fire for the warm satisfaction of igniting.

There's something else, too. The more you learn about survival at this time, the greater capacity you'll have for enjoying the pleasures of the farther places, until now too often disregarded. The individual equipped to take care of himself outdoors under stress will be far better able to turn the ordinary hardships of any trail into joys, for there is nothing more satisfying than the assurance that, no matter what emergency besets you in the open, you'll be able to meet both the outer and the inner challenges with ability and prowess to spare.

You may be in an auto, snowmobile, swamp vehicle, trail bike, or even a train that is stopped by mechanical failure, accident, or storm in an uninhabited region; common events that too often bring on needless difficulties or even death. Possibly you'll survive a plane crash or be set down in an unsettled area by a forced landing. Perhaps, whether in a canoe or ocean liner, you'll be shipwrecked.

Using the largely free methods of living off the land minutely considered here, anyone who is abruptly dependent upon his own devices for survival will have a considerably better chance to stay alive and even to turn what otherwise might have been a disaster into an enjoyable adventure.

The fundamentals considered in this volume take the mystery out of survival and put in the mastery. For survival is a positive thing. Mere endurance is not enough.

Untold numbers of North Americans are venturing into wilderness areas in every conceivable kind of motor vehicle. Most fail to realize that they can drive further into the wilderness in half an hour than they can walk out from, alive.

Just as important as the physical ones may be the psychological problems a man develops when he is suddenly forced to adapt to a primitive existence that's a far cry from the comforts of civilization. It's not always a question of survival of the strongest. It's more likely to be survival of the *thinkingest,* for man's brain is his best survival tool.

There's this, too.

"During World War II, when merchant ships were being torpedoed, it was noted that younger seamen did not survive when older ones did, largely because the inexperienced younger men gave up and perished." Doctor Stephen R. Elek, of the University of Southern California School of Medicine, told me, "In my opinion, the most important requirements for survival are high morale, emotional resistance, and an unshakable will to live, plus the knowledge of what to do.

"Many people live their lives without realizing how much stress and isolation they can endure. Learning your outer limits is excellent preparation for any survival episode."

As Thoreau said, "A man is rich in proportion to what he can do without."

Shelter 2

Shelter in softwood country is simple. In warm, fair weather you can get along very well — with the stars for company — atop a browse bed beside a long hardwood fire, with a log or ledge to reflect warmth on those parts of the body not turned to the blaze.

On a stormy night, when the climate is not too cold, you can satisfactorily augment these by making yourself a niche in a low spruce, fir, or other bushy conifer. Just a knife will do the job, although with the expenditure of more time and effort you can even strip off the boughs by hand.

Make an opening just large enough to accomodate you. Use the branches thus secured, perhaps supplemented with others from surrounding trees, to bush in the top and sides against wind and weather. Kindle a fire in front and you'll be snug.

Such a shelter is so easy to contrive that I often fashion one in stormy weather when I stop to boil the kettle at noon. Its comfort will conserve markedly more energy than its fashioning will entail.

THE REAL BROWSE BED

The traditional browse bed of the North Woods is laboriously thatched, a process that all takes upward of half an hour. The browse bed is not for heavily frequented camping spots on the fringes of civilization, but is ideal for survival usage.

Once you have picked your site, where a body-long night fire can be kindled, strip off a large quantity of the youngest, most thickly needled, bushiest fir, spruce, balsam, or other softwood boughs that you can find. Although a good knife or a hatchet will greatly speed the task, such branches can be torn off by the hands alone.

Carry them on a long stick, held upside down, at whose end a branch stub has been trimmed to form a large V. Center each bough over this stick. Then the interlocking needles will hold the mass in place.

Begin by putting down a thick layer of the resilient green branches at the bed's head. These are laid upside down, opposite to the way they grow. The butts, well covered by subsequent tiers, point toward the bottom of the bed. Lay down the second row, overlapping the first, in similar fashion.

The browse bed is so shingled with tier after tier of keenly smelling boughs until it is at least a foot thick. It is finally leveled and augmented by the poking in of soft evergreen tips whenever possible.

The first night on such a genuine browse bed is a soft, pungently fragrant, sleep-lulling joy that, it has long been my contention, everyone should experience at least once. On the second night you'll discover some slippery pits and hollows, but you'll still rest well. After the third night, you'll likely feel disposed to make some renovations with a fresh load of boughs.

FALLEN TREE

A fallen tree may be your answer in a number of ways, and some of my most comfortable shelters have been constructed around them. The roots of a toppled forest giant often provide a solid vertical bulwark against which, in the clearing left by the roots themselves, several poles can be set at a conservative forty-five-degree angle and a bough roof laced to them. One of the shelters I so fashioned nearly three decades ago, in one of my favorite hunting territories in the Canadian Rockies, is still habitable.

This raises a fine point. If you are physically capable of doing anything about it, should emergency shelters be left standing? Or should they be razed and scattered so as to mar environmental beauty in the least practical degree? In heavily frequented country, many would tend to lean to the re-blending motif. In real wilderness, such a shelter does not seem really out of place to most, and many leave them, partly because of the possibility that they may be used again.

The boughs of a fallen titan often come close in their natural state to providing shelter, in front of which a body-long fire can be kindled. Often all that's necessary is to cut away several of the blocking boughs. These

Even a fallen tree can provide comfortable shelter.

and others from the same tree can be used to thatch the roof and ends. Be careful, however, not to cut any of the underneath limbs that may be helping to support the tree in its new position.

PRINCIPLES OF THE LEAN-TO

These are a pleasure to make, and in a pinch the experience thus gained can mean the difference between life and death. There are so many common sense variations that lean-tos are suitable for almost any country. For instance, one or both ends of the horizontal top pole can be tied to or notched to standing trees, laid in the crotches of trees, in the crotches of other poles that are leaned against trees for support, or in tripods made by lashing three poles together at the top. Other variations, as for example those employing rocks, will readily come to mind, depending on the terrain in your location.

Once the top pole is in place, the framework can be rapidly completed by leaning other poles short distances apart along the back. These are often supplemented by horizontal poles laid in crotches or tied in position.

How long should the ridgepole be? How high should it be erected? At what angle should the back extend to the ground? The following facts may act as your guides.

First of all, the lean-to should be as long as your body. This is because you'll be most comfortable sleeping beside a fire that is as long as you are tall. Even when you have a companion, the two of you will be snugger sleeping lengthwise to the fire than with either your head or feet facing it.

Ideally, the lean-to should be high enough to stand in. On the other hand, a low lean-to will reflect heat more conservatively and is easier to build. For a satisfactory compromise, make the emergency lean-to just high enough so that the occupants can sit comfortably in its mouth.

The steeper the roof, the better the structure will both shed precipitation and reflect heat. A forty-five-degree slope is usually considered a suitable compromise between water-shedding efficacy and available interior space. If you have a sleeping bag, of course make the shelter wide enough to accomodate it.

The fourth basic variable has to do with the wind. The fundamental rule is to have the opening on the side away from the wind. In open snow terrain, however, drifts may form in that lee. Then the most satisfactory compromise is to make the entrance crosswise to the wind. This is also the thing to do when you are camped in a canyon beside a mountain stream or in some other location where the thermal air currents alternate with the time of day, in fair weather flowing downward in the early morning and then back upwards toward evening.

Suppose you may be stranded in relatively flat country for an extended period? Then you'll be influenced by the prevailing wind rather than by any momentary breezes. This prevailing wind will be indicated by such natural signs as leaning trees and the direction of the majority of the downfall.

BUILDING THE LEAN-TO

You're stranded and alone. It's dark, cold, and damp. The strength and energy expended in building a one-man shelter will be more than regained during a night of comfort.

The ideal time to start on such a bivouac is late in the afternoon while there's still plenty of light. If you have delayed longer than you should, however, the leaping companionship of a high fire will poke plenty of light into the forest's recesses.

An ax will make this job simple, a hatchet easy, and just a light, small knife feasible. In a pinch, you can get by with your bare hands. Let's assume that you have at least a good sheath knife.

You want a shelter seven feet long, to accomodate you lengthwise in its mouth. So you cut and trim a slim poplar sapling, say, at least two feet longer. Place this ridgepole four feet high in the crotches between limbs and trunks of two trees.

At each end, you slant a roughly trimmed sapling in a forty-five-degree angle toward the back. You'll want three or more additional poles the length

Roof a lean-to with evergreen boughs.

of the ridgepole. There are enough stubs of branches on the first two saplings to support these poles, parallel to the ridge, evenly spaced from the ground up. Now your framework is complete.

Birch bark makes your lean-to practically waterproof.

You'll want walls at least six inches thick. One foot would be even better. The back wall is the only problem. You bush in the ends by leaning there several thickly needled young fir.

A large quantity of fir boughs will cover your shed roof. Start with the bottom layer, just as if you were shingling a house roof. Hang the boughs close together over the pole nearest the ground. The next row will overlap these, and so on, until you have a substantial roof that will shed a fair amount of precipitation. The boughs are laid upside down, with the butts uppermost, then overlapped and covered by the tops of the next row.

Build a browse bed within. Extend your campfire until it is as long as your body, and lay in a towering pile of firewood so you will be able to replenish it during the long night without leaving your bed. You'll awaken several times during the blackness to find yourself shivering and the fire dwindled to just a few red coals. Build it up again and you'll soon be happily snoozing.

OTHER LEAN-TOS

There are innumerable other types of lean-tos, all made in the same general fashion by shingling a pole framework. For example, you might make a bivouac seven feet wide and five feet high in front by laying the crotches of two poles together. Hold this angle upright by leaning a ten-foot pole, which will serve as your ridge, from these crotches to the ground in back. Thatch this with available browse, preferably softwood boughs, or just lean a quantity of small leafy trees against it. Moss, bark, vines, reeds, grass, and other outdoor materials may be used, too. For that final master touch you might curl rolls of birch bark entirely across the top, extending down atop the shingled browse on both sides, to make the bivouac practically waterproof. This will make a fine den for the night.

The companionable way to put up a pair of lean-tos, when the party is large enough, is face to face with a cheery campfire between. Unfortunately, such a setup is as impractical as it is charming. No matter how you arrange things, the fire will tend to fill one of the shelters with smoke. You may have everything going along happily for an hour, and then a changing caprice of breeze will cause trouble.

One large lean-to, built so that all occupants will be sleeping parallel to its front and to the long fire, or two smaller ones side by side, will handily solve the problem.

DRAINAGE

You may wish to protect your shelter with a small but functional drainage ditch. Of course, if you are bivouacing on a ridge where moisture sinks almost at once into the forest floor, or if you are camping on sand, no such ditching will be necessary.

A furrow a couple of inches wide and deep can be quickly scratched with a sharp dead stick when no more likely tool is at hand. In front where this indentation is in the way of traffic, and also where the soil is such that it falls in readily, fill it loosely with pebbles.

Such a drain should be placed so that it will bear away any water cascading down the walls. If you are bivouacing on an incline, moisture will have to be turned away only from the upper portions of the shelter.

SUPPOSE YOU HAVE PLASTIC?

A rectangle of light plastic, large enough to roof and thus waterproof a lean-to, can be folded and carried in a breast pocket as easily as a handkerchief. For years I've always had such an eight-by-twelve-foot plastic sheet with me whenever I have been in the bush, even though my major use of it is as a rainy-day shelter when I'm stopping for lunch.

By the same criterion, parachute silk or wing covers insure excellent lean-to covering for downed airmen. These can be used alone, although they are better with a corollary sheath of evergreen boughs, bark, grass, moss, or such.

Which should go underneath? Light-colored manufactured products, used directly atop the framework, will cheerily reflect warmth and heat. Therefore, fabric beneath and browse above is the answer for very cold weather.

However, if there is melting snow or heavy rain, thatch the framework first with boughs. To keep these dry, cover them with a sheet of plastic or other material, perhaps held in place by a few scattered branches.

The best arrangement is fabric both below and above, if there is enough. Then with a shelter mouth no higher than the seated individual, a depth no greater than the width of the bed, and the full length of the body exposed to the fire, you can be surprisingly comfortable even when the colored alcohol shrinks forty or fifty degrees below zero — and the smoke of your lone campfire rises like a pillar to support the ceiling of frost that hovers at cabin level above a wilderness cannonading with cold.

SUSPENDED TEEPEE

With the vastly increasing myriad of private aircraft, there is the multiplying possibility that one day you may have to parachute to safety in an

An Indian-style teepee can be fashioned of parachute fabric.

unfrequented area. Your parachute, then, can be by itself one of the best of shelters, and with a minimum of effort.

Cut the shroud lines some two feet from where they join the fabric. Now you need to get the top of the chute into the air. You can do this by attaching a piece of shroud line around the cords in the apex of the chute, then throwing it over a limb or across a pole stretched between two trees, or tying it to a tripod fashioned of poles at least fifteen feet high.

Once the canopy is secured at the desired height, make a conical tent of it by rounding out the periphery with stakes, rocks, fallen branches, or sod. The circumference will be dictated by both your tastes and the number of inhabitants. The smaller the teepee, of course, the easier it will be to heat. Usually there will be several gores of silk that will not be needed. These may be cut out for other uses, or they may be loosely gathered to form the entrance.

If you desire a fire for warmth, companionship, or for the relative freedom its smoke will give you against insects, additional preparations will be necessary before the teepee is raised. If you are in open, windy country, the hole in the apex may be sufficient.

In the woods, though, this opening will be too small to allow for sufficient ventilation. Then slit the chute a few inches down the center groove of a gore seam. Keep this vent open by tying in a cross of sticks of the desired size. The width of the vent will vary according to local air currents, and the only way to determine its approximate size will be by experimentation. You'll find, too, that you can control the ventilation by propping or pinning open a side of the teepee, as the Indians used to do.

Kindle the fire in the middle of the teepee, beneath the vent. If it's fly season and what you desire is some degree of protection from the humming biters, use a quantity of damp or green wood and regulate the ventilation to your momentary satisfaction.

Pitching methods, of course, will vary in relation to your ingenuity and the materials at hand. If you have more prospective room than energy, just use the trimmed trunk of a tree as a center pole and rope the parachute around it at the desired height.

At the other extreme, the enterprising adventurer who may be stranded for a matter of days may choose to build his walls log-cabin fashion some three feet high, using easily handled logs up to eight inches in diameter. Such walls will support a framework of light poles over which the parachute material can be draped.

For a really superb roof, supreme in both water-shedding and insulative qualities, use a double layer of fabric with an air space between. Some of the Indian tribes employed the same principle in building their winter teepees.

AIRCRAFT SHELTERS

Where the weather is warm, the sufficiently intact fuselage and wing and tail portions of a downed plane can be turned into a snug shelter. The main concern will be danger from the fumes of spilled gas. In winter, however, the fuselage can be deadly as a shelter because of the rapidity with which the metal will conduct away what little heat can be contrived.

In the desert, on the other hand, the inside of the airplane may be far too warm during the day. Then seek the shade of a wing if you have no better shelter. When you stay with the plane, you can make a shady and functional shelter by tying an opened parachute as an awning to a wing. Then, using sections of the plane tubing for poles and pegs, fasten the lower edge of the chute at least two feet clear of the sand for air circulation. Make sure first that the plane is staunchly moored and the wing securely guyed to prevent movement in wind or storm.

During the winter, particularly during the hours of darkness, desert temperatures may plummet below freezing and heavy rains may fall. Then use the inside of the plane for shelter from cold and rain. Do your cooking outside, though, even when there is no danger from spilled gas. Otherwise the accumulation of carbon monoxide can be a menace.

SHELTER ON THE DESERT

A trench three feet deep, running east and west to avoid as much sunlight as possible, can result in a difference of as much as one hundred degrees in temperature between its shadowy bottom and ground level. Scooping out such a shelter for daytime use, when no natural shade is to be found, may save your life. Of course, always leave some sort of signal, such as a brightly colored shirt, so that rescuers can spot you.

If a sandstorm should blow up, take shelter at the earliest possible moment. Mark your direction with an arrow of stones perhaps, lie down with your back to the gale, cover your nose and mouth with a cloth, and sleep out the storm. If possible, seek shelter in the lee of a hill. Don't worry about being buried by the sand.

In fact, it's recommended that you get some protection from the sun in exposed conditions by covering your body with sand. Burrowing in the sand also reduces water loss. Some desert survivors report that the pressure of sand affords valuable physical relief to tired muscles.

If you have a parachute or other suitable fabric, dig out a depression and cover it; always leaving some clear signal outside. In rocky regions or where desert shrub, thorn shrub, or tufted grass hummocks grow, drape a parachute, blanket, or sheet of plastic over the protuberances.

Too, make use of natural desert features such as a tree, a rock cairn, or a tall clump of cacti for shelter or shade. The overhanging bank of a dry stream may offer a retreat, although after even a distant cloudburst your home may be abruptly flooded. Banks of valleys, dry rivers, and ravines are especially good places to look for caves, and maybe you'll find a deserted native shelter.

If you are unaccustomed to desert travel, a rule of thumb is to multiply your estimates of distance by three, as both the clear, dry air and the absence of land features are apt to make underestimation likely. The main objective in the desert during the hot seasons will be to keep cool and thus conserve as much body moisture as possible, so traveling at night and bivouacing during the day may be the best answer.

WHAT ABOUT CAVES?

"Who," asked Thoreau, "does not remember the interest with which, when young, he looked at shelving rocks or any approach to a cave? It was the natural yearning of that portion of our most primitive ancestor which still survived in us."

Such Stone Age shelters, found in wildernesses throughout the continent, still offer sanctuary for the wayfarer. Make sure first, though, that they are not already occupied, or overly damp, or drafty. A shallow cave, warmed by a leaping fire in front, is a fine thing when you've strayed or become lost. A bigger cave, composed perhaps of several dry and well-ventilated rooms, may boast all the comforts of a large camp.

Even a sturdily overhanging ledge can keep you dry and warm. Along many streams, floodwaters in the spring have undercut forested banks, offering many a shelter to the enterprising wayfarer.

Brooks bend in such a manner during high water that, when the current has dwindled, a niche is often provided in a bank. This can many times be speedily roofed with browse and a fire safely kindled on the rocks in front. Beware of building a fireplace in such an instance, though, as entrapped moisture often causes stream rocks to burst and splinter dangerously.

In country where run-offs are severe, never camp in a ravine, stream bed, or gulch bottom. A sudden storm far from you could wash you out even though the immediate weather, offering no warning, continues bright and sunny.

DOME DOMICILE

Even where a lean-to is not possible because there is no growth large enough, you can still fashion an extremely snug domical shelter from wood as slight as the very widely distributed willow. Begin by cutting a substantial quantity of the longest withes you can locate. Their length will determine the size of the bivouac because it will not be practical, for a short stay, to make this more than about a foot wider than the average length of the wands.

With this in mind, take a pointed stick and scratch on the ground an outline of the proposed structure.

The base most practically may be oval if this shape will give you enough room. Otherwise, make it rectangular and slightly longer than the length of your body. It will then take on the shape of a barrel that has been split lengthwise. The most functional procedure, in other words, is to build with rounded sides and top.

Commence the actual construction by shoving into the ground, deep enough to hold, the larger end of the first wand that comes to hand. Continue to follow the outline you have etched, which for the purposes of description may be considered to be a circle; set the bigger end of the next switch opposite the first one on the scratched line. You can then bring the two tops together in a semicircle and tie them with string, rawhide, vines, roots, or any other convenient substance.

Implant and curve two more wands, roughly bisecting the initial pair. Now lash all four together at the top. The arch of the now outlined dome roof will determine the curve of the subsequent pairs of wands.

The distance these are set apart will be governed by the covering material available to you. If this is to be plastic sheeting from your pocket, para-

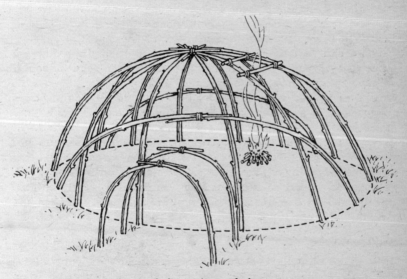

Saplings are the framework for a dome shelter.

chute silk, or animal skins, support members a foot apart will generally be sufficient. However, if you must weave moss, grass, or more willows through the basketlike structure, the wands will be better set as close as two inches.

One of these substantial, if seemingly fragile, finished domes can be bolstered with a plastering of mud or snow. If you are using the latter in subzero weather, give it an icy coating by throwing on water; perhaps snow melted over your campfire.

You may choose to give such a dome shelter a small, crawl-in entrance on the side away from the wind in order to conserve heat. Possibilities will be limited only by ingenuity, energy, and the materials at hand.

If you want a fire in your shelter, leave an opening near the apex. This can be strengthened if necessary by weaving withes into the structure at right angles.

HOW ABOUT A HUT?

Youngsters build their backyard huts without any prior instruction, and so an adult may proceed from his instincts and his observations, governed by the materials at hand. A ledge, the trunk of a fallen tree, or its dirt-encrusted root system may serve as the back of such a hut. Like some trappers' bivouacs regularly inhabited in the North during cold weather, this may be just large enough to crawl into.

Although spaces in the walls can be chinked with mud as in log cabin construction, in a small emergency shanty you may appreciate the additional warmth that can be acquired by heaping dirt, sod, or forest litter against them. If the walls have been built slanting in slightly from bottom to top, such insulation will hold itself more substantially in place.

The roof can be similarly reinforced, although in its case you'll be more comfortable if you first sheathe it with bark. Too, sod holds together better than loose loam and provides one of the most practical of all roofs. I have spent some comfortable seventy-degree-below-zero days in a log cabin roofed with sod, and I can therefore attest to its qualities of insulation.

If you are able to snare or otherwise collect a large animal for the commissary, its skin can serve as the door. Fabric, woven vines, and even a thickly needled young fir or spruce also will do.

So as to guard more easily against conflagration, you may choose to make a stone fire ring in the center of the dirt floor. A hole will then have to be cut in the roof to serve as a chimney. You may be able to regulate the smoke and fumes, too, by opening the door at various degrees. The chimney hole can be closed, by laying something over it, when the fire is not burning.

THE LOG CABIN

The ultimate in shelters in wooded country is the log cabin, and a consideration of its construction may give you an idea of the possibilities if you should ever be stranded below the timber line with plenty of time and, ideally, an ax or at least a belt hatchet.

No special skill is needed. The wool-shirted pioneers who hewed log homes out of the North American wilderness were, for the large part, inexperienced men, working with a maximum of haste with a minimum of tools. If there had been anything complex about log work, they would have turned to some other type of construction.

INGENUITY

The North American log cabin traditionally is a wilderness abode built with whatever tools may be at hand. The pioneers who hewed two great countries out of the unspoiled places north of the Rio Grande put up thousands by ax alone.

Where tools are few, ingenuity flourishes. The square, even if it be but the upper back corner of an ax head, should be kept busy. The measuring implement, perhaps a primitive notched stick, should be worked overtime to make the job easier in the long run.

A sharp stone, a soft-nosed cartridge, or the burned end of a stick can replace the carpenter's pencil. Any of these tied to a thong, or to a tough flexible vine or root, will make a compass. The butt of an ax or hatchet that has been driven into a stump becomes a backwoods anvil.

The builder not wishing to imitate that ever further tilting Leaning Tower of Pisa needs no expensive level. The bushman's plate of water will do. Or you can use a can or any flat-bottomed receptacle. The contrasting color of one of the wild teas, described in the portion on edible wild plants, makes this device even more satisfactory, while the long slim bottle of fluid with its telltale air bubble is too fine for any but the very good.

CHOOSING YOUR LUMBER

Building logs can be cut and used at any time, but if there is standing dead wood where you are, perhaps the result of a lightning-ignited fire, the sticks will be lighter to handle and, having already dried and shrunk, will make a stauncher cabin.

The straighter softwoods are usually selected. Cedar, balsam, tamarack, fir, pine, hemlock, redwood, and spruce are all good. Some other woods, such as oak and chestnut, have to be seasoned, then hewn into shape if the cabin is not to resemble latticework.

Quickly deteriorating species — for example cottonwood, buckeye, basswood, willow, and aspen — are not practical for long usage, although they'll do for a temporary structure.

Cedar is particularly advantageous for pillars and furniture. Osage orange has similar vigorous durability. So does locust, cypress, redwood, and chestnut. Iron oak resists ground decay and is a prime foundation and post wood. So is juniper. Birch, although too prone to rot to be used as cabin logs except in the most temporary of structures, is widely prized for furniture because of its adaptability and beauty.

Building will progress more happily if all logs are grouped according to their intended purposes before any are used. The straightest, soundest, and sturdiest will be reserved for the ridgepole.

The usual log cabin seldom takes more than fifty or sixty logs. The pick of available timber should certainly be used, therefore. Logs from six to twelve inches in diameter are a good general size. The larger sticks are eminently satisfactory, but their weight makes them harder to handle. The same consideration applies to lengths.

The slighter the taper, the easier the work. The sticks will be alternated, butts for tops, throughout to compensate for tapering. Walls can be kept reasonably level, that is, by laying one tier of logs clockwise butt to top, butt to top, butt to top, and butt to top. The next tier of the rectangle, also viewed clockwise will run top to butt throughout.

FELLING THE TREES

Even the greenest tenderfoot can fell his first trees in a given direction if he will follow the simple principles set forth here. Wind, incline, weight, and surrounding objects must, of course, be taken into consideration.

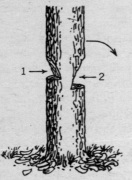

The safety notch (1) and cutting notch (2) form a natural hinge to control direction of fall.

A small safety notch is first made to minimize any possibility of the butt's kicking back or the trunk's splitting. Below this on the opposite side, where the tree is to fall, a wide notch is cut. When this indentation is about three-fifths through, a few strokes at the first nick should send the tree crashing.

The two notches are so placed that they form a natural hinge. This hinge controls the direction of the fall and lessens the chance that the butt may thrust backward. However, you should have your eye on a safe place, and you should hurry there when the moment comes for the solitary call of, "Timber-r-r-r!"

FOUNDATION DEPARTMENT

The cabin foundation may be as simple as you like, but it should be solid and level throughout if work is not to be unnecessarily prolonged. Four cornerstones, embedded with flat surfaces upraised, will suffice. None need be larger than what you can move easily.

Log cabins should be supported at the corners and at about every six feet. A cabin approximately twelve feet wide and eighteen feet long, to mention one in which I lived for five years in northern British Columbia, needs an additional bolster at the middle of each short span. Two more props should be spaced equidistant beneath each long sill.

SILLS

The sill logs are the wall logs that rest directly upon the cabin foundations. They should be surpassed in strength and straightness only by the ridgepole.

The sill logs should be based as solidly as possible on the foundations. It is frequently best to square them at points of contact for this reason.

WALLS

Log walls are complete in themselves. The builder does not have to bother with studs, shoes, girts, braces, or a dozen other complications. When these walls are chinked, all insulating and weatherproofing will be finished.

Many think log cabin building is a lot more difficult than it really is. A major reason for this error is that fanciful walls are visualized that fit with scarcely a crack. The opposite condition is more often true. This is as it should be. The spaces are valuable in that their variability permits the easy trueing and leveling of the structure.

The experienced log cabin builder, therefore, generally values crannies and crevices for the assets they can be. He realizes what a simple and effective matter it will be to close them later with moss and mud, both free for the using. He knows he need not worry about the spaces between logs except to limit them whenever possible to a maximum of two inches.

PLUMB

Log walls, along their interiors, should run as straight up and down as possible. Of course, no harm is done if the inside walls are not vertical along their outer contours. It's just easier to install shelves and arrange furniture, that's all, when one log bulges no further into the room than another.

It takes considerable skill to keep a wall in line by eye alone. Only patience and a certain amount of common sense are required if you have the assistance of a plumb line. For log work, an adequate plumb line can be made by knotting a piece of twine around a fishing sinker, a cartridge, or even a pebble. When this weighted cord is suspended free, gravity will of course straighten it into a perfectly vertical guide line.

HEIGHT

Cabins, by their very nature, best hug the warm, shielding earth from which the logs themselves have sprung. Many a cabin wall rises from the wilderness floor itself, and cabins partially subterranean are not uncommon in the North. Such practice saves heat, materials, and labor.

CORNERS

What type of corner are you going to use to hold the wall logs in place? There is plenty of room for choice, limited only by the fact that you'll probably be building without nails or spikes. Experiment with a jackknife and four lengths of sapling until you have a practical working knowledge of how your corner is made and fitted. You need have no misgivings. The log cabin, being characteristically low and rugged, requires no architectural perfection. Chinking will compensate for any technical shortcomings.

The saddle notch is simple. The two sill logs are in position. Now one of the shorter end logs is rolled into place. Its butt rests on the top of one sill log, and in turn its top angles across the butt of the other sill. The end log is now shifted until it lies most solidly.

The level is now laid along the top of the end log. Let's assume the log is already roughly level. The two notches, therefore, need to be half as deep as the respective thickness of each end of the log. Each notch will be as wide, of course, as that portion of the underneath log each will cover.

Log work being rough, you can estimate all this by eye. But suppose you want to come a little closer? First, mark the center of one end of the log. Say, for purposes of illustration, that the log is eight inches thick. The notch at that end will then be half of that, or four inches.

Let's assume you are using a thong with a sharp stone at the end of it for a compass. The string is held four inches from the stone. Now mark the width of the log beneath. Then, using the compass, approximate the curve of the log beneath. Do the same thing at the other end. Both notches are thereby plainly marked. All that remains is to cut them out. Roll the log over and go to it, fitting and cutting further if this should be necessary. Successive notches are so marked and so hollowed.

Now let's assume that when the level was laid atop the short log, it showed that the stick was lower at one end than at the other. Then move

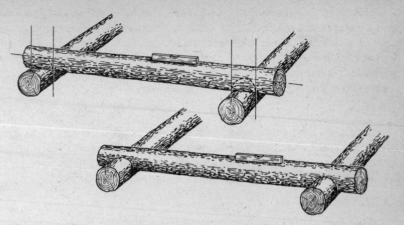

A simply constructed saddle notch forms the log cabin's corners.

the device until it is level. Measure the width of the angle. Say this is one inch. Then the notch will be one inch deeper.

The walls will go up quicker and easier if, as succeeding tiers are raised, each log is so leveled that it is about two inches from the log beneath at the farthest point.

LOCK NOTCH

Such a saddle notch will be adequate for temporary work, even without spiking, as the weight and roughness of the logs will hold it reasonably in place. For a more secure dwelling, though, the lock notch can be used.

This common notch is made by cutting both the upper and lower logs so that the sticks will lock one another in place when fitted. Instead of cupping the top of each lower log as in the case of the saddle notch, each lock notch curves into a similar hollow that is upturned on each lower log. This

Lock notches result in a sturdier cabin.

makes for a stronger connection but, if you are planning for the long run, is more vulnerable to dampness.

HANDLING THE LOGS

The ruggedest of men would have a time of it if forced to lift cabin logs into position by sheer strength. With some elementary knowledge, however, one or two individuals can do the job with little exertion.

Two or more gradually slanting poles, laid from the ground to the top of the cabin wall, can serve as a skid up which, perhaps with the aid of a line or with poles used as levers, logs can be readily moved. The usual procedure for the builder working alone is to raise one end of the log, secure it, and then lift the other end.

OTHER BASICS

Windows and doors present a problem to the builder not handy to a hardware store. But if the individual has enough resourcefulness to build a cabin he can be reasonably expected to be a successful hunter. Hides will provide both a functional door and soft, warm coverings for the dirt floor.

Cabin windows might be covered with thinly scraped deerskin, pioneer style. Or you can use that piece of plastic that should be in your pocket.

Rocks can be arranged for a center fireplace and a hole, which can be closed when not in use, left in the roof for a vent.

ROOF

Roof that log enclosure, and a cabin is created. Personal preferences, governed as always by the materials, once more hold the scepter. One of the sweetest joys in building a wilderness cabin lies not only in the satisfying of an instinct as old as life, but also in the fact that you can make it what you want.

The lower the roof, the easier the cabin will be to heat. You'll likely settle for a flat roof. These are more practical than one might think, although in heavy snow country you may have to keep it reasonably clear after storms. Sturdy construction and short spans will avoid any danger from ordinary winter weather, however. Slant this roof slightly, say one inch for every ten feet, to take care of drainage.

Just construct the front and sides of the cabin to the desired height, but have the front, say, one log higher than the back. Lay poles across for the roof. This will leave a space at the sides that can later be handily filled with hewn poles or with moss and mud.

Shingle the roof with bark if you can, starting with the lowest row and overlapping each successive tier so that water will run over them to the ground. Then insulate the roof with moss, mud, or sod.

A roof shingled with bark and sealed with moss and mud gives the finishing touch to your log cabin.

CAULKING AND CHINKING

Log walls must be closed against wind and weather before the wilderness home is habitable. This is so simply and easily accomplished that most builders take little heed of the spaces that remain between logs as the cabin rises except to limit them to a maximum of two inches.

Log construction is sealed by caulking and chinking. Caulking generally refers to the setting of some elastic material, such as moss, in the crevices. Chinking characterizes the subsequent blocking in of this filler by a substance such as mud.

Chinking should be forced into crevices until it reaches the caulking material. It is important for reasons of warmth, however, that an insulative air space be left between the outer and inner chinking. A heavy core of caulking will assure this. Ancient Ojibwas, who habitually spent the cold months in teepees whose double walls were stuffed with moss, never dreamed that in later years insulation would be considered a modern building development.

Caulking by its elastic nature may be done at any time. Chinking should be delayed as long as possible unless the logs used throughout are already well seasoned. Sticks that have not dried out entirely continue to shrink diametrically when in place, widening cracks between one another. Plastering, therefore, may have to be redone periodically.

Sphagnum moss, which can be gathered by the armfuls from swamps and muskegs over thousands of square miles in the northern United States and in Canada, is excellent for a cabin's initial insulation. So are other long-fibered mosses.

Caulking is often strung liberally between logs and bedded in joints as the cabin is built. Each stick is fitted first, then rolled aside a final time while caulking is spread along the log beneath. This procedure is advanta-

29

geous when abundant materials are at hand, if only because of the time it saves that otherwise would be spent driving in the filler. Caulking so applied is tamped more firmly into position, and any excess can be torn away upon completion of the building.

It is well to cradle, at the very least, all but the most tightly fitting notches with caulking as they are built. This will do away with some otherwise vagrant air currents.

TOOLS

A spud, a long piece of wood flattened on one end like a chisel, is generally used for driving the caulking into place. Its softer, yielding surface grasps moss better than metal. A spud can be whittled from a piece of seasoned hardwood in a few minutes. A blade of about two inches at the end of a twelve to fourteen-inch handle is a convenient tool for ordinary work. A rock

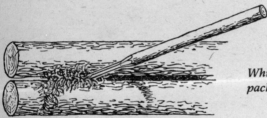

Whittle a hardwood spud to pack caulking between logs.

or malletlike piece of root may be lighter to use with this than the back of an ax.

You can whittle a trowel out of wood, or use your bare hands, to smooth chinking into place. The chinking material, often clay moistened to the consistency of very soft putty, can be transported in any kind of a container or on a hewn slab. One method of application is to slap the mud into crevices with the left hand, then smooth it with the makeshift trowel held in the right hand. This is best done during a warm spell, as freezing and thereby expanding moisture will force this insulation out of cracks.

SHELTERS IN THE SNOW

Snow is a good insulator. Shelters during cold weather are, therefore, many times more easily achieved than during more temperate months. I have bivouaced during the snowy season along northern Canada's Peace River more easily than I've been able to do this at other times of the year.

Here, as on many wilderness rivers, there is a scattering of huge boulders interspersed with driftwood of all sizes. Whereas during the warmer months it is understandably drafty among these rocks, snow had closed the crannies. It proved necessary only to find several such boulders with a reasonably level place between, roof the wider end by piling several young spruce across it, and build a fire in the narrower portion. Driftwood kept this easily fueled all night. All in all, the experimental camp was an unusually agreeable one, even though I found out later that the temperature had dipped more than forty degrees below zero during the darkness.

You need neither boulders nor drifted snags to enjoy such a snug shelter in deep snow. Just open a rough hole from the top down, by tramping, by digging with snowshoes or gloved hands, or by a combination of both. The result may be in the form of a crude triangle. Floor the wider end with evergreen boughs. Roof it with more boughs or with whole small trees. Kindle a small fire in the apex, so that it will be reflected about you as you lie or sit in secure comfort.

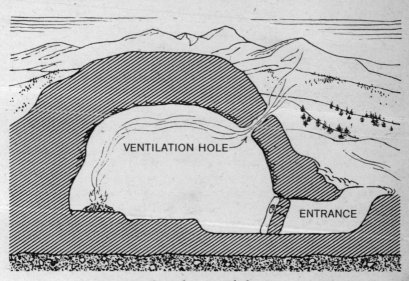

In deep, firm snow a tunnel can be your shelter.

If the snow is deep and firm enough, you can also find warmth and shelter by tunneling into it, being careful to do this at right angles to the wind to avoid drifting.

DANGERS OF DRIFTING

Always take care to keep from situating your snow camp where there are perils from overhang, slides, or dangerously amassing drifts.

Beware in open country of fashioning a snow shelter on a slope that is shielded from the wind. This is a precaution diametrically opposed to the way you'd proceed in a forest. It is important to heed, nevertheless, because in open terrain such sheltered sides collect drifts that could bury and suffocate you.

SLEEPING ON SNOW

Although snow is an excellent insulator, you should never sleep or even sit directly on it. Snow is then too prone to melt, and wet clothing, so susceptible to freezing and so difficult to dry at subzero temperatures, is one of the major dangers in snow country under survival conditions. As slight a substance as a thin sheet of plastic or a strip of bark should be used between body and snow. Unexcelled is a thick browse bed.

THE SNOW HOUSE

Building a snow house is another survival stratagem that harks back to the instinctive play of childhood. It is none the less effective for all that.

All you need do when the weather is cold and you require shelter is to pile a mound of snow a bit larger than the bivouac you wish. Tamp down the surface. If water is available scatter it over the mound until you have an icy glaze. Otherwise, allow the pile to compact as hard as it will in the air for upwards of a half hour.

Then, cutting an entrance at right angles to the wind, tunnel into the mound. Continue to scoop out snow until you have a shell, making any repairs that may be necessary by smoothing and pressing fresh snow in place.

Finally, kindle a tiny fire inside the snow house. Any meltage, you'll find, will be quickly absorbed by the remaining snow. When the fire has burned down, carefully cut and then shove out a ventilation hole in the roof, close the entrance with browse or even a large snowball, and leave the shelter to ice.

You won't credit, until you try it yourself, how small a blaze within will, supported by the heat of your body, keep you snug. As a matter of fact, you'll likely discover that the tendency is to overheat. Of vital importance, because of the smoke and the carbon monoxide fumes that would otherwise accumulate in such an impervious shelter are the establishment and maintenance of good ventilation.

ARCTIC SHELTERS

A long-bladed snow knife or the combination snow knife-saw — a long, saw-toothed blade with a crooked handle for convenient handling — is essential to survival during the cold months in country above the widely varying timber line. One should be in the survival kit of anyone who is traveling in such country.

Snow suitable for construction has a number of characteristics seldom found below timber line. For example, the best of it is sufficiently strong that a cubic foot will support the weight of a man. Still, it can be sawed, cut, split, and shaped with ease.

Even in the arctic regions of Alaska and northern Canada, only a minor percentage of the snow is suitable for the building of block shelters. Initially, you should seek terrain where it is possible to cut your blocks from the vertical face of a drift. Such a drift, therefore, should be at least two feet deep. It should be able to carry your weight and be nearly impervious to footprints. Ideally, probing should prove that it is uniformly firm, free of softer or harder layers built up by former storms. Next, be sure that the drift is large enough for your purposes. Eskimos feel it is worth an extra hour of searching to find such a spot.

Otherwise, the blocks will have to be cut from the flat horizontal surface. This consumes time. A considerably larger area of hard snow is required. Finally, the shelter will have to be built higher rather than being dug snugly into the sheltering drift.

TRENCHING IN SNOW

When there is not enough time to build an igloo, a snow trench may be the answer. You'll find yourself capable of contriving one easily and speedily, with maximum results in return for minimum efforts.

Excavating snow blocks to build a trench shelter

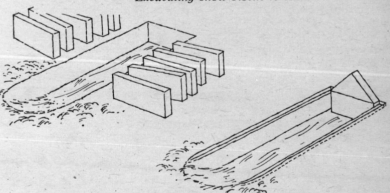

Triangular blocks support the roof.

When you can come upon a large drift of snow at least three feet deep, you can provide the roofing materials for the shelter as you excavate it, cutting large blocks vertically from a scratched outline just wide and long enough to accomodate you and perhaps one companion. Stand these blocks in equal numbers on both sides of the trench.

Once the trench is finished, cut a notch the length of each side, as shown in the illustration, to support the roof. Then stand a triangular block of snow at one end of the trench to support the initial roof block.

This first roof block is cut narrower than the one slanting into it from the other side. This is so that the second block will overlap it at the side, thus providing a projection to support the third roof block, and so on. The remainder of the blocks are slanted into position in similar fashion, as shown.

Positioning the roof blocks

An entrance can be situated at the middle of the trench opening into a square-roofed pit which is roomy enough to provide an area for cooking and for removing your clothing before entering the sleeping bag. You'll also want to poke a ventilation hole in the roof and to have a substantial snow block handy with which to close the entrance.

If no deep snow drift can be located, you're still in business. Then erect a walled enclosure with a square pit at one end. Roof this with large slabs, hollowing them a bit inside after they are in place to form an arc.

Such trenches, while providing fine emergency shelters, are too cramped for permanent camps. Too, it is soon impossible to move more than slightly without dislodging the frost accumulating on clothing and sleeping bag. You therefore become damp, a dangerous condition in the freezing temperatures of the Arctic, without a good way to dry out. The answer? An igloo.

THE IGLOO

This traditional Eskimo cold-weather home is the supreme winter shelter in the American and Canadian Arctic. Large enough for long-term comfort, it is also staunch, wind-resistent, and soundproof. Once you have made one on your own, the igloo will almost invariably be the shelter you'll seek in an Arctic emergency.

Once you have found a suitable drift, in which the snow tests out favorably by the methods suggested previously, scratch the outline of your igloo. For one man, the circle should have an approximate diameter of eight feet. Nine feet will do for two men, ten feet for three, twelve feet for four, and thirteen feet for a quintet.

Next, begin to accumulate your snow blocks, cutting them from the face of a trench as shown in the illustration.

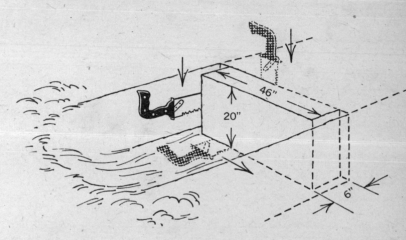

Begin igloo construction by cutting blocks of firm snow.

Start by excavating a clear vertical face. The blocks should be about forty-six inches wide and some twenty inches deep. You'll only waste time with smaller blocks. Although they are a little easier to cut, construction is more protracted and arduous with them.

Using your snow knife or snow knife-saw, cut a slot at both ends of each block. Make this two inches wide for the full depth of the block.

Now cut under the block, releasing it from the drift at the bottom. Then make a groove parallel to the face, scoring this so that the final block will be approximately six inches thick.

If you have a snow knife, deepen this indentation by running the point to and fro along it. Then several gentle stabs, followed by a firm central stroke, will break it off. If you are using a knife-saw, merely saw along the mark then break off the block with a firm push in the center.

Stand the snow block to one side and start another. When you have accumulated ten or twelve, you can commence the actual building.

IGLOO CONSTRUCTION

When the bottom row of the blocks reaches the trench from which they are being excavated, temporarily replace one block in the trench so that you may build the wall atop it.

It is important to note the slope of the first row of blocks. All end joints should point, like radii, toward the center of the igloo. If they don't, you are in for difficulties.

The bottom row of blocks slopes toward the center of the igloo.

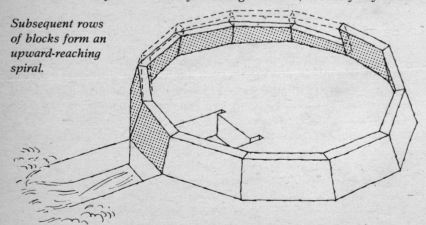

Once the bottom row is completed, start the spiral which will be culminated with the key block. When you are right-handed, cut away any of the

Subsequent rows of blocks form an upward-reaching spiral.

To prevent them slipping, blocks must bear only at areas A, B, and C; not at areas D and E.

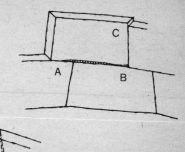

lowest blocks diagonally, slanting down from left to right. If left-handed, cut the slope the other way.

Then fit the next block, leaning it inward so that its interior follows the curve of the dome-to-be. Even during this primary stage, the block would probably fall in except that it is held by the face of the notch and by the tops of the lower blocks. Look at the drawing. The block must bear only at areas A, B, and C. It should not bear at D and E lest it pivot and slip. The joint can be inches apart at these points, or it can almost touch.

All the blocks from this stage on, up to the final central block at the apex, are set in this fashion. Continue to cut them from within the igloo center, fitting them in place as you go.

You'll soon become familiar with the A, B, C method illustrated. Each block is lifted into position. The joint is first fitted roughly while the block is being supported by the left hand in the case of the right-handed individual. If the blade is run between the newest block and the one previously fitted and the slit pushed shut, then a minor uppercut on the underneath face at the end nearest the previous block will leave the block holding at A and C only.

Then a firm downward tap at C, as indicated by the arrow, will ease the block into its final position where it will no longer have to be held in place. It will then hold, as discussed before, at A, B, and C.

The shape of the igloo will depend, of course, on the slope of the blocks. It is best to keep the curve of the walls as symmetrical and reasonably low as possible. In all events, try to avoid a pointed igloo. So much heat would accumulate at the top that your bed would remain cold. With the spiral technique it is amazing how flat an arch can be achieved. The last few blocks will lie almost horizontally; however, if you continue to use the A, B, C fit, they will remain in place.

Continue erecting your igloo, block by block. You will discover, as you expected, that the steepening slope of the wall will increase the pull of gravity on the blocks. However, this is compensated for by the heightening angle between the A—B axis of successive blocks, as the width of the opening decreases. The blocks will jam firmly into place as you go on, making the building actually simpler and easier toward the finish.

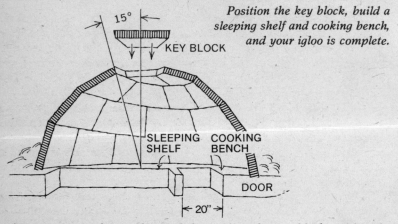

Position the key block, build a sleeping shelf and cooking bench, and your igloo is complete.

As soon as you have exhausted the cutting of snow blocks within the enclosure, carefully cut a small hole as far down the wall as possible, tunneling beneath the wall at this point so that you can get more building blocks from the outside.

When the remaining aperture in the roof is small enough, the key block is fitted. This is a surprisingly easy procedure. The hole should be rectangular to allow the key block to slide easily up through it. Then cut the block to fit and let it settle slowly into position. You have constructed your igloo!

FINALITIES OF IGLOO CONSTRUCTION

Igloos, like log cabins, have to be chinked. This is easily enough done by pressing and patting snow in all outside cracks. Here it will soon harden, preventing drafts and the loss of warm air. If you are only going to use any particular igloo for a short time, such chinking will be sufficient. But for the tighter job that will be more practical during longer sojourns, chink the inside cracks as well.

When you can not reach the top of the dome, insulate it by tossing powdery snow on it. Don't add too much weight by carrying this to extremes, however.

Also as with log cabins, it is sound practice to bank the bottom round of blocks. With igloos, this guards the base from the erosion of wind-driven snow. The wind can quickly deteriorate an igloo, cutting into the blocks with gale-impelled snow pellets that, at times, reach the comparative intensity of sand blasted with compressed air. Then a wall of snow blocks should be stretched to the windward to cut off the drifting snow. Pack loose snow and any broken blocks against the wind-beleaguered side of the igloo to protect it as much as possible against the cutting proclivities of the drift.

LIVING IN AN IGLOO

About a third of the way back from the door, make a snow wall about a foot-and-a-half high both to conserve warmth and to build the front of your sleeping shelf. This sleeping shelf will elevate you into the heat caught above the door. Push all the loose snow behind the wall to floor the shelf, breaking up lumps to make your bed soft and to achieve better insulation. Level the top of the shelf carefully for the sake of your own comfort.

At either side of the doorway, leave or build small benches, leaving some twenty inches of leg room between sleeping shelf and each bench. This is the kitchen and furnace room. If you situate it reasonably close to the sleeping shelf, you will be able to tend to cooking without leaving your bed.

You'll find that pots can be hung from pegs driven securely into the wall above the fat lamp, the Eskimo's koodlik, or the primus stove.

Drying racks can be arranged by shoving sticks into the wall above. Clothing can be dried here after all possible ice, snow, and frost have been scraped away. Too, this is the place for the long process of thawing frozen food that is going to be eaten without cooking.

A block of snow, the Eskimo's kovic, may be left on the floor for use as a bedchamber vessel. The standard practice is for the user to take care of its sanitary disposal in the morning.

Now that the igloo has been chinked, the door and the entrance tunnel completed, and the sleeping bench finished, you can set up housekeeping as soon as you have cleared away the last of the loose snow. The bench is initially covered with skins or other insulation if possible, then the sleeping bags stretched side by side with their heads toward the entrance. It is important to note that all ice, snow, and frost must be beaten and scraped off of hides, bedding, and clothing before any are put on the sleeping platform.

THE KOODLIK

Any flat can or other stone or metal container will serve as a koodlik. When you have fat to burn, the only other thing that is necessary is a piece of cloth, absorbent cotton, or moss for a wick, plus a sloping surface to support it.

Lubricating oil can be burned in a koodlik, but the wick will have to be trimmed more precisely to keep the flame below the smoking point. Then as the level of the oil decreases, the flame may follow it down the wick to cause additional smoking. A primitive damper, fashioned from a piece of sheet metal from a can or made of foil, will prevent this, allowing closer control of the flame.

Naturally, gasoline can not be used in a koodlik except perhaps two or three drops to ease the lighting of the wick. As Canadian Armed Forces survival experts warn their students, "Don't be the first man to burn down an igloo!"

IGLOO ROUTINE

If more than one individual is using the igloo, the usual practice is for anyone coming into the dome for a lengthy stay to scrape any ice, snow, or frost from his clothing, then to get up on the sleeping bench out of the way.

The cook, customarily at the right-hand bench unless he is left-handed, has the primus stove or its equivalent. He tries to set this on something like a piece of cardboard from a ration container to keep it from melting into its shelf and toppling.

The Eskimo koodlik is an easily assembled stove for cooking in an igloo.

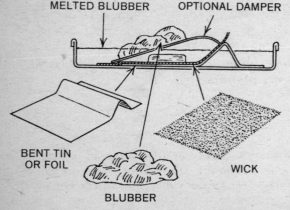

MELTED BLUBBER   OPTIONAL DAMPER

BENT TIN
OR FOIL

BLUBBER

WICK

He may also be using a koodlik for slow cooking, if fat is available. This requires relatively little attention as compared to the burning of lubricating oil, which is prone to smoke and to require frequent wick-trimming. If you are using lubricating oil, you'll find that a little animal fat mixed with it will bring about a notable improvement in the flame.

You'll find that you will be boiling or stewing most of your food. Too, it's best to use a pressure cooker or tightly lidded pot, whenever possible, to avoid steam. Frying, grilling, and baking are out of place in igloo living.

Igloos are amazingly warm; in fact, you'll probably find yourself wearing a minimum of clothing during the day. If the inner walls begin to glaze, ice, and drip, you are getting too much heat, and should adjust it before general icing develops. The inside temperature can be regulated to some degree by either shaving the outside of the dome or by banking additional snow around it.

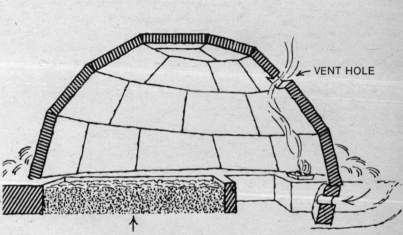

VENT HOLE

SLEEPING BENCH

Ventilation in an igloo, as in any shelter, is extremely important because of danger of carbon monoxide poisoning.

IGLOO VENTILATION

Ventilation is all important. It becomes a delicate balance in keeping the vent holes in dome and door, indicated by the drawing, large enough to permit the ingress of adequate fresh air, yet not so open that freezing will become a danger.

41

The door is left open during the day. At night, however, it is closed by a snow block. Patting snow in around the cracks will make the block fit more securely. It is important, however, that a ventilation hole is cut in the upper part of this door. The more fumes are being accumulated, the larger the door and roof apertures must be. It is dangerous in the extreme to wait until the fire will not burn as it should, and you begin to feel lightheaded and dizzy, before letting in more air.

Sometimes the wind is such that the hole in the dome does not draw properly. Then a snow chimney can be set up by placing a perforated block over the opening.

SNOW AND CHUTE

Although not nearly as effective as an igloo, a parachute or other shelter-sheet can be combined with snow to make a bivouac. Smooth off a circular area some ten feet in diameter. On it erect a round wall of snow blocks at least four feet high. Centrally in the snow circle, construct a pillar of snow blocks higher than the wall. Stretch one or more parachute canopies over wall and pillar.

Drape excess material over the outside of the wall for additional insulation. The excess can then be anchored by piling snow and blocks atop it. Even more efficient is the digging of a trench around the outside perimeter of the snow wall. Push the edges of the fabric into this trench and secure them snugly by tamping back the snow.

For the door, tunnel and cut an opening under and through the wall at right angles to the prevailing wind. This is best screened with a tunnel or L-shaped entrance of snow blocks. Such a shelter will be adequate for up to five individuals. As with the igloo and all other shelters, tents included, there must be a chimney hole and adequate ventilation if there is to be an inside fire.

ICE ALONE

Suppose you are afloat on a floe in the polar regions. Snow may not be available. Then make a similar shelter, as nearly as you can, of ice slabs. Keep this shelter as small as possible because of warmth, using the lee side of a pressure ridge if the ice seems old and solid. You can build such a shelter with hands alone if necessary.

Fire

Fire is often the survivor's most basic need. With it he can warm himself, dry clothing which in a cold climate can of itself mean the almost immediate difference between life and death, enjoy a safe and comfortable night, cook his meals, and even signal for assistance. No one should ever travel in the wilderness at any time without the means of lighting a fire in an emergency.

PRINCIPLES OF FIREMAKING

Although campfires can be built in innumerable ways, the principles of firemaking are always the same. The fire proceeds from spark, to tinder, to fuel. It is in these three essentials that the differences lie. An understanding of the fundamentals will add sureness to your ability to kindle a fire under every practical circumstance.

For one thing, firewood itself does not burn directly. It is a combustible gas, driven from the fuel in sufficient quantities by heat, that combines with enough oxygen in the air to give you your warmth.

The starting fire, in sequence, must be hot and long-lived enough to light more and more gas from progressively larger amounts of fuel. In other words, firemaking under extreme conditions is much more likely to be successful if it is approached deliberately and with thoughtful concern, not haphazardly and helter-skelter — the way you see too many individuals trying to light their blazes.

MATCHES

The easiest way to light a fire is with a match, and it follows that it is only sensible to keep a supply in a waterproof and unbreakable container whenever you are in the unfrequented places. Even though you may momentarily have sufficient matches, it is still best to get in the habit of making that first match count. Such gradually acquired skill may one day mark the difference between a snugly warm camp and a miserably damp and chilly one.

If you can carry them, common wooden, strike-anywhere matches are best. The trick is to hold them so that the fire can feed down the wood. You'll do this in the most practical method of the moment. For example, you may face the breeze with your hands cupped before the lighted match. You may kneel between the wind and your methodically piled wood with your body serving as a shield. You may use your coat or any other convenient thing, perhaps a big sheet of bark, to guard the first wavering flames.

If possible, you should carry an unbreakable waterproof case kept filled preferably with substantial wooden matches whenever you are in the farther places. At the very least, you should have such a container filled with safety matches and a strip on which to strike them.

The match case I carry has a top ring by which it can be pinned inside a pocket. In deep wilderness, too, I consider it inexpensive insurance to carry a second filled case. For everyday use, so that you don't have to disturb the emergency supply, it's a convenient idea to scatter other matches throughout your clothing, most safely one to a pocket with the strike-anywhere variety.

If you find that your loose matches are damp, rub them through your hair. If your hair, too, is wet at the moment, rub the match to and fro between the palms of the hands with its head protruding slightly.

With any container filled with strike-anywhere matches, you have to be careful not to light a match accidentally and thus set off the whole batch. Always close the container gently and carefully. It's a smart dodge, too, to pack the matches with their heads about half and half in both directions. That way you can stow away more, besides.

Paper matches are not reliable enough to depend on for emergency use, although you may have several folders distributed among your pockets for casual use, particularly if you are a smoker. If you ever find yourself in a situation where your life may depend on your ability to light fires and you've nothing more dependable with you than a folder of paper matches, do everything you can to protect it from dampness, whether this is from rain, melting snow, or perspiration. Wrapping the pack in foil or a convenient bit of plastic to keep dry the heads and stems, in addition to the vulnerable striking surface, is sound procedure.

It's short-sighted practice to use a limited supply of matches to light cigarettes or a pipe. Smokers should do their best to wait until the campfire is crackling, then to ignite their tobacco with the end of a burning or glowing stub. Or in bright sunlight you can use a burning lens.

METAL MATCH

This ingenious invention will start a very great number of fires without matches and will remain intact despite most survival hardships. A metal match may be purchased inexpensively and should be a part of every survival kit. Just scrape a twinkling of the dark metal into the tinder, hold the short metallic stick against it, and strike it briskly with your knife.

WHEN IT'S SUBZERO

Have the fuel ready and everything else set to go before you bare your hand. If the fire does not catch with the first match, warm your hand before proceeding further, perhaps by shoving it under an armpit or inside the shirt. As soon as enough stiffness has left the fingers, the attempt can be made once more as swiftly and surely as possible.

SAVING ENERGY

Although a hatchet, knife, or other cutting tool will be an asset in gathering firewood, it's easy enough to make small sticks out of big ones by the hands alone. You can break them over a knee, by wedging one end against rocks or roots and pulling or pushing or by bridging two high points with a dead branch and dropping a stone on its middle.

It's a whole lot easier, though, to burn the large sticks in two. Another backwoods stratagem is to place the ends in the blaze, continuing to push them further in until they are consumed.

LIGHTING A FIRE WITH WATER

If the water is frozen, find a clear piece of ice. Experiment with shaving this with your knife, then finally smoothing it in the warm hands, until you have a lens capable of pinpointing the sun. This method works surprisingly well.

If the weather is warm, you're still not beaten. Hold the curved crystals of two watches of similar size, or even such compass crystals, back to back. It does not matter if these are made of unbreakable plastic instead of glass so long as they are clear. Fill the space between the crystals with clear water. Then hold this contrived enlarging lens so as to converge the sun's rays in a point hot enough to start tinder glowing. Blow the glowing tinder into fire in both cases, and you're in business.

FIRE FROM GLASS

Forest fires are occasionally started by the sun's shining through a discarded bottle, especially if this has been partially filled with rain or melting snow, and from broken segments of such a bottle, particularly the ends. It follows that you can often find in your outfit such a bottle to use with clear water, or a bottle whose sides or bases contain sufficient distortions to pinpoint the brightly shining sun.

Lenses taken from binoculars, telescopes, telescopic rifle sights, and cameras are excellent for magnifying the sun to produce fire. A little pocket magnifying lens will also turn the trick.

WHAT ABOUT PLASTIC?

I've been experimenting with a nine-by-twelve sheet of plastic, sometimes called a full page magnifier, which is obtainable from mail-order houses.

Even with somewhat clouded sunlight this starts a fire in short order. It is thin, light, flat, and unbreakable, making it a likely candidate for a personal survival kit.

FLINT AND STEEL

The flint and steel of buckskin years still work today. The spark may be made by striking the back of your knife against a piece of flint, perhaps the top or bottom of a match case. If there is no recognizable flint in your vicinity, experiment with other hard stones. Quartzite, jasper, nephrite, obsidian, iron pyrite, jadite, and agate are among the rocks that will work.

You don't even need a knife, of course. Any steel or iron will work. Holding your hands closely over your dry tinder, strike flatly with your knife blade or other small piece of satisfactory metal with a sharp, downward scraping motion so that sparks will skitter into the middle of the tinder.

SPARKS FROM TWO ROCKS

The Eskimo in northern Canada often carries two fist-sized chunks of fool's gold. This iron pyrite is easily recognizable because it looks more like flecks of gold than many a piece of gold-bearing quartz itself. To get a spark, just strike the two rocks together.

If no fool's gold is at hand, try to find two other rocks that will give sparks when briskly stroked together. Many have this property.

SPARKS FROM A BATTERY

Sparks for beginning a campfire can also be generated by bringing together, as with wire, the positive and negative poles of a battery. You can even do this with little flashlight batteries. Better is the more highly developed electrical system of a downed plane, stalled automobile or boat.

Be careful in these latter instances, though, of spilled gasoline. Yet with care a small amount of gasoline can be successfully used in starting a fire with an electrical spark, as for example when a gasoline-soaked rag or clump of moss is used as the tinder.

USING A LIGHTER

A cigarette lighter is tops for firemaking—as long as the flint and fuel last. A glowing cigarette lighter from the dashboard of a stalled car will, while battery power remains, readily start a blaze.

AMMUNITION

If you have ever shot a firearm at night, you may have been startled by the tongue of flame issuing from the barrel. Here is another firemaking technique that will work, although you may have to try several times. Modern progressively burning powders, particularly when they lack the resistance of a projectile which you will have removed and replaced with a dry shredded bit of cloth, perhaps from your clothing, have the tendency of blowing out

Start a flame by firing a shell in which a dry bit of cloth has replaced the shot and wadding.

of the gun barrel partially unburned in lieu of lighting either the top portion of the charge or the tinder.

The bullet may be removed before you make the first campfire attempt. You can loosen it by laying the cartridge horizontally on a hard surface and tapping the neck all around with the back of your knife. If you have a shotgun instead, uncrimp the top of the shell and remove both wadding and shot or other projectile. Stuff the cloth in either's place.

If you are at first unsuccessful, try to use the same cloth in subsequent attempts, as the charring it will likely initially receive will make it easier to light. It will help, too, to pour about half of the powder, cordite, or nitrocellulose into the tinder.

Shoot straight upward. The rag will most likely not be burning when it falls to the ground nearby, but it may well be smouldering sufficiently that, when shoved into the midst of the tinder, it can be blown into flame.

GUNPOWDER AND STONES

Place the powder from several shells or cartridges in tinder at the base of a pile of firewood. Take two rocks, sprinkling a little powder on one of them. Then grind the two rocks together immediately above the powder at the base of the fire-makings. This will ignite the powder between the rocks and, in turn, the larger quantity in the tinder.

PYROTECHNICS

These are an excellent fire source although care must be exerted in their use both for reasons of safety and in avoiding needless waste. A signal used for starting a campfire is one that can not be used to attract help. A railroad fusee or the night end of a day/night signal will produce an instant flame.

If you have a fusee signal flare in your outfit, light it by striking the self-contained flint and steel. Although this may mean wasting a signal, you can ignite a campfire from the flame.

CANDLE

A longer, hotter, more substantial flame can be obtained from a candle than from the match that is needed to light the wick. Also, a candle burning in a tin can will give both effective heat and light in a small shelter in moderate weather. One, too, may be effectively added to the survival kit.

THE BOW AND DRILL TECHNIQUE

Fire can also be started by friction as with the bow and drill technique or the fire thong, although these are the most difficult methods of all. But you may be in a spot sometime when you have to rely on a bow and drill to save your life.

Make a strong bow, strung loosely with a shoelace, thong, or string. Use this to spin a soft, dry shaft in an easily handled block of hardwood. This will produce a powdery black dust which eventually will catch a spark. When smoke begins to rise, you should have enough spark to light your fire. Then lift the block, add tinder, and begin blowing on it. Sound easy? Then let's consider the details that are important to success.

THE WOOD TO USE

In North America, both the drill and the fire board are often both made of one of the following woods: fir, balsam, cottonwood, white or red cedar, linden, tamarack, cypress, basswood, yucca, poplar, and willow.

THE DRILL

The drill can be a straight and well-seasoned stick about one-half inch thick and about twelve to fifteen inches long. A longer drill is too difficult to press effectively into position for twirling by bow alone.

The top end of the drill should be as smoothly rounded as possible so that it will turn in the socket with the least possible friction. On the other hand, a maximum of friction is desirable at the other end. This end consequently will be blunter.

It is interesting to note that a longer drill, perhaps one three feet in length, is sometimes used when it is to be rotated between the palms rather than by a bow. The hands, pressing downward as much as possible, are rubbed rapidly to and fro over the drill so as to spin it with the utmost strength and speed. If you are ever in a position where you can not somehow fashion a thong, if only from your clothing, this method is one to remember. But it is less effective than the technique with bow and socket.

THE SOCKET

The sole function of the socket is to hold the top of the turning drill. Inasmuch as it is grasped with one hand, it may be an easily held knot of wood with a hollow formed in its underneath. It may also be a block made for that very purpose. Or if you are near water, it is often possible to find a slick stone with a smooth depression eroded in one side.

The socket may be oiled or waxed with native materials such as animal fat or bayberries to permit the drill to rotate more freely.

THE BOW

The bow may be made from a limber stick which, if strung more tightly, could be used to shoot arrows or darts. More often, however, you would use

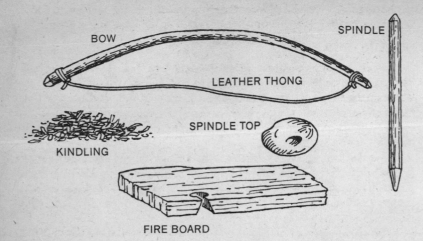

Implements of the bow and drill method of firemaking

a substantial segment of branch with a natural crook already in it.

One end of the bow may have a natural crotch or branch stub that will make the tying on of the thong easier. Or the bow can be notched for this purpose. If you are using one to experiment with by the fireplace, a heavier stick can be drilled to allow the insertion of the then knotted cord.

The bow string, which may be anything from a shoelace to tightly braided strips of clothing fabric, is tied at both ends with enough slack remaining to permit it to be wound once about the drill.

This works well with rawhide, but when cord, especially that of nylon, is used, the cord mostly slips on the drill. A second loop of the cord around the drill makes the bow want to twist out of position. A solution might be to use two cords, one tied to the drill at the top and one at the bottom, wound on the drill to meet in the middle.

THE FIRE BOARD

The fire board can be split out of a dry log and then split again, and may be whatever size you can handle easily. You'll want it to be long enough to be held under one of your feet.

Using a knife, hatchet, ax, or even a sharp stone, begin a hole some three-fourths of an inch in from the edge of the fire board. Round out this hole, at the same time fitting it to the end of the drill, by turning the drill with the bow.

Finally, cut a notch through to this cup from the edge of the board. The sides of this slot generally slant so that it is noticeably wider at the bottom, permitting the hot black powder that is produced by the drilling to fall as rapidly as possible into the tinder that is laid at the base of the notch.

DRILLING FOR FIRE

Tinder is massed beneath the slot in the fire board. If you are right-handed, kneel on your right knee and put your left foot as securely as possible on one end of the fire board. Take the bow in your right hand. Loop the string once around the drill or perhaps, as suggested above, use two cords to avoid slippage. Place the drill in the concavity made in the fire board.

Hold the drill in position with the socket which you grasp in your left hand. You'll likely discover that you can maintain more steady pressure on the drill by hugging your left leg with your left arm, keeping your wrist against your shin. Press on the drill, not enough however to retard it, when you begin spinning it to and fro with the bow.

Draw the bow back and forth in smooth sweeps, making these as long as the string will conveniently allow. At this stage you might try dropping a few grains of sand in the hole to build up the friction. In any event, the

Using the bow and drill technique to start a fire

hole will eventually start to smoke. Spin the bow even more rapidly now, never ceasing the swift even motion. Press down more determinedly on the drill.

Hot black powder will start to spill into the tinder. Continue drilling, for the stouter a spark you can start reddening there, the more speedily you'll be able to blow it into fire.

Everything finally will seem ready. Then carefully remove the drill. Blow gently into the slot until you can see a glow. Then lift both tinder and fire board if that is easiest. Press the tinder easily about the gleam. When the spark finally begins spreading, lift the board out of the way so you can fan and blow on the heat more freely. Gently continue feeding air to the area until the tinder bursts into flame.

FIRE THONG

The thong can be a strip of dry rattan, preferably about one-fourth inch in diameter and some two feet in length. You'll also need a dry stick.

Prop the stick off the ground on a log or rock. Split the elevated end of the stick, holding this open with a wedge. Place a small wad of tinder in the

Starting fire with a thong

split, leaving enough room behind it to insert the thong. Then, securing the stick with your foot or knees, work the thong rapidly back and forth until the tinder starts to glow, whereupon it will be possible to blow it into the flames.

CARRYING FIRE

Especially if you have to depend on such primitive friction methods to build your blaze, you'll want to carry the makings of the next fire with you if possible. This can be done by igniting dry spongy wood that, similar to the punk sold for setting off firecrackers, smoulders for a long time. You can wrap this fire stick and bring it with you, ready to be blown into flame when the next campfire has been laid.

TINDER

The fire, particularly if the spark for it has been hard won, should be started in some fine, dry, highly inflammable material. Cotton fluff from your clothing will do. So will lint from unraveled clothing, cotton, twine, rope, or first aid gauze bandages. Absorbent cotton works well. So do gasoline-impregnated rags if you stay well away from the main source of supply.

Nature affords even more tinders. Pulverized Arctic cotton grass tops are fine. So is dry dead grass or so-called witch's hair. The dry fluff from pussy willows, available autumns and winters as well as spring in many localities, makes a good tinder. So does the down from such edible plants as milkweed and fireweed.

A handful of extremely dry evergreen needles, especially if they have been rubbed and broken together, will do. So will a part of a forest tree that has dry-rotted and can be powdered. Dry lichen and moss are frequently ground into powdery substances for use in fire-starting. Dried mushrooms and other fungi can also be pulverized for such a purpose. The edible giant puffball has dry spongy threads that provide excellent tinder.

Dry evergreen needles, twigs, birch bark, wood shavings, and fuzzsticks provide tinder for speedy firemaking.

The Indians often turned for tinder to the dried pith from the insides of elderberry shoots, which, incidentally, is poisonous to eat. Other suitable desiccated substances may be obtained from bird nests. The down found in these nests, as well as the undersides of certain birds you may be securing for food, is also efficacious. So are fine bird feathers. So are the dry powdery droppings of bats, often at hand if you have taken refuge in a cave.

Strips of birch bark can be pulled apart in the thinnest of layers and shredded for firemaking. The dry barks of some of the cedars is also utilized in this fashion. You can use the fluff of the eminently edible cattail, as well as many a dried and pulverized wild vegetable fiber.

Field mouse nests make excellent tinder if they are bone dry. So will the fine wood dust produced by insects, often prevalent under the bark of dead trees.

You may be able to make your tinder even more volatile, when the time comes to use it, by spattering it with a few drops of gasoline or by mixing it with a few grains of the powder from a carefully dismantled shell or cartridge. Even a bit of pulverized charcoal scattered among it will help to hold the spark.

Once you have fire, you can ready tinder for future fires by charring a bit of cloth in some such closed container as a lidded can or even a ball of mud. Then for the next fire, as soon as your primitive apparatus starts a portion of the cloth glowing, place it hurriedly into a bed of tinder and breathe and blow it into flame.

KEEPING YOUR TINDER DRY

The tinder must be absolutely dry. This property is not always easy to find, as tinder is prone to absorb moisture readily from the atmosphere. It is a good idea in humid country to carry a supply of tinder on your person, in such a manner that it will not be dampened by outside wetness or by perspiration. Expose it to sunlight on bright days.

Man has been doing this since he came groping out of the cold of fireless eons. Many of these tinders were carried, and some still are, in special containers such as the antique shop's tinderboxes, horns, pouches, and other such receptacles. I use a little rawhide bag, with a leather drawstring, originally intended to encase a fishing reel.

Suppose you have had to swim a river. You are soaking wet, and you need a fire in a hurry. Then, especially if materials are scarce, be sure to hold the tinder high enough when you light it so that water won't run down from your clothing and your body to nullify all fire-starting attempts.

FUEL

Having considered the many ways of achieving a spark and the numerous tinders in which this can be blown into flame, we come to the third ingredient of the lonely campfire — fuel. These, too, are almost limitless.

Wood is the most common fuel by far in the wilderness and if you are starting your fire with it under emergency conditions — when if you are using matches, you must almost always do the job with one — it will pay you to make fuzzsticks, firesticks, feathersticks, or whatever you call them.

These are surer and more effective than just bare kindling, and with practice you'll be able to manufacture three or four of them in half as many minutes. In the North I use them every morning to start the fire in my log cabin stove, and it is a mark of courtesy in these regions always to leave kindling, firewood, and a few fuzzsticks when you quit a cabin in the bush.

The fuzzstick is made by shaving a stick of dry kindling again and again, leaving the ribbons of wood attached so that they curl away from the parent stick in a sort of fan. You'll need at least three of these, and if conditions are drastic I commonly add another one to start the blaze with even more sure swiftness.

You can lay your fire with the fuzzsticks at the bottom, angling these upward for better draft and so that you can get the match under them. Atop of these will be progressivley larger fuel, crisscrossed or peaked so that plenty of oxygen can reach the upward-licking flames. This way takes a little more time, but it is a surer method, and the heaped firewood also serves to protect the light against the wind although, it should be noted, it is generally most satisfactory to light your fire from the windward side.

Or, if you are in a bit more of a hurry and are an old hand, have the fire materials at hand. Light one, then another of the fuzzsticks, and lay them in a well-ventilated pile, building the fire as it is burning with larger and larger fuel. This way, too, you can control the starting fire better.

WHICH WOOD TO USE

The numerous softwoods, particularly when time is taken to split them, will quickly laugh into a cheery campfire, not good for most cooking but satisfactory for boiling a kettle and for rapid toasting or grilling.

For steadier and less flamboyant heat, the hardwoods are more long-lived. Coals are best for most cooking, and for a glowingly enduring bed you'll likely select such wood as oak, ash, and hickory whenever possible. Split green birch, which burns with such a sweet black smoke that it is sometimes used in the tanning of leather, is particularly effective.

The difference between hardwoods and softwoods is a matter of botany, not of hardness, some of the softwoods being markedly more solid than some of the so-called hardwoods. Softwoods, such as the familiar evergreens, have different sorts of scales or needles rather than flat leaves.

The resinous softwoods, if they are dry, make the quicker kindling. However, they are short-lived, smoky, and prone to snap sparks. The dry hardwoods, as well as a few living hardwoods like the ash and birch, make a slower, longer, and steadier fire. These serve best for your night fire, for instance. Too, these fall apart into the glowing expanses of red coals that are best for most cooking.

Sparking can be a danger, particularly at night. The worst culprits include both softwoods and hardwoods. In order, they are: white cedar, red cedar, alder, hemlock, balsam, the spruces, the softer pines, basswood, box elder, chestnut, tulip, sassafras, and the ubiquitous willow. It may well be noted in passing that some of these trees are particularly valuable for shelter-making and for eating.

You often have to use one of the above woods because no other is readily available. Then don't make the mistake of adding fresh fuel to the fire in front of your bivouac and leaving the scene even for a couple of minutes. Sparks don't usually do more than char a tiny circle of canvas, so if you have a pack cover or tarpaulin, throw it over your precious sleeping bag. A parachute is also valuable in this respect. So is a woolen blanket if you happen to have it.

In windy weather be careful that a spark does not start a quickly leaping grass or forest fire.

Hickory is the leader among North American woods in heat-generating properties. Oak is a close second. Beech follows, succeeded by the birches and hard maples, the sap and inner bark of both of which are valuable foods as well. Ash is favored by many. Likewise is elm. Then trail locust and cherry.

The above woods are fifty per cent again as effective as short-leaf pine, western hemlock, red gum, Douglas fir, sycamore, and soft maple. They are twice as hot as cedar, redwood, poplar, catalpa, cypress, basswood, spruce, and the decorative white pine.

Many of the barks, such as that from the hemlock, are notable for the steady warmth they will impart. Others, particularly the birch, are hard to excel for starting the fire.

Birch bark is so inflammable that it will light even after being freshly dipped in water. But even in the deep woods, there is no need to scar a birch tree unless you need great strips of the bark for some use other than for firemaking, such as to waterproof a lean-to or to roll a horn by which you can call in a bull moose. To start your fire, just a handful of the wisps that are fluttering on all birches will do.

In wet weather, you can often get things going better if you lay your campfire materials on a dry sheet of birch or other bark and angle more sheets above it to keep the moisture away until the fire is safely crackling.

Even when there is no birch bark in your country, if there are softwoods in the vicinity, you are still well away. The small, dead twigs that characterize the bottoms of all spruce, pine, balsam, fir, and the like are filled with resin and will burn like torches. Just gather a handful of the smallest, straightest stuff, snapping it off with the fingers. Light this and shove it beneath a pile of heavier, equally pitchy dead branches. Then, unless you want just a brief hot fire, you'll probably add some hardwood limbs.

Experimenting with whatever fuel is at hand is often wisest, especially as some species vary among themselves in different parts of the continent because of the prevalent soil and atmosphere. Too, there are numerous separate varieties in every family group, each with its own individual characteristics.

There is a general rule that you can use in selecting firewood if you don't know the various species of trees. The heavier a wood is, the more heat it will throw. This works with green woods, too, an excellent reason for mixing green wood with dry, particularly when you want a long-lasting fire such as at night.

STANDING DEADWOOD

You'll ordinarily want dry fuel. For this reason, you'll normally avoid fallen wood except during prolonged dry spells because it has absorbed too much moisture from the ground. If you have a choice, you'll ordinarily only use this when you want to hold a fire and when excessive heat is not important, as with the night fire in mild weather or with the cooking fire you wish to hold, buried, until you return to camp in the later part of the day.

Standing deadwood is generally the choice, although there are exceptions. Dead birch, for example, rapidly loses most of its heat-generating qualities if the bark has remained around it to hold in its abundant moisture. Such easily toppling dead birch can even be a hazard, and should be pushed over if you are making your camp nearby. The bark will still be good.

A rotten stump is generally of no use except to hold a fire. Again there are exceptions, and a decayed softwood stump may kick apart into tough knots or a hard pitchy core that will burn as if saturated with oil, as indeed they are.

FUEL WHERE NO TREES GROW

Driftwood is often the best fuel in country where no trees are growing. Above the timber line, you can usually find sufficient bush to make your small fire, perhaps in a heel-dent to protect it from the wind. On this continent's great central plains, you'll find yourself using small brush such as the traveling tumbleweed, roots of plants such as the mesquite, knotted clumps of grass, and the dry cattle droppings which are to the modern wayfarer what the buffalo chip was to the earlier frontiersman.

In parts of the far north where driftwood is not at hand, dried chunks of fuel from the great northern muskegs, which are actually peat bogs in the making, are sometimes available. There is also fully developed peat and even coal which, as I can attest, burns with a fine hot flame. In the continental northwest, there are also vast quantities of oil-rich shale and oil sand which burn with a heavy black smoke.

In the Arctic, too, brush and roots are often yours for the collecting. Moss and the numerous lichens can be used for fuel. The small heatherlike evergreen known as Cassiope is so resinous that it will burn while green and wet. If necessary, all these can be secured from beneath the snow.

Fuel in some deserts is so rare that when you find suitable plant growth you'll find yourself utilizing all twigs, leaves, stems, and underground roots. Dry animal dung gives a very hot flame.

No matter where you are, when fuel is scarce, it is sound practice to gather a supply whenever you can.

ANIMAL FAT

Animal fat and bones can be used as fuel, but never make the mistake of burning either of these if rations are short. Fat is surpassed by no other food in caloric strength. As for bones, extremely nutritious marrow can often be extracted from them.

If you do have more than ample food, lay chunks of fat on a framework of bones or sticks, or on the top of a perforated can, with a wick of sphagnum moss or of some greasy fabric beneath. Then just light the wick.

Too, a simple fat lamp can be built Eskimo-style. Fashion a wick of rag, rope, string, moss, or even a cigarette and rest it on the edge of the receptacle.

Blubber from the seals you may be catching for food in the Arctic will make a satisfactory fire without the need of a container if a little gasoline

A large can provides a good makeshift stove.

is at hand to provide an initial hot flame. A square foot of blubber, to give you an idea, will flame for several hours. Then you can eat the shriveled husks of the blubber.

The smoke from a blubber fire is heavily black but not nauseating. The flame is very bright and can be seen for several miles. But although blubber cracklings and even the carbon from seal-oil lamps are edible, the nourishment from them is nowhere near that of the unburned fat, something to remember in an emergency.

OIL

In cold weather, drain the oil from a crashed aircraft or stranded automobile and store it for fuel. Even if you have no apparent means of storage, get the oil out before it congeals, letting it drip on the ground if necessary, as it can be used in the solid state. Too, rags, paper, wood, and similar substances will burn more intensely if they are first soaked in oil.

An Eskimo-style fat lamp will burn this oil, particularly if it has been primed with a few drops of de-icer fluid or gasoline. De-icer fluid itself, incidentally, can be burned in the lamp.

PETROLEUM GAUZE DRESSINGS

If these are in your emergency kit and if you urgently need fire rather than first aid, open at the center, pull up a small portion to serve as a wick, prime with a few drops of something such as insect repellent, and light.

After it has burned dry the wrapper can be used to cook a small bit of meat or fish. Fold the container air-tight. A grill? Bend the wire splint in the first aid kit into any desired shape.

INSECT REPELLENT

If it is winter and you won't be needing your supply of insect repellent, it may provide some heat. Try burning it in a small flat receptable, with a match stick or wooden sliver as the wick.

GASOLINE

Be extremely careful at all times with any gasoline. If you are with an aircraft or automobile you can safely improvise a stove to burn gasoline, lubricating oil, or a mixture of both. Sourdoughs use an improvisation of the same idea, often with a bed of ashes, to warm their vehicle motors before trying to start them on subzero days.

Place one or two inches of sand, fine gravel, or ashes in the bottom of a can or other container and add gasoline. Even with this device, you have to be careful when you light it, as it may initially explode. Make slots at the top of the can to release flame and smoke. Punch holes just above the level of the solid to provide a draft. To make the fire burn longer, mix in oil.

Suppose you have no can or other satisfactory receptical? Then just dig a hole in the ground. Fill the hole with sand or gravel, pour on the gasoline, and light it, always taking care to protect yourself from the usually explosive start.

Remember, a little gasoline poured on balky or damp fuel before it is lighted will help it to begin burning. Never pour gasoline on a fire that is already started, even though it may barely be smouldering. Very severe burns and often death have followed the neglect of this prime safety precaution. Incidentally, no matter where you are or what are the circumstances, keep any gasoline apart from all other liquid fuels in a very plainly marked container.

WAXED CARTON

You can also make a stove from any empty waxed ration carton or, if you have it, from a waxed milk container. Just cut off one end and punch a hole in each side near the unopened end. Stand the carton on its intact end. Stuff an empty sack, or other paper, or dry moss into the carton, leaving an end hanging over the top.

Light this end. Effective? Surprisingly. Burning from the top down, such a carton will boil more than one pint of water or soup.

FORESIGHT

Even if fuel and tinder are so easily available that you need not gather them as you proceed, it is always a good idea to keep an extra supply of both dry in case of storm. Stow this under cover in a handy place near the fire. Once the fire is going well, dead wood that is wet only on the outside will burn readily.

The most desperate condition you'll likely ever come across in wooded country is when every twig, branch, and trunk is sheathed with ice. The solution? Start your fire with birch bark or the dead evergreen stubs that usually remain dry in the bottoms of all softwoods.

Split logs always burn better, and it is interesting to note that you can split many a log with no tool of civilization other than a small knife. Not even that is absolutely necessary. You can utilize a sharp stone, instead. For the splitting, whittle hardwood wedges. Start a division with knife or stone. Then keep driving the wedges into the crack with a rock or club.

DRAFT

Although it does not make so much difference with the ordinary campfire, when you are building a long fire for cooking or for sleeping it's advantageous to lay it in line with the prevailing wind. When you use two logs to confine your fire, perhaps placing them close enough so that pots and pans can be set across them, it's sound practice to lay these in a slender V with the open end toward the existing air currents.

There is something else about campfire draft that is many times even more compelling, especially when you're beset by survival demands. That's the smoke that actually does follow you, not just seem to, as you move around the blaze in an effort to escape it. The reason is that smoke tends to be attracted into the partial vacuum formed by any nearby large object, in this case your body.

One way to get around this is by kindling your blaze against a boulder, ledge, or sandy bank. If you're camping in the open, there is still a way around. Pound two rugged stakes into the ground some twelve inches behind the fire. Against them heap a two-foot wall of logs. Then with any ordinary wind the smoke will climb straight upward, and you'll be able to work in front or at either side of the fire without the nuisance of getting smoke in your eyes. The tier of logs, which may be green, can act as an auxiliary supply of firewood, especially valuable when you want to hold the blaze overnight.

REFLECTOR

If you have an ax and the time, an excellent reflector can be made by leaning green logs against several stout stakes, driven into the ground at

For extra warmth sleep between your fire and a reflector.

an outward slant. If you keep your blaze going long enough, these logs will eventually burn, furnishing more heat. The reflector, too, can be a safe ledge or bank. If the weather is extremely cold, situate yourself between the fire and the reflector.

SINGULAR OR PLURAL?

A single large blaze for warmth is not always too effective unless you build it so that you are between it and the reflective surface, perhaps a ledge. Otherwise, the answer may be two or more strategically placed blazes. Too, the heating fire and the cooking fire, being different in character, are often separate.

The cooking fire and the heating fire may be different in character.

NIGHT FIRE

If you build up your campfire before turning in, you may be able to keep it going all night. It will then afford warmth while you drowse and, in the morning, a carpet of coals that will do for cooking breakfast. There is no certain formula, though, for keeping such a fire alive throughout the dark hours without attention. Sometimes it will hold. But if the heat is necessary for comfortable sleeping, more often than not someone has to pile out around two a.m. to freshen it.

This is not too much of a chore to an old woodsman. He lays on some logs that are already cut, and perhaps he stays hunched up on an elbow for a few minutes. Never does smoke smell so sweet. A coyote yelps. The sparks and fumes go straight up to heaven where gleams Polaris. It's fine to be awake at such a time.

NO BEDDING?

Suppose the night is frosty, but you have no bedding. Then build a large long fire, rake it carefully to one side when you're ready to turn in, and then lie on the warmed ground, or atop a browse bed.

If you ever decide to heat rocks as substitutes for hot water bottles, avoid stones that have been in or near water. The alluringly smooth rocks from brook and river beds are especial offenders, the moisture often caught within them evaporates to steam, thus precipitating splintering explosions.

IN SNOW

The only provision you normally have to make in snow is to scrape or stamp out a depression large enough for your blaze. In extremely deep snow, though, it may be necessary to provide a loose platform of green logs. Snow ordinarily makes things even easier, for you can stop and build your fire wherever there's fuel, at the same time obtaining your water for soup, tea, and such by melting undisturbed snow.

IN THE MOUNTAINS

Here the problem is often a combination of sparse fuel and howling wind. Make a small depression in the ground, narrow enough so that your cooking container will bridge it. Build your little fire in the bottom of the shallow hole. This way you'll be using all the heat with the utmost efficiency.

SAFETY

The ideal place for your campfire is on mineral soil or solid rock. The hazard of fire is always present with campfires on pine needles, muskeg, dry grass, leaves, or even dead roots.

Even after you've extinguished your campfire, a subterranean root can still be burning. This smouldering can continue slowly underground all winter, to burst into flame and possibly a devastating forest fire in the hot days of spring. Roots will sometimes continue to burn in this fashion even if you've kindled your blaze in snow near the bottom of a wind-scoured tree.

When you break camp, make sure your fire is dead out if there is the slightest chance that it may spread. Drown it with water if possible, stir the coals, and drown it again. Pay particular attention to the vicinity where sparks may be glowing.

It is a good idea to break matches once they are used. If they're cold enough to be handled this way, they are safe.

Speaking of safety, open fires are prohibited in some regions during the dry season. If there is a lookout your campfire may be spotted and men, who'll be your rescuers, dispatched to the scene.

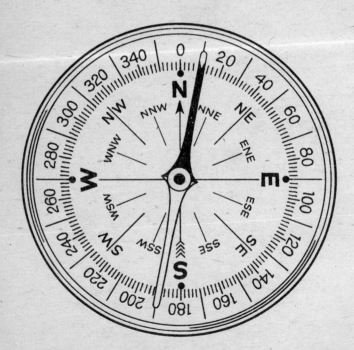

Your compass is one of your most valuable survival tools.

Direction 4

The greenest tenderfoot who utilizes the direction-maintaining methods considered in this section will, from the first, be able to find his way through any wilderness at any time far better than the Indian or other native who tries to rely on an abstract sense of direction, which scientific studies have shown doesn't exist in man. Instead, the usual native everywhere relies on the familiarity of surroundings, the explanation of why native guides have customarily deserted explorers when faced with country that is new to them.

COMPASS DEGREES

Every circle can be divided into 360 degrees. It is this way, too, with the compass. Compass degrees can be most easily pictured in your mind as 360 possible paths extending like the spokes of a wheel from where you chance to be. Compass degrees are ordinarily numbered clockwise, beginning at north.

East is one-quarter of the way around the dial. In degrees, in other words, east is regarded as 90 degrees. The distance between each of the four cardinal points — north, east, south, and west — is likewise 90 degrees apart. Therefore, south is often thought of as 180 degrees and west as 270 degrees.

Halfway between north and east is northeast. In degrees, therefore, northeast is half the distance between 0 degrees and 90 degrees or 45 degrees.

There will be times when you'll want to designate directions even more closely. You can do this by splitting the already determined eight points, giving you sixteen in all. Named with equal logic, halfway between north and northeast is north-northeast. The nearest of the four cardinal points always comes first in the nomenclature. Halfway between west and southwest, for example, is west-southwest.

Some compass dials are broken down into thirty-two points. Halfway between north-northeast and northeast, for example, becomes northeast by north, and so on.

YOUR COMPASS

It needn't be expensive, but it should be rugged enough to withstand ordinary hard usage if necessary. By all odds, it should have a luminous dial. If not, the night may sometime come when you have to waste unnecessary time and matches to keep located. I like a small compass that pins on so that the face is horizontal, always ready for a quick check. Too, this sort of compass has the advantage of being attached to the clothing and thus being less easily lost or mislaid.

Despite the preponderance of natural direction signs, it is always assuring in sheer wilderness to have a second compass with you, perhaps as mine is, in the hilt of your knife. A spare compass may prove almost as vital under survival conditions as an extra waterproof case filled with matches. Both only cost around a dollar apiece and are worth far more than that in reassurance alone.

The time may come, too, when you seriously question the accuracy of one of your compasses. Then place or hold both compasses level. Keep them well apart and as far as reasonably possible from any metallic objects. See to it that the needle or dial of each is wavering freely on its pivot.

If there should be any marked difference between the two, travel by the instrument whose indicator quivers more freely, in gradually shortening arcs, before oscillating to a stop. If you still have doubts, pinpoint north to your own satisfaction by one of the methods discussed later, and compare that to the compasses.

In winter particularly, ample time must be allowed for the needle to complete its swing. It will do this slowly and sluggishly, but taking a bearing can not be hurried if it is to be accurate. If you'll keep the compass warm, this will speed the taking of bearings.

An important point to remember, though, is always to make sure that no iron or electrical field such as a gun or transistor radio, is close to your compass. Iron ore, too, can throw you off. You can check this by observing whether the distance from compass to rock will change your compass reading.

WHICH NORTH?

There are two norths, true north and magnetic north, the first situated at the North Pole and the second located at the magnetic pole some fourteen hundred miles away near the shallow Northwest Passage. We're interested in true north, but our compasses point to magnetic north.

This problem is further complicated by the fact that the magnetic north isn't stable but is drifting all the time. Yet for all purposes of everyday travel in the unmarked places, an ordinary little compass costing perhaps a dollar or two is entirely sufficient. The only allowance you usually have to make is to allow for the difference between the two norths in a particular region, so as to follow more easily the maps of that locality. This declination is generally noted on the map itself.

Despite the fact that the above is not technically accurate, it is exact enough for day by day travel. As a matter of fact, the whole whirling earth is magnetized, causing the compass variation to differ at various localities. In some spots this magnetic shift may be as much as twenty-five degrees from the declination shown on your everyday map.

In northern latitudes the horizontal magnetic field is weaker than it is farther south. For this reason, it is most important to make certain that the compass is not affected by the iron mass in the ground, by nearby equipment, or by magnetic objects on the observer such as a battery-operated watch.

CHECKING YOUR COMPASS

Only in a narrow strip that passes through the Great Lakes does the compass point to true north, yet allowing for this declination when reading a map is simple in the extreme. Just lay the map flat on the ground or other flat surface. Orient the map roughly by placing your compass on it, then turn it until the north-south grid lines are parallel to the compass needle and north coincides with compass north.

Finally, turn the map again until the needle on the compass indicates the amount of magnetic declination for the area. For example, if the decli-

Note the difference between true north and magnetic north.

nation is fifteen degrees east, true north is not where the needle is indicating but fifteen degrees to the right of the needle.

It's easy enough to find the compass declination at night by seeing how closely the dial or needle points toward the North Star. If your compass does not have a luminous dial, point the way from you to the North Star with a scratched line or an angled stick. Then in the morning make your comparisons. If your compass is working reliably, the difference between the North Star and where your compass indicates will be the local magnetic variation.

It is a good idea to note this variation and to check it with the declination indicated on your map. If the difference is less than three degrees, check again before noting the change on the map. If even a small difference of slightly more than one degree is constant, however, it will be a good idea

Using the North Star to check magnetic declination

to adjust your reading of the local map to correspond with your observations.

Checking magnetic declination can be very important to the traveler who's suddenly stranded in the wilderness, especially if he has been covering vast distances by plane. Much of North America, particularly in the Far North, has not been accurately mapped magnetically. Small local variations that would not mean much to a swiftly flying pilot can be of great concern to the man travelling twenty-five miles a day on foot.

If you're neither using a printed map nor paying any particular attention to such natural signs as the sun, it's entirely feasible to travel all day from the direct readings of the compass, not taking declination into account. If

you head out by compass north from a river, for example, you'll return by
compass south, although for practical reasons you'll like to return either
slightly west or east of south so that when you reach the river you'll know
precisely which way to turn.

POLARIS

In the Northern Hemisphere one star, the North Star, is never more than
roughly one degree from the Celestial North Pole. In other words, a line from
any observer north of the equator will never be but slightly more than one
degree from true north. This single night star has saved more lives than
any other.

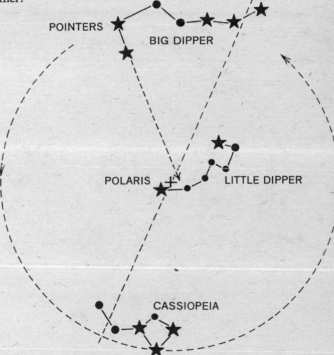

To find the North Star, first locate the Big Dipper or Cassiopeia.

The easiest way to locate Polaris is by finding the Big Dipper, usually
prominent in the northern heavens. The two stars on the outer edge of the
Big Dipper, called the pointers, lead the eye upward almost exactly to where
the Pole Star twinkles by itself.

No matter when the Big Dipper is seen, a line joining the two stars forming
the side of the bowl of the dipper farthest from the handle, if extended five

69

times its length, will end near the North Star. This guiding star is about the same brightness as the pointers, and there are no bright stars between. The pointers are about five degrees apart.

Suppose the Big Dipper is obscured by cloud cover? Then find Cassiopeia, the big M or W, depending on its position in the northern skies. The North Star is always the same angle away from Cassiopeia. It is a sound idea to memorize this relationship.

LITTLE DIPPER

You can check your find as the North Star by the fact that Polaris is the bright star at the free end of the handle of the much dimmer Little Dipper. This constellation, not as easily found as the Big Dipper and easily missed

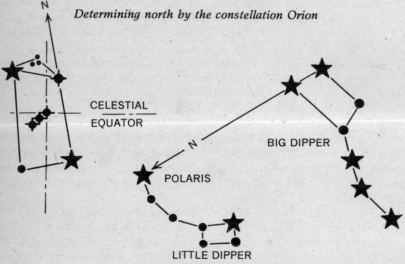

Determining north by the constellation Orion

Polaris in relation to the Big and Little Dippers

in slight cloud cover or in the brilliance of bright moonlight, or northern lights, pours its imaginary contents into the Big Dipper and vice versa. Seven of the eight stars forming Ursa Major outline a dim but definite dipper.

ORION

The belted brightness of the constellation Orion is made up of seven stars. It is the three which are close together in the middle of this group that make up the Belt of Orion.

The one of these stars on the end nearer the shorter height of Orion, indicated by the north-south line of the illustration, lies directly on the Celes-

70

tial Equator. This means that no matter where you are on earth, this star will rise due east of you and set due west.

DIRECTION FROM THE SUN

The sun, of course, rises in the east and sets in the west. The only trouble is that it does this in different positions every day of the year, depending not only on where you are, but on the geography of your location. At the same latitude, that is, you'll see the sun earlier and later on the prairies than in a mountain valley. The difference will differ greatly, too, depending on whether you are in the south or north in the Land of the Midnight Sun.

The sun rises precisely in the east and sets exactly in the west, over the ocean or flat country, only two days every year. These two annual events, known as the equinoxes, fall approximately on March 21 and September 23. Then the equator bisects the sun's center, and day and night are therefore both twelve hours long.

At any time of the year you can, with a little help, find north by observing where the sun rises and sets. The table on the following pages shows the true bearing of the rising sun and the relative bearing of the setting sun for all the months of the year.

For example, on January 26 your position is 50 degrees north and 165 degrees, 6 minutes west. Entering the table at that date and under 50 degrees latitude, you find that the azimuth or true bearing of the sun is 120 degrees. Inasmuch as the sun is rising, you know that this is the true bearing of the sun from north. Therefore, north will be 120 degrees to your left when you are facing the sun.

Suppose you want to find north from the setting sun? Then consider the same problem as above. However, in this case, the azimuth of the sun is not the true bearing. It is, instead, a relative bearing. Since the sun sets in the west, north must be to the right of the sun. Therefore, north will be 120 degrees to your right when you face the sun.

The table does not, of course, list every day of the year, nor does it tabulate each degree of longitude. If you desire accuracy to within one degree of the true bearing, you'll have to do some figuring from the comparative values listed. For all practical purposes, though, using the closest day and the nearest degree of latitude listed in the table will give you an azimuth which will empower you to hold your course.

For example, if you are at 32 degrees north latitude on April 13, the azimuth of the rising sun is actually 79 degrees, 22 minutes. However, by entering the table with the nearest day listed, April 11, and the closest latitude, 30 degrees, you get 81 degrees as the true bearing of the rising sun. This value is certainly accurate enough for purposes of foot travel.

AZIMUTH OF THE RISING AND SETTING SUN

Latitude	Jan 1	Jan 6	Jan 11	Jan 16	Jan 21	Jan 26	Feb 1	Feb 6	Feb 11	Feb 16	Feb 21	Feb 26	Mar 1	Mar 6	Mar 11	Mar 16	Mar 21	Mar 26	Apr 1	Apr 6	Apr 11	Apr 16	Apr 21	Apr 26	May 1	May 6	May 11	May 16	May 21	May 26	Jun 1	Jun 6	Jun 11	Jun 16	Jun 21	Jun 26
60	141	140	138	136	133	130	126	123	120	116	112	108	106	102	98	94	90	86	81	77	74	70	66	63	59	56	52	49	47	44	41	40	39	39	39	39
55	133	132	130	129	127	124	121	118	116	113	109	106	104	100	97	93	90	87	82	79	76	72	69	66	63	61	58	55	53	51	49	48	47	47	47	47
50	127	127	125	124	122	120	117	115	112	110	107	104	102	98	96	93	90	87	83	80	77	74	72	69	66	64	62	60	58	56	54	53	53	53	53	53
45	124	123	122	120	119	117	115	113	110	108	105	103	101	98	96	93	90	87	84	81	79	76	73	71	69	67	64	63	61	60	58	57	56	56	56	56
40	121	120	119	118	117	115	113	111	109	107	104	102	100	98	95	93	90	87	84	82	80	77	75	72	70	68	67	65	63	62	61	60	59	59	59	59
35	118	118	117	116	115	113	111	109	108	106	103	101	100	97	95	92	90	88	85	82	80	78	76	74	72	70	68	67	65	64	63	62	62	62	62	62
30	117	116	115	114	113	112	110	108	107	105	102	100	99	97	95	92	90	88	85	83	81	78	76	75	73	71	69	68	67	66	64	64	63	63	63	63
25	116	115	114	113	112	111	109	107	106	104	102	100	99	97	94	92	90	88	85	83	81	79	77	75	73	72	70	69	68	67	66	65	64	64	64	64
20	115	114	113	112	111	110	108	107	105	103	101	100	99	96	94	92	90	88	85	83	81	79	78	76	74	73	71	70	69	68	66	66	65	65	65	65
15	114	113	113	112	111	109	108	106	105	103	101	99	98	96	94	92	90	88	86	83	82	80	78	76	74	73	72	70	69	68	67	67	66	66	66	66
10	113	113	112	111	110	109	108	106	105	103	101	100	98	96	94	92	90	88	86	84	82	80	78	76	75	73	72	71	70	69	68	67	67	67	67	67
5	113	113	112	111	110	109	107	106	104	103	101	99	98	96	94	92	90	88	86	84	82	80	78	77	75	74	72	71	70	69	68	67	67	67	67	67
0	113	112	112	111	110	109	107	106	104	103	101	99	98	96	94	92	90	88	86	84	82	80	78	77	75	74	72	71	70	69	68	67	67	67	67	67

Month	Date													
July	1	39	47	53	56	59	62	63	64	65	66	67	67	67
	6	40	48	53	57	60	62	64	65	66	66	67	67	67
	11	41	49	54	58	61	63	64	65	66	67	68	68	68
	16	43	50	55	59	62	64	65	66	67	68	68	68	69
	21	45	52	57	60	63	65	66	67	68	69	69	69	69
	26	48	54	59	62	64	66	67	68	69	70	70	70	70
August	1	51	57	61	64	66	68	69	70	71	71	72	72	72
	6	55	60	63	66	68	69	71	73	71	73	73	73	73
	11	58	63	66	68	70	71	72	75	74	74	74	74	75
	16	61	65	68	70	72	73	74	76	75	76	76	76	76
	21	65	68	71	72	74	75	76	78	77	77	77	77	78
	26	68	71	73	75	76	77	78	78	79	79	79	79	79
September	1	73	75	77	78	79	80	80	81	81	81	82	82	82
	6	77	78	80	81	81	82	82	83	83	83	83	83	83
	11	81	82	83	83	84	84	85	85	85	85	85	85	85
	16	84	85	85	86	86	86	87	87	87	87	87	87	87
	21	88	88	88	89	89	89	89	89	89	89	89	89	89
	26	92	92	92	91	91	91	91	91	91	91	91	91	91
October	1	96	95	95	94	94	94	93	93	93	93	93	93	93
	6	100	99	98	97	97	96	96	96	95	95	95	95	95
	11	104	102	101	100	99	99	98	98	97	97	97	97	97
	16	108	105	104	102	101	101	100	100	99	99	99	99	99
	21	112	109	107	105	104	103	102	102	101	101	101	101	101
	26	115	112	109	108	106	105	104	104	103	103	103	102	102
November	1	120	116	113	110	109	108	107	106	105	105	105	104	104
	6	123	119	115	113	111	110	109	108	107	107	106	106	106
	11	126	121	117	115	113	111	110	109	108	108	108	107	107
	16	130	124	120	117	115	113	112	111	110	109	109	109	109
	21	133	126	122	119	116	114	113	112	112	111	110	110	110
	26	135	128	124	120	118	116	114	113	113	112	111	111	111
December	1	138	130	125	122	119	117	115	114	113	113	112	112	112
	6	140	132	126	123	120	118	116	115	114	113	113	113	112
	11	141	133	127	124	121	118	117	116	115	114	113	113	113
	16	141	133	127	124	121	118	117	116	115	114	113	113	113
	21	141	133	127	124	121	118	117	116	115	114	113	113	113
	26	141	133	127	124	121	118	117	116	115	114	113	113	113
	31	141	133	127	124	121	118	117	116	115	114	113	113	113

NOTE: When the sun is rising, the tabulated azimuth is reckoned from North to East.
When the sun is setting, the tabulated azimuth is reckoned from North to West.

FINDING NORTH ANOTHER WAY

You've no compass. You've no watch. The sun is bright. You want to find out exactly where true north lies.

Push a short pole into the ground, making sure that it is vertical by holding a weighted string beside it. Then loop the string, lace, thong, vine, etc. around the base of the pole.

Holding this taut, measure the length of the pole's present shadow. Then tie or hold a sharp stick to the line at this precise point. Draw a half circle,

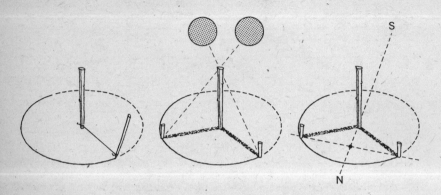

Its easy to find north with no compass or watch.

either starting at the tip of the present shadow or marking this point with a stake.

The shadow of the pole will shorten until it is noon by local standard time. Then it will commence lengthening again. Watch for the moment it once more meets the arc. Mark this point with a second stake.

A line connecting the pole with a point halfway between the first and second marks will run north and south. South, of course, will be toward the sun.

USING THE SHADOWS ONE MORE WAY

Again sometime before midday drive a rod vertically into the ground, checking the alignment of the stick with a makeshift plumb bob. Mark the end of the present shadow with a peg or stone.

Keep on doing this while the shadows shorten, then begin lengthening again. The shortest shadow will run north and south. It should be noted, however, that even with this method you often have to compromise and find your north-south line by selecting a point halfway between two shadows of equal length.

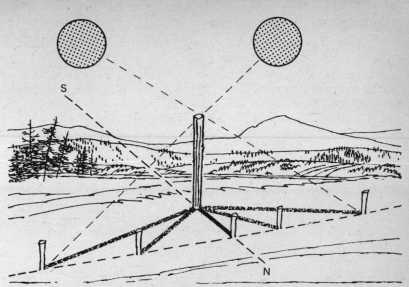

Using the sun's shadow to find north

NORTH OR SOUTH?

Whether the sun is north or south of you at midday will depend, of course, on your latitude. North of 23.4 degrees, the sun will always be due south at noon. Its shadow, therefore, will point north. South of 23.4 degrees, on the other hand, the sun will always be due north at noon local time, and its shadow will point south.

WHERE IS WEST?

There is an even swifter method of telling direction from shadows. All you need is sunlight or moonlight strong enough to cast its shadow. Press or drive your pole or stake into the ground as before.

Mark the top of the shadow, perhaps with a pebble or twig. Five or ten minutes afterward, mark the tip of the new shadow. A line joining the second mark with the first will, in the Northern Hemisphere, point generally west.

With the sun this method is surprisingly accurate during the middle of the day. The line runs a bit south of west in the morning. Afternoons it tends somewhat north of west. During a day of travel by this method, however, these inaccuracies will average themselves out.

TELLING DIRECTION BY ANY STAR

Stars, because of the earth's rotation, seem to swing across the heavens in great east-to-west arcs, like the moon and sun. The way in which any star at all is moving at the moment can, therefore, give you a fairly accurate indication of direction. This can be important if the sky is nearly clouded over, and only a few stars are visible.

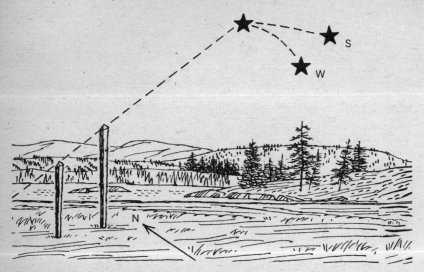

Determining direction by the stars

Begin by taking a sight on any star. The brighter ones will be easier to follow. The orb's movement will be too slow, of course, for anyone to detect just by glancing at the sky. You'll need two fixed points over which to look. These may be two pegs, driven into the ground for the purpose, their tips lined up accurately. If you watch a star over these markers for several minutes, it will seem to be falling, rising, or swinging left or right.

If your star appears to be falling, it is situated just about west of you. If the star gives the appearance of looping flatly toward your right, you are facing approximately south.

If it appears to be rising, you're heading just about east. If it gives the impression of swinging flatly toward your left, then you are facing north.

Make your check with several stars if you want to be sure. Then mark north with a slanting stick or scratched line so that you can head in the right direction in the morning.

LATITUDE FROM POLARIS

Knowing your latitude when you're shipwrecked or down in an aircraft may vastly add to your chances of reaching safety. Even under everyday conditions the process, like many others in this section, can provide some engrossing experiments which, one day, may save your life.

You can find your latitude in the Northern Hemisphere north of ten

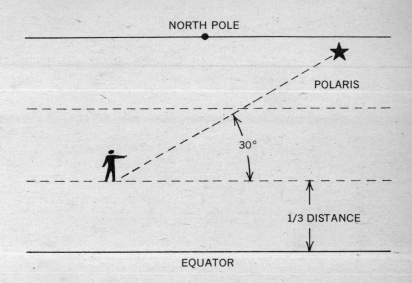

Using Polaris to find latitude

degrees north by measuring the angular altitude of Polaris above the horizon. This works both because at the pole Polaris gleams almost precisely at a ninety degree angle above the horizon, and because at the equator the North Star lies on the horizon at zero degrees.

As shown by the drawing, if you are a third of the way between equator and north pole, a sight on Polaris will reveal that this star lies almost exactly at a thirty degree angle from you.

That's also your latitude, for at whatever angle the North Star lies from you, that is also your nearly precise degree of latitude.

DETERMINING LATITUDE EVEN MORE ACCURATELY

If you have a Weems plotter or some other inexpensive protractor, it will be possible to become amazingly accurate with this Polaris method of determining latitude.

Begin by attaching a thread or string from the center hole of your plotter or protractor. Tie some weight, perhaps a pebble or bit of ice, to the end of the string so that it will serve as a plumb line, giving you an exact vertical.

Now sight along the edge of the protractor at the North Star, holding the protractor so that the thread or string crosses the scale in the zero-degree — ninety-degree section. Subtract the reading of the point where the string crosses the scale from ninety degrees to get the altitude of the North Star.

The figures indicate the angles of zero degrees, forty-five degrees, and ninety degrees between the vertical and the line through Cassiopeia and the Big Dipper. The intermediate positions of the angle may be estimated and the correction taken from the following table. Try it!

DECLINATION OF SUN
IN DEGREES AND TENTHS
OF A DEGREE

Declination is tabulated to the nearest tenth of a degree rather than to the nearest minute of arc. To convert 1/10° (0.1°) to minutes, multiply by 6. (i.e. 27.9° = 27° 54')

DAY	JAN	FEB	MAR	APR	MAY	JUN	JUL	AUG	SEP	OCT	NOV	DEC
1	S 23.1	S 17.5	S 7.7	N 4.4	N 15.0	N 22.0	N 23.1	N 18.1	N 8.4	S 3.1	S 14.3	S 21.8
2	23.0	• 17.2	7.3	4.8	15.3	22.1	23.1	17.9	8.1	3.4	14.6	21.9
3	22.9	16.9	6.9	5.2	15.6	22.3	23.0	17.6	7.7	3.8	15.0	22.1
4	22.9	16.6	6.6	5.6	15.9	22.4	22.9	17.3	7.3	4.2	15.3	22.2
5	22.8	16.3	6.2	5.9	16.2	22.5	22.8	17.1	7.0	4.6	15.6	22.3
6	S 22.7	S 16.0	S 5.8	N. 6.3	N 16.4	N 22.6	N 22.7	N 16.8	N 6.6	S 5.0	S 15.9	S 22.5
7	22.5	15.7	5.4	6.7	16.7	22.7	22.6	16.5	6.2	5.4	16.2	22.6
8	22.4	15.4	5.0	7.1	17.0	22.8	22.5	16.3	5.8	5.7	16.5	22.7
9	22.3	15.1	4.6	7.4	17.3	22.9	22.4	16.0	5.5	6.1	16.8	22.8
10	22.2	14.8	4.2	7.8	17.5	23.0	22.3	15.7	5.1	6.5	17.1	22.9
11	S 22.0	S 14.5	S 3.8	N 8.2	N 17.8	N 23.1	N 22.2	N 15.4	N 4.7	S 6.9	S 17.3	S 23.0
12	21.9	14.1	3.5	8.6	18.0	23.1	22.0	15.1	4.3	7.3	17.6	23.1
13	21.7	13.8	3.1	8.9	18.3	23.2	21.9	14.8	3.9	7.6	17.9	23.1
14	21.5	13.5	2.7	9.3	18.5	23.2	21.7	14.5	3.6	8.0	18.1	23.2
15	21.4	13.1	2.3	9.6	18.8	23.3	21.6	14.2	3.2	8.4	18.4	23.3
16	S 21.2	S 12.8	S 1.9	N 10.0	N 19.0	N 23.3	N 21.4	N 13.9	N 2.8	S 8.8	S 18.7	S 23.3
17	21.0	12.4	1.5	10.4	19.2	23.4	21.3	13.5	2.4	9.1	18.9	23.3
18	20.8	12.1	1.1	10.7	19.5	23.4	21.1	13.2	2.0	9.5	19.1	23.4
19	20.6	11.7	0.7	11.1	19.7	23.4	20.9	12.9	1.6	9.9	19.4	23.4
20	20.4	11.4	0.3	11.4	19.9	23.4	20.7	12.6	1.2	10.2	19.6	23.4
21	S 20.2	S 11.0	N 0.1	N 11.7	N 20.1	N 23.4	N 20.5	N 12.2	N 0.8	S 10.6	S 19.8	S 23.4
22	20.0	10.7	0.5	12.1	20.3	23.4	20.4	11.9	0.5	10.9	20.1	23.4
23	19.8	10.3	0.9	12.4	20.5	23.4	20.2	11.6	N 0.1	11.3	20.3	23.4
24	19.5	9.9	1.3	12.7	20.7	23.4	20.0	11.2	S 0.3	11.6	20.5	23.4
25	19.3	9.6	1.7	13.1	20.9	23.4	19.7	10.9	0.7	12.0	20.7	23.4
26	S 19.0	S 9.2	N 2.1	N 13.4	N 21.1	N 23.4	N 19.5	N 10.5	S 1.1	S 12.3	S 20.9	S 23.4
27	18.8	8.8	2.5	13.7	21.2	23.3	19.3	10.2	1.5	12.7	21.1	23.3
28	18.5	8.5	2.9	14.0	21.4	23.3	19.1	9.8	1.9	13.0	21.3	23.3
29	18.3	8.1	3.2	14.4	21.6	23.3	18.8	9.5	2.3	13.3	21.4	23.3
30	18.0	...	3.6	14.7	21.7	23.2	18.6	9.1	2.7	13.7	21.6	23.2
31	S 17.7	...	N 4.0	...	N 21.9	...	N 18.4	N 8.8	...	S 14.0	...	S 23.1

EXAMPLE: On December 10 the declination of the sun is 22.9° S., so an observer who measures the zenith distance as 0° would know that he is at latitude 22.9°S. If he measures a zenith distance of 5° with the sun south of this zenith, he is 5°north of 22.9°S, or at a latitude 17.9°S; and if the sun is north, he is 5° south of 22.9°S, or in latitude 27.9°S.

LATITUDE FROM THE SUN

You can also use this same Weems plotter or other protractor in determining latitude with the sun.

On any day there is only one latitude on this earth where the sun will pass directly overhead, through the zenith, at noon. In all latitudes south of this, the sun will pass to the north. In all latitudes south of this, the sun will loop to the south.

For each one-degree change of latitude, the zenith distance will also change by one degree.

With a Weems plotter or other protractor, you can use the maximum altitude of the sun to find latitude. This is accomplished by measuring the

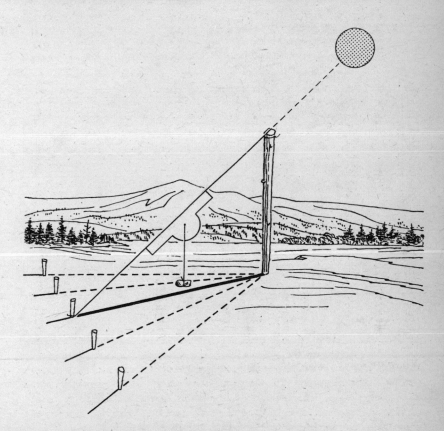

Determining latitude with a Weems plotter

angular distance of the sun from the zenith at noon. To ascertain the exact time of the local noon, use one of the stake and shadow methods previously described.

Easier than trying to hold the protractor at the exact angle is to drive a second pole at the end of the shortest shadow of the first pole, indicating noon. Sighting over the first and shorter pole, either drive the second pole to a distance exactly in line with the sun or make a scratch on it in line with the sun. Connect these two points with a string, as shown Now the angle of the sun can be estimated with the protractor at your leisure.

ANOTHER OBSERVATION FOR LATITUDE

On prairies, desert, or on a large body of water you can find the length of the day from the instant the top of the sun appears above the flat eastern horizon to the exact moment it wheels below the western horizon. Write down these precise times of sunrise and sunset. They alone determine your latitude.

But suppose mountains are to your west and the great plains are to your east. Then write down the exact moment of the sunrise according to your watch. Determine local noon by one of the shadow methods. The length of day will be twice the interval from sunrise to noon. If you're situated differently, with your flat horizon to the west as on the Pacific coast, the length of the day will be twice the time from noon to sunset.

Knowing the precise length of the day, you can find the latitude by using the nomograph illustrated on the endsheets of this book.

FINDING LONGITUDE

You'll also be able to determine the longitude, those vertical lines on maps and globes that run between the North and South Poles. Longitude is represented by either degrees or time, both figured from zero degrees, the longitude of Greenwich, England.

To find longitude, you must know the correct time. If your watch gains or loses, you should know the rate of gain or loss. If you know this rate and the time you last set the watch, you can compute the correct time. Then change the zone time on your watch to Greenwich time, as indicated by the chart if you do not already know it. For example, if your watch is on Pacific Standard Time, add eight hours to get Greenwich time.

You can find longitude by timing the moment when a celestial body, such as the sun, passes your meridian. Determine this moment by stick and shadow as previously described.

Mark down the Greenwich time of local apparent noon. The next step is to correct this observed time of meridian passage for the equation of time —

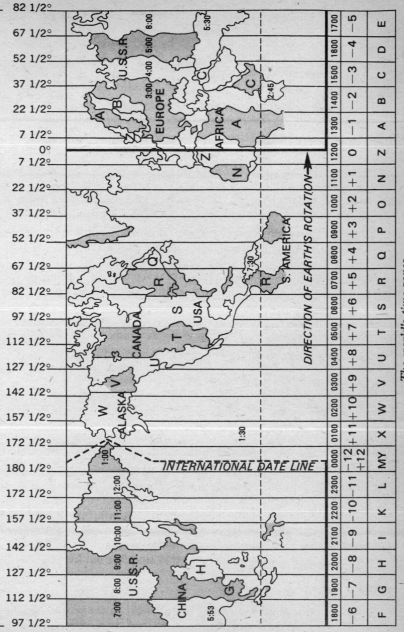

The world's time zones

in other words, the number of minutes the real sun is ahead of or behind the mean sun.

The phrase "mean sun" was invented by early astronomers to simplify the problems of measuring time. It wheels along the equator at a constant rate of fifteen degrees an hour. The real sun, not as considerate, changes its angular rate of travel around the earth with the seasons.

The accompanying table gives the value in minutes of time to be subtracted from or added to the mean or watch time to get the sun time.

Now that you have the Greenwich time of local noon, you can find the difference of latitude between your location and Greenwich by converting the interval between 1200 Greenwich and the local noon from time to arc. If you'll think this over for a minute, you'll see that it isn't as complicated as it may seem at first. Just remember that one hour equals fifteen degrees of longitude. Four seconds, then, equal one minute of longitude.

For example, your watch is on Eastern Standard Time. It normally loses thirty seconds a day. You haven't set it for four days. On February 4, you time the local noon at 15:08 on your watch.

Watch correction is 4 x 30 seconds or plus 2 minutes. Zone time correction is plus 5 hours. Greenwich time is 15:08 plus 2 minutes plus 5 hours or 20:10. The equation of time for February 4 is minus 14 minutes. Local noon is 20:10 minus 14 minutes or 19:56 Greenwich. The difference in time between Greenwich and your location is 19:56 minus 12:00, which comes out 7:56. This 7:56 of time equals 119 degrees of longitude.

Since your local noon is later than Greenwich noon, you are west of Greenwich. Your longitude then is 119 degrees west.

If such a procedure is carried out at 9:00 in the morning standard time, then a line drawn from the center of the dial outward through 10:30 will point south. It is interesting to note that if your watch is accurately set, then the direction will be true within eight degrees, depending upon where you happen to be within any of the 15-degree-wide time zones.

Suppose your watch is set to daylight saving time? Then there is no need to reset it. Just find your north-south line between the hour hand and one o'clock.

If you ever have any difficulty in remembering which end of the line is north, then all you have to remember is that in the Northern Hemisphere the sun swings in an east to west loop to the south. Above the equator, north has to be at the end of the imaginary line that stretches out from the watch.

SETTING YOUR WATCH

You can do that in the wilderness, too, although unless you know where you are in any of the fifteen-degree-time zones and do a little figuring, the time you get will be sun time rather than Greenwich. But, even at the extreme, it won't be far off.

It's easy to set a watch in this manner if you have a compass. Whereas in the previous examples your watch had to be set accurately to determine direction, it is your compass that must be accurate when you are telling time. Therefore, local magnetic declinations must be reckoned with. If your maps do not give this, you can use the North Star as previously considered.

If you are in British Columbia or Wisconsin, for example, and want to set your watch, find due south with your compass. Then, using a twig and shadow to keep the hour hand of your watch pointed toward the sun, turn the hands until south is midway between the shadow and twelve along the shorter arc. Your watch will then be set to within a few minutes of the local standard time.

If you are stranded in the bush with your watch but no compass, you can still proceed in the above fashion by previously determining south, either by one of the previously described shadow methods or from the North Star.

WHO NEEDS A COMPASS?

With all these ways of determining north, who needs a compass? The answer to this question is the same as that to the query, with all the ways there are of making fires who needs a match? Both compass and matches will save you a lot of time.

You may have traveled later than you expected. The overcast night is about a half hour away. From a knoll you can see the chimney smoke curling

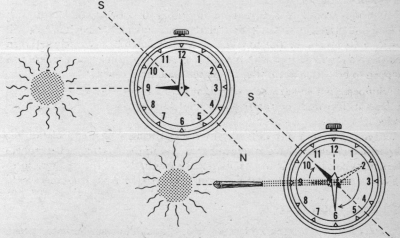

Use your compass to set your watch.

up from your camp, some two miles away through thick spruce. Your compass indicates that camp is due south. So by repeatedly referring to your compass you travel there in a straight line during the remaining dusk, something you'd have found impossible to do unaided in the time remaining. You're home safe, and you've avoided the injury you might have incurred by trying to get through the thick stuff in darkness.

Even where most of the time vision is extraordinarily good, as in much of the mountainous West, you still need a compass. For example, you've climbed the predominant peak after pictures. A cloud blots out all visibility before you can get down. You know that dangerous cliffs suddenly fall away from the slope on all sides but the north. With a compass you make the descent safely.

MAKING YOUR OWN COMPASS

You can even make a temporary compass if you have a small, thin length of steel such as a needle. Stroke the needle, for example, a minute or two in a single direction with a piece of silk or with a magnet.

Next, place the magnetized needle so that it can move freely. To make this a bit easier, rub the needle lightly between thumb and forefinger, first getting these extremities a little oily by passing them over the nose.

Then find some still water, perhaps a sparkling little pool caught in a rock. Take two threads, two thin lengths of grass, or some such thing and double them to make two loops in which to cradle the needle. Lower the needle cautiously into the water. You'll see the top of the fluid bending under the weight of the needle, but the surface tension will still support it.

The floating needle, left to its own devices, will revolve until it extends north and south. If you have stroked the needle from eye to tip, the eye end will point north.

MAP BUT NO COMPASS

Perhaps you'll be able to climb a tree or hill, then turn the map until the rivers, peaks, or swamps look as if they are in the same places on your map as they are on the terrain. Then the map will be turned in the right direction.

In real wilderness, though, it is more likely that you will have to determine north by some direct method such as one we've already considered or are about to consider. Then unless the particular map indicates otherwise, the top of the map will be north, the bottom south, the left west, and the right east.

NORTH IN THE ARCTIC

In the actual Arctic, the North Star is too high above the Pole to help in determining direction. Other constellations must be used, or an extremely accurate determination can be made by shadows.

Hang a rock from the end of a stick slanted into the ground or snow at a forty-five-degree angle, as shown in the illustration. Some time before noon mark the spot where the rock's shadow falls.

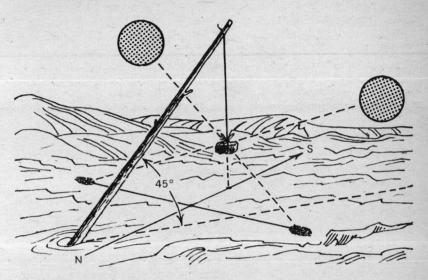

Finding north in the Arctic

Approximately six hours later mark the spot where the rock's shadow is cast by the afternoon sun. Draw a line from the point precisely beneath the suspended rock through a point halfway between the morning and afternoon marks. This line will point to within three degrees of true north.

NATURAL SIGNS SHOWING DIRECTION

In open country, snow and sand drifts are usually on the lee or down-wind side of protruding objects like knolls, high banks, rocks, trees, or clumps of willow. If you know in which direction the wind was blowing when the drifts were formed, you'll have a direction-indicator directly in front of you as you travel. In any event, the angle at which you continue to cross drifts will serve as a check point in maintaining a course.

The snow on the south side of knolls, ridges, and the like tends to be more granular than on the north. You can thus maintain your direction by the sun even when it is not shining, if no new snow has fallen since it shone last.

Snowdrifts and sand dunes also accumulate in such a way that they are lower and narrower to windward. This, too, will help to orient you if you know the direction of the prevailing wind. Even if you don't, this phenomenon can keep you traveling in a straight line.

Knowing the direction of the prevailing wind can also be valuable in country where there is considerable deadfall, perhaps after a lightning-started or man-made fire. You have to take into account, though, the results of unusual storms and the air deviations caused by hills, gorges, and the like.

In the barrens and semi-barren lands of eastern Canada, wind-blown trees point to the southeast because of the prevailing wind. The prevailing wind will also blow away the snow at the bases of drifts to give these anvil-like shapes. These snow anvils point to the northwest.

There is the compass plant, sometimes called pilotweed or rosinweed, whose alternate leaves, attached directly at their bases instead of by stems to stalks five to twelve feet high, hold their edges vertical, generally pointing north and south. The yellow flower heads, several inches across, resemble those of a wild sunflower.

The compass plant's leaves point north and south.

Willows, poplars, and alders tend to lean toward the south unless, of course, the prevailing winds turn them in another direction. Similarly, the tops of such trees as pines and hemlocks naturally point to the east.

The age rings revealed in standing stumps are generally widest on the southern side if, as under ideal conditions, this has been the sunniest side. To make sure of your direction, it is wise to select several stumps of trees so situated that they would have been in the full warmth of the noonday sun and to average the results.

Too, pines, spruces, hemlocks, and other softwoods tend to be bushiest on the south side. Look for single coniferous trees growing apart from others.

The bark of poplar trees is whitest on the south side and darkest on the north side.

Ant hills are always found on the warm south side of trees and other objects.

All vegetation also tells its own tale, growing larger and more open on northern slopes, and smaller and therefore denser on a southern exposure.

Then there is the story told by moss. It does, indeed, thrive most thickly on the shadiest side of trees which, if these are sufficiently in the open where the sunlight can touch them all day, will be on the north. However, certain lichens somewhat resembling moss to anyone who does not examine them closely grows best on the sunniest portions and could cross you up.

FOLLOWING A STREAM

This usually works in well settled country if you take the very important precaution of skirting any swamps on the upwater side. You'll usually find that you can travel more swiftly and with greater ease if you keep to the better going instead of holding to each curve and crook of the stream, following the water's progress as well as you can with your eyes and cutting back occasionally to check it.

In sheer wilderness, though, following even one of the larger streams can take you through some mighty rough going, particularly in country where such running water digs almost impassible gorges, only to bring you to a desolate lake or muskeg miles from any habitation.

As a matter of fact, using any but well mapped water for landmarks in strange country should be only part of the process of establishing one's whereabouts. Small streams in particular loop around so much that you're apt to come upon them flowing in apparently the wrong direction and read the wrong story. Or a similar stream may parallel the first before flowing into it. I spent a confused hour one late afternoon when unwittingly I cut directly across a stream that had gone underground for a mile or so.

WATERSHEDS

In big country a better way to orient yourself than by paying much attention to small streams is by keeping track of the entire watershed. You can go gravely wrong with this system, though, in places near the Continental

Divide where often only a few feet separate waters that on the west may flow into the Pacific and on the east eventually reach the Atlantic.

This happened to me one autumn in Idaho and could have been serious if I hadn't been also using a compass. I had my tent on a river and, having no set destination any day, got into the habit of following some stream down out of the mountains late afternoons until I'd reached a recognizable part of the river.

What happened on this particular day, when I reconstructed the facts, was that I crossed a saddle so low that I paid it no particular attention. But when I started to follow a rill downward that afternoon, I soon saw that something was wrong. That water ended up in another stream fifty miles from where I wanted to go. When I rerouted my way by compass, I saw that particular saddle, insignificant though it was in those high mountains, marked the division of the local watersheds.

THE IMPORTANCE OF MAPS

You can't travel intelligently for any distance in the wilderness without a map even though this map may be one you're sketching as you go or, if you are more of an old woodsman, are keeping mentally.

It is only reasonable foresightedness, therefore, to study whenever possible during any trip a map of the region through which you're journeying. Besides being sound procedure in case you suddenly find yourself afoot and on your own, for some reason or other, such a practice enhances anyone's enjoyment of the drive, cruise, flight, or whatever.

Excellent maps are, as a general rule, remarkably easy to obtain. The multitudes of maps offered free by service stations, oil companies, and the automobile clubs give a good general idea of what to expect where you're going.

If you are flying, there will likely be a map in the pocket in front of your seat, or you can pick up a supply at almost any airport. Knowing what you're flying over will make any flight more interesting, while even cursory knowledge of this sort could save your life if you should walk away from a forced landing.

If you are on an extended hike, you should be armed with one of the maps available from clubs, the government, and other sources. When you plan to camp a few days in one spot, it's a good idea at the very least to have a local inhabitant or someone who's been there before draw a map of the region for you.

Before entering sheer wilderness anywhere it's profitable practice, even when you have what seems to be a good map, to have some old timer correct and supplement it, particularly if you're in one of the vast northern areas where even the most diligent and ambitious surveying crew can do only a sketchy job in the short summer season when they can work. Aerial mapping in many such sections has turned out vastly improved maps, but country looks a lot different when one is afoot.

No matter where you get your map, either be sure of the basic topographical details or do not rely on them. The road you were planning to cut after the day's activities may have come to an abrupt end shortly after you left it. A high ridge you've been using as a landmark for miles may, ahead, dwindle to a level. Even prominent streams sometimes vanish underground just where you've been expecting to spot them.

WHERE TO GET MAPS

They're extraordinarily inexpensive in almost every case. Sectional maps are obtainable from the Superintendent of Documents, U.S. Government Printing Office, Washington, D.C., 20402, and are frequently supplied below cost. This source as well as other suppliers of government maps will generally furnish detailed lists of the availabilities at no charge.

Maps of regions east of the Mississippi River may be secured inexpensively from the U.S. Geological Survey, Map Information Office, Washington, D.C., 20242. This office also handles topographic maps, aerial photographs, and geodetic control surveys for each state, Puerto Rico, the Virgin Islands, Guam, and American Samoa. Most valuable are this agency's contour maps which indicate mountains, valleys, gorges, and other such features in terms of elevation.

For area coverage west of the Mississippi, including all Minnesota and Louisiana, address the Geological Survey, Federal Building, Denver, Colorado, 80225.

Requests for maps of Alaska, originating in that Forty-Ninth State, may be addressed to the Geological Survey, 310 First Avenue, Fairbanks, Alaska, 99701.

Concise maps of all units of the National Park System may be obtained from the Office of Information, National Park Service, 18 and C Streets N.W., Washington, D.C., 20240. Price lists are free.

Nearly three million charts and maps, thirty thousand atlases, several hundred globes and models, and a fifty thousand-card bibliography of cartographical literature are to be found in the Map Reading Room, Library of Congress, First Street and Independence Avenue S E, Washington, D.C., 20540. Information regarding the ordering of both priced and free maps and other publications will be found in the *Library of Congress Publications in Print,* revised annually and obtainable without charge from the Office of the Secretary of the Library at the address given above.

Canadian maps may be had from the government publicity offices in the provincial capitals, from the Government Travel Bureau in Ottawa, and from the Map Distribution Office, Department of Mines and Technical Surveys, also in Ottawa, Ontario.

STAYING FOUND

Just as darkness is merely the lack of light and cold the absence of warmth, getting lost is also a completely negative circumstance. You get lost not because of anything you do but because of what you fail to do.

You stay found by keeping track of approximately where you are. Far from being complicated in practice, this becomes, instead, an ever intriguing problem of angles and distances. Anyone can do it.

At the very least, you can stay located by means of a map, compass, and pencil. Every quarter hour, or whenever you change your direction, will not at first be too often to bring that map up to the moment. You don't have a map? Then sketch one as you proceed.

This is the entire secret. As you gain in experience, you'll do more and more of this mapping in your head.

HOW TO MEASURE DISTANCE

A watch is of particular value in the wilderness, especially under survival conditions, not only because you can tell direction with its help but because it affords the best method of measuring distance. Any watch adjusted to a reasonable speed will do for this latter purpose, although if you wish to be in closer ratio with the sun in determining direction, you can set the watch by one of the previously suggested shadow methods.

Miles as such mean little by themselves in wilderness travel, for a stretch may be across open level country, or it may wind and twist the same distance up and down gorges and through downfall.

Suppose a prospector sets you right one early morning after you've been wandering aimlessly. Where you stand, two trails lead to the road where you're camped.

You ask how far it is along either trail to your camp. His laconic answer, "Ten miles apiece," still leaves you at a loss. If he says instead, "The left trail is an easy three hours. I suppose you could get there along the right path by nightfall if you rustled right along," you'd know precisely what to expect.

Suppose you are stranded on a river shore after a plane crash and decide to stay with the aircraft and its supplies until you find a sure way out. Leaving a note telling exactly what you are going to do, you head generally north for four hours, marking the trail as you go. You probably won't know how many miles you have traversed. But you can be certain that the return trip over the same ground at the same general pace will take another four hours.

THE VALUE OF TELLING WHERE YOU'LL BE

It's a common thing to come across where a lost man has been camped a night or two before, only to find no indication of his present whereabouts. Anyone who's lost or stranded should always leave behind him, before quitting any camp or wreck, the exact information of where he's headed and what he has in mind. The more explicit this data, the better. But even an indicative arrow scratched beside the remains of a campfire may save your life.

The only way to keep from becoming lost is, as we've already considered, to stay found. One preliminary safeguard in the wilderness anywhere is never to go anywhere without making your plans known to someone else or, if you are camping alone, by at least a marker indicating where you are heading. Members of hunting groups would get into trouble far less often if they just observed this primary precaution before leaving camp en masse in all directions each morning.

Even if you park your automobile along a wilderness road for an hour's fishing, it's a sound idea to leave a note under the windshield telling of your plans.

HOW TO FIND A LOST HUNTER

The most practical advice that I have ever seen on this subject was written by Leon L. Bean.

"In case one of your party does not show up at camp when night falls, as has previously been his custom, do not get excited and do not do a thing until 6:00 p.m. If you started signaling before 6:00 p.m. other hunters, who have not gotten into camp, are likely to butt in and make it very misleading.

"Eat your supper and see that the lantern is full of oil. Then go outside with rifle, lantern and flashlight. At exactly 6:00 p.m. fire two shots. Listen a moment for a reply. Not hearing any, walk about one-quarter mile and repeat your signal. If you get a reply, see a fire or note any odor of smoke, continue the signals, always walking in the general direction that you believe your man is located.

"In the meantime what is the 'lost' hunter to do? If, in the late afternoon, he realizes that he is lost or so far from camp that he can not get in, he selects a sheltered spot where dry wood is handy, starts a fire, and collects a lot of wood before dark. At exactiy 6:00 p.m. he listens for a signal. On hearing it, he answers and the signals continue, the same as in daytime. Hearing no signal, he wastes none of his shells but pounds a signal at regular intervals with a club on a sound, dead tree. If there is no dead tree available, select a live tree and peel off a spot of bark where he wants to pound.

"In the morning, if not sure of the direction to camp, he is not to leave the spot or to shoot except to answer his party's signals. Keep a smoke going and pound out a few signals about every ten minutes.

"The party at camp should not stay out too late. Notify a Game Warden or Sheriff during the night and continue the search at daybreak.

"By following these simple rules the lost hunter or his party have nothing to worry about."

THE BIGGEST SECRET IN GETTING BACK

There are, as with every other pursuit, various time-saving shortcuts. The biggest one involving finding one's way back to camp has to do with knowing exactly which way to turn when you reach a broadside such as a road, river, lake, mountain range, etc.

Let's take an example. You're camped, say, on the south shore of a wilderness river which flows from west to east through the backbone of the Canadian Rockies. Such a broadside, incidentally, is the place where under normal conditions you should always try to camp. Then even in a heavy snowstorm you'll be able to find your way safely back.

You take your camera and telescopic fishing rod and walk generally south for four hours. Straight lines, of course, are only a figure of speech in the bush. But by compensating for swings around such obstacles as beaver ponds and by occasionally checking your compass, you can keep traveling in a single direction.

If you return generally north for four hours at the same speed, you know you'll be close to your river. Then camp will be only a short distance away. Perhaps you're acquainted enough with your surroundings to head in the right direction without any delay. But suppose you've never been in this country before. Darkness is filling the swamps and coulees, and you want to be back in camp before there's the danger of walking over a cut bank or getting a dead stick in an eye. What do you do?

The correct procedure of return starts back at your noon campfire. You look over the country. To the west are open poplar benches. To the east are the occasional muskeg and spruce swamp. So you decide to bear west. By heading slightly west of north, say north northwest, you will still reach the river in slightly more than the same four hours. But now you know that camp definitely lies downriver to the east a short distance. The two comparative illustrations make this even plainer.

LOCATING A TRAIL GOING AWAY

The above, wherever applicable, is the biggest secret of finding your way through the wilderness. You can even use it in locating a trail going directly away from you.

You're still camped on the south side of that river, for example, but where the country is thick with fallen burn. So when you leave camp, you head due south along a horse trail that surveyors have cut a year or so previously. You follow this for three hours, then walk another hour at the same pace generally south by compass.

When the time comes to head back, you want to hit that horse trail again. You know that it is an hour generally north. What do you do?

You could travel north by compass for an hour in the hope of blundering on the trail. If you didn't hit it at first, you could begin zigzagging in gradually lengthening traverses, northeast and then northwest, until you did.

Both of these possibilities, however, leave too much to chance. Instead, you head north northwest from the campfire, because that's easier going than north northeast. After a conservative hour and a half, you can be sure that your horse trail lies directly east of you. So you head that way and bisect it after a few minutes.

WHAT ABOUT BLIND CAMPS?

Suppose instead you're camped, alone or in a party, at a spring in dense forest. There are no trails or landmarks. You must find your way back after a day in the bush. How do you do it?

Once more the solution is positive. You first make your own landmarks by blazing a line north and south, and another one east and west, for a mile, say, each side of camp.

During the day you keep general track of your whereabouts so that, when the time comes to return, you can cross one of these lines. Some method of marking, perhaps cutting the higher blaze on the side of the tree nearer camp ("h" for high and for home), can prevent your following any of these radii in the wrong direction.

STAYING ON A TRAIL

There are trails and trails. Even game trails can be useful to a lost man, making for easier going if nothing else. In dry country, such trails may lead to water. In areas where water is no problem, deepening and widening game trails usually lead around comparatively impassible sections. If you're lost, therefore, you'll do best to take the fullest possible advantage of the often centuries-old game routes when they're going in the same general direction you wish to travel, then to leave them when they divert.

A blazed trail is very apt to go somewhere, even if only to a distant trapper's cabin, and will be well worth following if one is lost and wandering aimlessly. When these cuts are old, you'll have to pay particular attention to which marks are indeed blazes and which are made by antler-shining deer, eating moose, or spring bear hungry for the laxative bark of the spruce.

You can often feel the flatness of even a burned ax cut, while in some the telltale flap of bark still remains at the bottom. Too, a trail is ordinarily blazed both going and coming, and you'll be able to check a blaze by the presence of a companion blaze on the other side of the tree.

If you ever find yourself off the trail, be sure to mark the starting point of your search to regain it. Then circle or zigzag out from that particular spot. That way you'll never wander very far from the trail.

When a blazed trail seems to stop, stand still and look forward and backward. Usually you can find the blaze again by determining where you'd have gone if you had been blazing the trail in the first place.

STARTING POINT

When you do not know where you are, establish a starting point from which to begin your search. This may be an oddly shaped boulder or tree, or it may be just a branch or bush that you break on the spot.

This way when you suddenly realize you are lost, you can stay, by retracing your footsteps to this new starting point whenever necessary, within the same general area which usually is not too far from where you are supposed to be. Too many lost individuals walk right out of the country that is being searched.

If your starting point is in totally unknown country, as when you are walking away from a crashed plane, you'll at least be able to keep track of your new position and thus proceed with some method.

LOST NEAR CIVILIZATION

In settled country, where traveling in any one direction, usually downhill and around the upper sides of swamps and such, will bring one out, the lost individual who keeps his head seldom has much of a problem. If he has a compass, he's well away even though he may have to camp out overnight. If he has no compass, he can keep going straight by always keeping two trees or other objects lined up ahead. In mountainous country, all he may have to do is keep a certain peak at his back.

Sound may play a part: a distant locomotive whistle, factory siren, car horn, or even a man chopping wood. As the weather becomes colder, so proportionately does the hearing range increase.

As cold intensifies, one is able to see farther, too. In such regions distant smoke, perhaps viewed from a hilltop or safely climbed tree, with one's keeping as close to the trunk as possible for additional security, will usually mean habitation.

When you're lost, don't make the all too common and often fatal mistake of rejecting a road or power line just because it doesn't seem to be the one you're seeking.

Travel Weather 5

The squirrel, so delicious to a hungry man when broiled over the ruddy coals of a campfire, can be of even more value as a short-term weather prophet. During the winter if you see him and his kin working in front of their houses on a fresh heap of cones, it's going to storm, and you'd better be thinking of making a snug camp rather than traveling — depending, of course, on the circumstances. The bigger the pile, the longer the storm!

But not even the squirrel is of any value as a long-term weather fore-caster. Old wives' tales that if his fur grows especially thick in the fall, it's going to be a hard winter — or if he stores a larger supply of food, the cold weather is going to be prolonged and severe — are just folklore, despite their seeming logic.

Scientific research has found no basis in fact for any of the tales, how-ever charming, that give nature the ability to forecast weather over a long term. The thickness of hickory nuts or the staunchness of goose bones give no clue as to the approaching weather. The thickness of an animal's fur carries no portent weatherwise.

The depth of a bear's den is no indication of what the winter will be. Even when bruin comes out earlier than usual in the spring, only to waddle back to his bed, it doesn't signify more cold blasts but merely that there isn't yet enough fodder for his huge appetite.

When the groundhog doesn't glimpse his shadow on February second, the cold and snow are not necessarily gone for another season. When fat-cheeked chipmunks are particularly industrious in filling their winter caches, it is no true indication that a severe winter will follow.

If such migrating birds as geese, swans, cranes, and ducks could sense the weather for more than a few hours ahead, such great flocks would not be entrapped and decimated by storms or by returning north to their nesting grounds too far ahead of the tardy spring.

SHORT-TERM WEATHER SIGNS

Even if such easily observed natural signs have no bearing on the long-term weather, their short-term value is an entirely different matter. Animals do have built-in barometers which let them accurately forecast the weather a day or two in advance.

Particularly when you consider two or more of these signs together, they can be lifesaving in that they'll give you an accurate idea of when to remain securely in camp and when it will be safest to make that attempt to walk out. Even then, the following two associated proverbs should always be taken into consideration. In dry weather all signs fail. In wet weather it rains without half trying.

Even the smoke of your lone campfire has its story to tell. If it rises steadily, fair weather will be with you. On the other hand, if the smoke is beaten downward after rising a short way with the hot air, it's a reliable sign of an approaching or continuing storm.

If the morning is gray, it will be a good day to travel. The thus-signified dry air, lying above the haze caused by the collection of dew on the lower atmosphere's dust, prognosticates a fair day.

On the other hand, a red sky or red sun at dawn forecasts approaching storm. A red sunset indicates that the atmosphere holds so little moisture that rain or snow within the next twenty-four hours is highly unlikely.

An evening sky that is overcast and gray shows that the moisture-bearing dust particles in the atmosphere have become so laden with water that the state of affairs favors rain.

When sudden green light blinks from the afternoon sun as it descends below a clear horizon, fair weather is likely for at least the next day.

A rainbow or sundog late in the afternoon is a sign of fair weather ahead. However, such refractions and reflections of the sun in atmospheric drops of water, pellets of ice, spray, or mist in the morning are a survivor's warning.

The corona, the usually colored circle appearing around either the sun or moon when one of these is glowing behind clouds, is a dependable weather sign. When this circle expands more and more, it shows that the drops of moisture in the atmosphere are evaporating and that the day or night likely will be clear. A shrinking corona is a sign that the water drops in the clouds are becoming so big that rain is almost certain to descend.

When thin but tight cloud cover slowly enshrouds the moon, the span of good weather is coming to an end.

A night sky bright with stars is a favorable sign. When only a few stars twinkle, the favorable weather is nearly finished.

The loftier the clouds, the better the weather. Indications are even more favorable when only scattered clouds, especially when they are decreasing in numbers, are separated by bright clear blue.

The consolidating of clouds does not foretell as favorably, particularly in an already milky sky.

Frost and dew blanket the ground, bush, and grass in sparkling abundance only when the atmosphere is so dry that snow or rain can hardly fall. On still nights, either frost or dew, depending on the temperature, fail to precipitate only when conditions favor wet weather.

As stormy weather nears, hemp rope, shelter canvas, and wooden-handled ax and hatchet heads tighten with the increasing dampness. Any salt that you may have in your outfit picks up moisture. Curly hair, both in humans and animals, becomes more ungovernable.

The appearance of morning mist lifting from ravines and gorges in hilly or mountainous country is an ideal sign of fair weather. In fair weather, you hunt upward when you leave camp in the early morning and downward when it's time to return to your outfit. This is because thermal air currents drift down hillsides and streams in the early forenoon. They begin flowing back near sunset. Any reversal of these air currents warns of approaching stormy weather.

When distant sounds, like the hoot of an owl, become more audible, wet weather is on the way.

When sounds are audible more clearly, and you can hear distant noises such as the hoo-ho-ho-hooing of a far away owl more distinctly, wet weather is coming your way.

Another sign of a nearing storm is the increase of high winds and their gradual extension to lower and lower climes, causing the mountains to roar and even the forests to murmur.

Insect-eating birds such as swallows feed higher when the weather is to be fair, lower when a storm is approaching.

You can also forcast stormy weather by your sense of smell in that ground, muskeg, swamp, marsh, and tideland odors become more preceptive.

Finally, anyone who has a touch of rheumatics, ulcers, corns, or other such ills can forecast the weather by his sense of feeling. Increasing discomfort will mark the approach of bad weather.

BAROMETER

If you have been flying or cruising before becoming lost or stranded, or if as a dedicated fisherman you have been watching for the rising needle which augurs the most productive casting days, you may have a little aneroid (fluidless) barometer with you. The following table will help you read it.

Barometer	Wind	Weather
High, steady	SW to NW	Fair with little temperature change for one to two days
High, rising steadily	SW to NW	Fair with warmer weather and rain within two days
High, falling rapidly	E to NE	Summer, rain in 12 to 24 hours Winter, snow or rain with increasing wind
Very high, falling slowly	SW to NW	Fair, with slowly rising temperatures, for two days
High, falling slowly	S to SE	Rain within 24 hours
High, falling slowly	E to NE	Summer, light winds and fair Winter, precipitation in 24 hours
High, falling slowly	SW to NW	Rain within 24 to 36 hours
High, falling rapidly	S to SE	Rain, with increasing wind, in 12 to 24 hours
Low, rising rapidly	Shifting to W	Colder and clearing
Low, rising slowly	S to SW	Clearing soon and fair for several days
Low, falling slowly	SE to NE	Rain for one or two more days
Low, falling rapidly	E to N	Northeast winds with heavy rain or snow, followed in winter by cold

CLOUDS AS SIGNPOSTS

Clouds are among the most reliable of the survivor's weather-forecasting procedures. You have to keep watching them, though. Even more important than the formations predominating at the moment is the way a cloud cover changes.

What actually is a cloud? Water molecules condense on dust and other particles in the atmosphere when moist air cools. As more and more of these molecules amass, they become drops of water or pellets of ice. When enough of these drift together, they collect into a cloud. The type of cloud this is prognosticates the weather.

CUMULUS

The familiar cumulus cloud is the fair-weather cloud. Moreover, clear nights generally follow days during which cumulus clouds march graphically and spectacularly across the heavens.

Cumulus clouds are formed by warm air soaring skyward and condensing its water vapor in the increasing coolness of the upper atmosphere, heaping these drops of moisture into flat-based mounds. In late afternoon, when this process slows, such clouds become small or even nonexistent, whereas during the day they measure from about one thousand feet to over a mile high from puffy tops to flattened bottoms.

Cumulus cloud formations

FRACTOCUMULUS

Fractocumulus clouds indicate the presence of high wind, being formed when lofty gales tear the gently amiable cumulus cloud into tatters and hurtle these across the skies. Their speed helps you to differentiate between them and young clouds that have not yet reached maturity. In late afternoon and at dawn when the winds calm, fractocumulus arrays also dwindle to leave a clear, fair sky.

STRATOCUMULUS

Light showers may filter down from stratocumulus clouds. Yet these arrays ordinarily dissipate to cumulus or fractocumulus by the middle of the afternoon, later disappearing entirely to leave a clear night sky. They also form at sunset, however, when cumulus clouds blend into each other before thinning and disappearing. Stratocumulus clouds, spreading in irregular patches or layers, are now as puffy and fluffy as cumulus.

STRATUS

Although stratus clouds often bring light drizzles, they seldom develop rain. On the other hand, when stratus clouds form thinly during the night to cover the morning sky, they generally augur a warm clear day.

Flat on both top and bottom, stratus clouds are layers of water particles. When one nears you, its edge seems to be almost straight and nearly of equal thickness all the way through. Some cover all that can be seen of the sky. Others are small. The thickness of these formations varies, too, from nearly one quarter of a mile to a few luminous feet.

The high coastal fogs of Newfoundland, Maine, and California, compounded by the mixing of cold and of warm moist air above the swirling ocean currents, are stratus clouds that develop nearly one thousand feet above the water and thicken downward. Such fogs ordinarily dissipate in sun-warmed skies.

Yet stratus clouds are predominant when the center of a low-pressure area is approaching. Then the stratus is usually succeeded by the denser nimbostratus, characterized by rain or snow. While the low is passing, the thick nimbostratus may change again to stratus or to wind-broken fractostratus. This latter generally vanishes to leave a clear sky alive with cirrus tufts.

Fractocumulus

Stratocumulus

Stratus

NIMBOSTRATUS

Nimbostratus clouds seventy-five per cent of the time mean rain or snow within four or five hours. The lengths of such storms vary. During the winter months snow often slants down from them for about eight hours.

These layers of dark rain or snow clouds, greying the day, often blanket the sky for miles. Some nearly scrape the treetops, although their average height is some 3,500 feet, while others sail almost three miles above the damp earth. Bits of cloud that surge beneath them are called scud.

CIRRUS

When the morning sky is vividly blue above cirrus clouds, the formations will likely disappear into clear skies before noon. This occurs when the warmth of the morning sun meets the floating ice of these clouds, which take shape some five to seven miles above the earth, turning them to vapor.

Cirrus clouds are like thin wisps and curls of soft hair, some elongated by the wind until only a twist remains at one end. Others seem caught in silvery mesh that nearly encloses the heavens. Those that are blown into wisps are known as mares' tails.

CIRROSTRATUS

When instead the heavens above the cirrus clouds are grey, rain or snow is probably in the offing. Then the formations will probably soon thicken to cirrostratus, indicating that a storm is no farther than a day away.

Cirrostratus clouds, also made up of particles of ice, resemble white veins, often embellished with milky scraps and stains. Both the moon and the sun, gleaming mistily through them, form hazy rings of luminosity known as halos. Such clouds may soar as high as the loftiest cirrus. The largest and thickest of them, however, are generally no more than some eighteen thousand feet above the earth.

ALTOSTRATUS

While the storm area is nearing, the cirrostratus formations thicken and lower to altostratus which either completely envelop the moon and sun or let their brightness through in formless blobs of light. Altostratus clouds resemble grey or dull blue haze, spotted or striped with dense streaks or patches. The snow or rain that generally follows is ordinarily steady but not particularly hard. These formations range in elevation from some two to three and one-half miles.

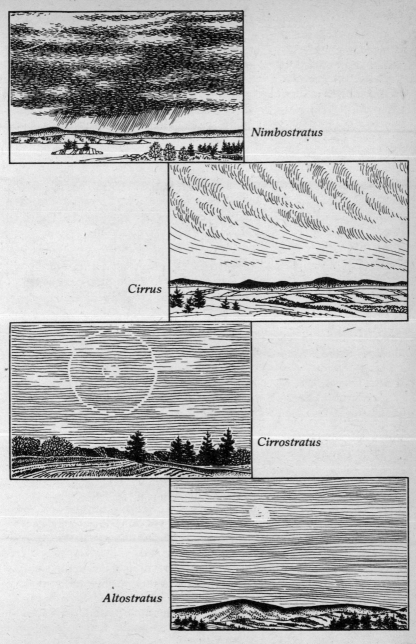

Nimbostratus

Cirrus

Cirrostratus

Altostratus

103

CIRROCUMULUS

Nearly always an omen of fair weather, cirrocumulus clouds generally show up the first or second morning after a storm, commonly dissipating that forenoon to leave a brilliantly blue sky.

The well-known mackerel sky, resembling the colorations on that fish's back, is composed of scudding rows of cirrocumulus. Composed of ice and at heights of three to five miles, cirrocumulus formations are about halfway between the puffy cumulus and the wispy cirrus. They are frequently in the neighborhood of cirrus and cirrostratus. They are so thin that sunlight diffuses through them brightly.

ALTOCUMULUS

Another fair-weather cloud, the altocumulus ordinarily reveals itself on the first day after a storm or comes into being above dissipating stratus. On the other hand, when such altocumulus clouds pile up in towers and castles, it is generally an indication of showers some eight hours away.

The sky often seems packed with the clustered white mounds, so tightly do these high, small, white clouds follow each other. Drifting from one to four miles high, they are occasionally beset by vertical air currents that cut them into flakes not unlike that of a mackerel sky. The underneath parts of these clouds are often gray, however, and the bigger ones dart their shadows across ground and water.

CUMULONIMBUS

Ordinarily forming on hot moist days, these towering mounds of rain clouds often drop hail as well as raindrops. Inasmuch as they also contain thunder and lightning, they are known, too, as thunderheads even when they do not result in precipitation.

Thunderheads begin as puffy cumulus clouds some two thousand feet above the earth, piling and towering into spectacularly portentous mounds reaching upwards of seven miles or higher. When these dazzling white piles are toward the southwest, they can be expected to approach steadily, darkening colorfully as they do so. Blankets of rain also can be seen in the distance. Then the day abruptly darkens and chills.

Later the precipitation abruptly slackens. The thunder again becomes ominous in the distance. Invigorating wind, cool and fresh, drives out of the west.

Even under survival conditions, it is far safer to be in the farther places during the height of the most dramatic thunderstorm than it is at home

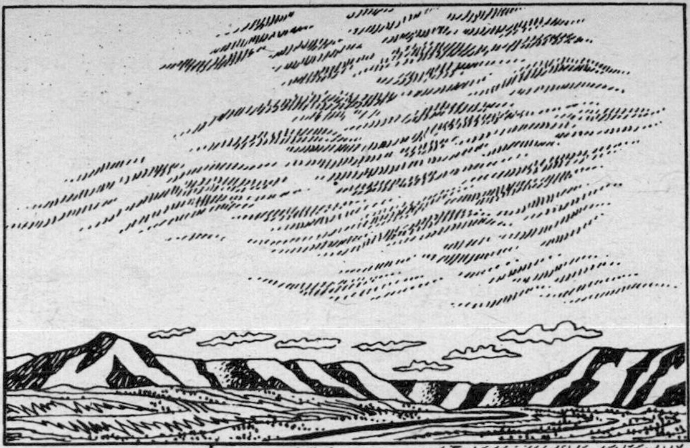

Cirrocumulus

Altocumulus

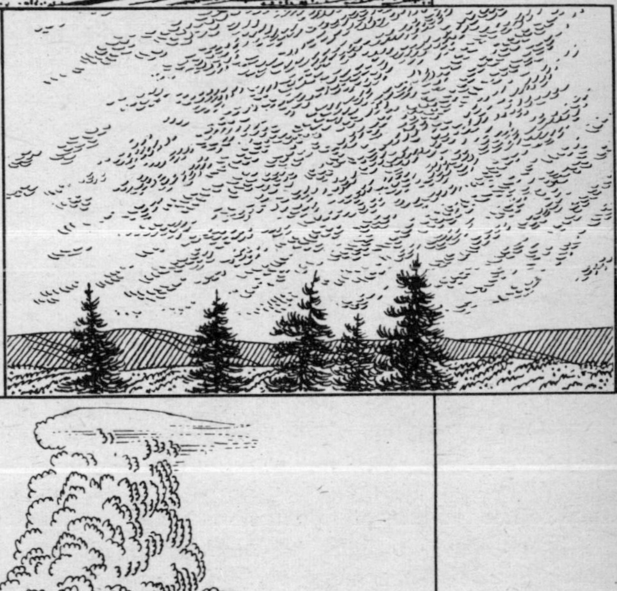

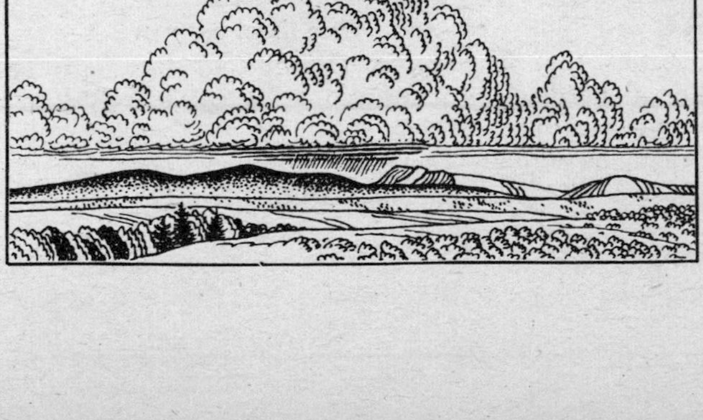

Cumulonimbus

to drive down to the neighborhood grocery. Observing a few safeguards will minimize even this very small degree of peril.

When you seek shelter during a sudden storm, keep away from tall, lone trees which are prime lightning attractions. Small evergreens offer much drier, as well as comparatively safe, cover. So does a cave, a stable over-hanging bank, or even a niche among boulders.

If you happen upon a large airy building such as a barn, keep out of it, as the volume of warm, dry air invites lightning bolts. It is safest to lay down such natural lightning rods as metal fishing poles. If you are caught in the open, your safest course will be to lie prone, perhaps taking your emergency plastic sheet from your pocket and anchoring it over you.

Secrets Of Staying Warm ⑥

Exposure can kill you far more quickly than thirst or starvation. A man in good condition to begin with can last, under favorable conditions, up to about a week without water and a month or more without food, but no longer than a few hours in severe weather unless he takes positive precautions against it.

We have already considered in detail the elemental problems of shelter and fire. What remains is clothing, both what you have the choice of wearing at the onset of your emergency and what you are able to improvise on the spot. One or more of these latter techniques may save your life, while a thorough understanding of the subject as a whole will provide a sound basis of surviving when the weather is cold.

WARM FEET

If your feet are cold, clap on your hat. This may sound jocose, but to those who realize how the human body functions in a cold environment it is a simple statement of fact.

The human body is actually a machine, continuously producing heat through the burning of food or food-storing tissues and then losing this heat so as to maintain a constant temperature within itself.

One way this heat loss is regulated is by the reduction, in ratio to the outer cold, of the blood supply to both skin and extremities. Because the head has such an abundant blood supply, and because it is the only part of the body where this flow is not reduced in frigid weather to conserve the available warmth for the vital organs, it is the major radiator for excess body heat.

If you want to shunt this heat down to the feet, you must make certain it is not lost through the head and, incidentally, through the unmittened hands. Therefore, you put on your hat if your feet are chilly. In this regard, a parka hood is more effective than even a stocking hat because of the way it also protects the neck.

HEAT PRODUCTION

We are actually tropical animals, able to survive in cold climates — where, as a whole, we are actually more productive and efficient — only because our ingenuity enables us to maintain our body temperatures within the limits set by our systems. To do this, we must constantly produce heat.

Our heat comes only from two general sources: our food which, under survival conditions, may be severely restricted; and from absorption of radiant energy from the sun and our lone campfire. There is an important ratio between the food available to you and the extent of your activity, which we'll consider later.

HEAT LOST BY RADIATION

The body must continually lose heat if it is to maintain its necessary constant temperature. There are five major ways it does this, two of them involving perspiration. The other three, accounting for more than three-fourths of the total heat loss, are radiation, conduction, and convection.

Heat loss from radiation on a winter day comes to only about one-twentieth of the total loss. Under a clear night sky, however, the heat loss from the surface of your sleeping bag can be greater than that.

Yet the only heat that can be lost by radiation is that which reaches the outmost layer of the clothing or bedding. The higher the temperature of the radiating surface, as when you're needlessly perspiring, the more rapid will be the loss of heat. If you have good convective insulation, which we'll discuss in a moment, the outer layer will remain cool and there will be little heat lost by radiation.

HEAT LOST BY CONDUCTION

Inasmuch as heat rushes from hot things to cold things, and since the greater the temperature differential the faster the flow, the sole way to prevent conduction from your body is to separate all parts of it from the cold by a non-conductive material.

A non-conductive layer is one that when heated on one side remains cool on the other. For clothing and sleeping bags, the most ideal non-conductive material today is plain, free air. The difficulty with air, though, is that it is always circulating. For example, when the air next to the skin absorbs a bit of heat, it expands and rises. Because nature abhors a vacuum, new and cooler air rushes in to take its place. This is known as natural convection.

Induced convection, on the other hand, takes place as a result of wind and breezes, as well as the bellows effect of clothing as it pumps air back and forth when you move around. Air in all cases, despite its being a poor conductor of heat, becomes a sometimes all-too-active heat transfer agent because of its mobility.

The feet are a major target for heat loss by conduction. So is the body even when you're in a down sleeping bag that, depending only on its own insulation for protection, compresses to an ultra thin layer between your person and the ground because of body weight. So are the unmittened hands while you are engaged in such hurry-up tasks as fire lighting.

HEAT LOSS BY CONVECTION

The air directly next to the body has the tendency to adhere to that surface, which is the reason it's not particularly uncomfortable to hurry from and to a warm sleeping bag on a subzero night with nothing on but shorts and boots. This insulative sheath is about one-eighth inch thick. Therefore, any material which confines air at intervals of one-eighth inch or less will stabilize it so that it becomes an effective insulation.

This principle is important because it emphasizes that there is no miracle insulation. Eiderdown, cotton, Dacron, wool, kapok, and even sphagnum moss, which you'll find by the thousands of tons in the northern wildernesses of this continent, insulate only by the amounts of dead air each contains. One substance, down or moss, is no better than another. Convective insulation depends on the substance's thickness.

For this reason, a cold man trying to survive can keep going a good while farther by buttoning something such as evergreen tips, dry leaves, or thick dry moss inside his shirt.

TWO KINDS OF EVAPORATION

The final two forms of human heat loss concern evaporation. The first of these is sweating. The second is the so-called insensible perspiring, the steady drying out of the skin which accounts for one-fifth of the body's total heat loss.

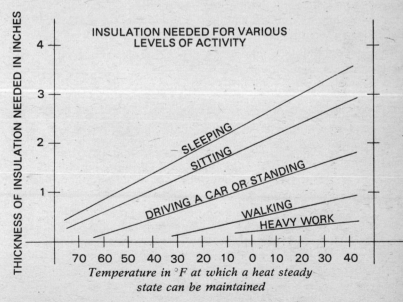

Even when the survivor in a cold environment has plenty of food and fire, sweating should be avoided by every reasonable means if only because of the way it undermines the convective insulation efficiency of the clothing and bedding. An error to avoid, no matter what, is the extremely common mistake of dressing too warmly in cold weather.

Not only is the rate of sweating increased by clothing that is too warm, but unless the garb is loose and open enough to permit the escape of this moisture, it can in a cold environment freeze within the garments. The result at best will be uncomfortable, while at worst it can so offset the qualities of insulation as to be fatal. Just plain wet clothing, too, is far less warm than when it is dry.

It follows that in frigid weather one's clothes should be shaken and brushed as free as possible of both external and internal frost before one approaches heat. When you can do so, clothing under such conditions should be removed and dried each night. As for your down bag or blankets, they'll be considerably warmer if allowed to dry and fluff when not being used.

MAINTAINING YOUR HEAT BALANCE

Heat production and heat loss, therefore, must remain in balance one way or another. When the heat loss is less than the heat production you become uncomfortably warm; dangerously so if the temperature is much below zero. When the heat loss is more than the heat production and the weather is cold, you're in trouble, too.

If you are to survive, you must get them back in equilibrium. You can do this, under favorable conditions, either by increasing your heat production or by cutting down your heat loss.

CALORIES

Your rate of metabolism — the burning of food in the body to provide the energy for the vital processes and activities — can be increased vastly more than your radiant absorption from, say, your campfire. This, of course, means more food must be consumed.

It is not possible to pinpoint this necessary food intake too closely, for body thermostats vary, this being one reason why some can not seem to become adjusted to the tropics, while others are proportionately just as miserable in polar and subarctic regions.

An office worker undergoing very little physical exertion requires some two thousand to twenty-five hundred calories daily depending on his weight. It is reasonable to generalize that a man undergoing the often rugged work of survival needs at least twice as many of these energy units. This is especially true if he is in a cold region such as Hudson Bay where for reasons of warmth alone he will need some two thousand more calories than he would require, for example, along the Gulf of Mexico. Any of these calories not furnished directly by food will be taken from the body's own carbohydrates, fats, and proteins.

Muscular activity can increase your metabolic rate as much as seven or eight times for short periods of time. Even stamping your feet or bringing the arms back and forth across your chest will help.

But suppose you wake up cold, and you're too sleepy to bother with the fire. Then either shivering or muscular tension exercises, when you merely

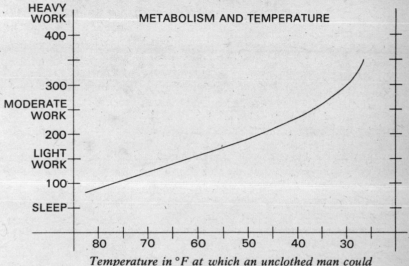

Temperature in °F at which an unclothed man could maintain a heat steady state

strain one muscle against another, will warm you even more efficiently than if you had risen and chopped some wood. With such external activity, only a portion of the expended energy is realized as body heat. The rest is lost to the surrounding cold. When you lie and strain one muscle against another for ten or fifteen minutes, nearly all the heat thus generated immediately warms the body.

Another way to get warm at night is to eat something. Even at worst, there are generally sufficient wild foods available that, if recognized and used, will let you conserve a decisive amount of energy the rest of the time by taking it as easy as possible.

The point is that the basal energy requirements of the human system decline but little even when one is starving. It may be important to you, therefore, to realize that by lounging comfortably before your campfire you may consume only about one hundred calories per hour, whereas when struggling through the bush you can burn six times as much.

INVOLUNTARY HEAT-LOSS ADJUSTMENTS

Since your body must keep its warmth and its heat losses in equilibrium, it takes care of many of the latter functions automatically. You may sweat, for instance; but as we have already considered, you should control sweating in cold weather.

Another involuntary adjustment is the familiar goose pimples, which bring the body hair erect and thus add to the thickness of the insulative still air next to the skin.

The body's other involuntary way of keeping your warmth and your heat loss in balance is by vaso-constriction. This simply means that the blood supply to your arms, legs, and skin surface is reduced so as to conserve the available heat for your heart and other vital organs deep in your body. The head is the sole region where the blood supply is not reduced. Therefore, although vaso-constriction is not controllable, its complement, vaso-dilation, one of the major means of keeping your extremities warm, is indirectly within your power to control.

When both your metabolism and torso insulation are more than sufficient to keep your heart and other vital organs at the proper temperature, the first place your blood circulates the extra warmth is to your skin surfaces. Any excess after that hurries to your hands and feet.

Low body heat, along with cold fingers and toes, will activate the vaso-constriction mechanism and close down the blood supply to your extremities. Incidentally, nicotine also has this effect; so if your feet are cold, don't reach for a cigarette.

THE IMPORTANCE OF WARM FEET

When you're on your feet, these are being compressed by the weight of your body and of anything you're carrying. They are not only vigorous sweat producers, but they are also usually the hardest to ventilate. They are the farthest part of your body from the vital heat-producing sources. If there is any moisture about, it has generally reached its lowest level which means that you are standing in it. Is there any wonder why feet are so frequently cold?

As we have seen, there is a completely different manner by which to fight cold feet and a particularly effective way, inasmuch as the limits of practical insulation on the feet themselves are rather quickly reached. Your answer to cold feet, therefore, may not be warmer and thicker footwear, but an additional shirt or some other extra insulation around the torso.

FOOT COMFORT

If you are ever caught in the wilderness in city shoes, you are in for a hard time of it if you have to do very much walking to get out. In fact, if at all possible, you'll be best off in most cases if you build a fire, camp, and set up signals. Trying to hike out in snow and ice might well mean frozen feet if you make it at all. Staying by a fire, though, and quickly making a shelter, you'll remain snug.

The shoe size you wear on pavement is all right for two or three miles of walking, but beware of this size for a daily tramp of eight or more miles over woodlands, particularly if they are hilly.

Just one such trip in city-size footwear will almost surely lay you low with blisters and bruises. After three or four miles of hiking over rugged terrain, your feet swell markedly because of the repeated and varying pressures. The footwear you select must be sufficiently big to remain comfortable when your feet are in this enlarged condition.

DRYING YOUR FOOTWEAR

Everyone knows that wet leather footwear can be quickly ruined if dried too near a campfire. Not so many are aware that even the top of a heated shelter can be too warm for damp boots. Their proper care is important, for if you are traveling out by walking, your life may depend on them.

The safest procedure is to wash, brush, and scrape off any mud and dirt, wipe off as much free moisture as possible, and then allow the garb to dry slowly in the open air.

If the environment is cold, however, they will freeze into stiff articles that will be like shells of ice to draw on in the morning. Under such circumstances, you'll want to keep them at least close enough to the fire to remain barely warm. If the lowers are leather, too, the shape will be better maintained if the whole boot is first worked and pulled into shape, then stuffed with some dry substances such as moss or even evergreen sprigs.

When bivouacing without a fire, you can make do by sleeping with your wet boots, located most comfortably beneath your legs, between sleeping garments and your bed. Preferable to risking damage to the leather with too-rapid drying, it is best at the end of a wet day to be philosophical about the whole thing, figuring that you'll soon be soaked again in the morning anyway.

WATERPROOFING LEATHER IN AN EMERGENCY

When you are surviving, especially if it is a long struggle, you may be forced to treat your boots with melted animal fat, always presuming that you have enough left to keep you amply supplied with food. However, although this is the normal practice of many northerners, many of whom prefer bear fat for the purpose, the fact remains that oils and greases soak into the leather and thus reduce its natural insulating qualities. This may not be a consideration, though, if you are in the wilderness under survival conditions; you can always get another pair of boots when you get out.

MAKING YOUR OWN FOOTWEAR

You can improvise footwear by wrapping four or five layers of parachute fabric, or perhaps wing cover cloth, around your feet. The canvas seat upholstery of a military vehicle, as well as that of some jeeps and cars, can also be used when improvising boots, as can the seat pad cover of a pilot's parachute. Burlap will do, too, in an emergency, as will almost any fabric.

For added protection, the improvised footwear should be lined with dry fine grass, feathers — especially down, kapok from your boat or plane cushions, or even some dry sphagnum moss.

Rectangles of heavy cloth can be cut from a mackinaw and stood upon, then drawn up around the ankles and tied. Strips cut or ripped from a shirt

Almost any fabric or fur can be used to improvise footwear.

and then, preferably covering the tops of the footwear, wound around the legs, will protect these extremities from snow, sand, sharp branches, thorns, and forest litter. All this may seem almost too basic to discuss, but more than one lost man has been found fully clothed except for long since bare feet that have actually been worn through to the bone in places.

The heavy canvas of large-enough packsacks make them ideal candidates for tough footwear material. Sometimes two bags or other containers are available which will make mukluks by themselves when stuffed with some soft, warm filler.

If you lose your shoes or if they wear out, you can improvise a practical pair of sandals by using the side wall of a jeep or plane tire, or a piece of bark, for the soles; with canvas or parachute cloth for the uppers and heel straps.

Used together with other materials, say between stockings and boots, the gentleness of rabbit or hare pelts can be enjoyed while their warm fragility is being guarded.

Other pelts can be similarly used, usually with the fur turned in toward the skin. The more durable bird skins, especially the breasts of ducks and geese, are soft and warm when worn between the skin and other covering. This latter can be manufactured if need be from bark or even wood, held on by wide straps or similar bindings.

The point remains, however, that if you are having such drastic foot trouble, you'll ordinarily be best advised to camp and set up signals. But there are exceptions, of course, as when you're seeking help for a comrade.

MAKING MOCCASINS

If you have animal skins and the time, you'll find it a comparatively simple matter to fashion moccasins. These normally will wear far better than the fabrics just discussed, although fragile skins, like those of rabbits, are not worth the bother.

Soft, tanned hides afford a lightly comfortable, easily worked material for moccasins and mukluks, but wet or rough going soon wears holes in them. In those parts of the North where such footwear is common, the practice is to protect the feet with larger, exterior moccasins, store-purchased rubbers or overshoes, and often both. You can travel warmly all day in the cold snow with such a combination.

Especially under survival conditions when no outer shell of thick rubber or plastic is at hand, it is best to use for your moccasins as tough a flexible hide as is available. In readying the raw skin, if you start with that, you should not attempt to soften it in any way. The hair or fur can be left warmly inward. Not only is it best not to tan such a skin, but it should be scraped only enough to level off any irregularities that might otherwise hurt the feet.

A moccasin pattern that is as functional as it is simple is shown in the accompanying drawing. To fit the pattern to your feet, stand on a corner of the hide you will be using or, if possible, on a more manageable cloth sample that can later be utilized as a liner. Draw an oval around the feet. Do not try to trace closely about the toes but allow space for easy movement.

Then add at least three inches all around for the moccasin sides. If you have ample leather, it's even better to bring these high above the ankles and shins in two broad flaps that can later be tied with three or four turns of lacing.

As soon as the two parts of the moccasin are cut, slit or punch holes around the edges as indicated. Rawhide or leather laces can easily be made

By using the pattern below, you can fashion moccasins from animal skins.

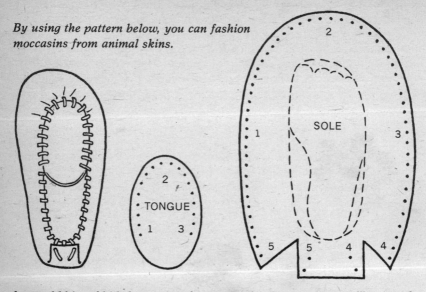

from odd bits of hide by cutting them around and around, as we'll consider next. These thongs, or some other lacing, should be run through the holes to join the two moccasin parts as marked.

CUTTING THE LACING

A lace or thong can be swiftly and simply cut from an old shoe top or a random piece of rawhide. If you have a sharp knife, just find a smooth

Cutting rawhide lacing for moccasins

log with a branch stub sticking up for use as a guide. Or whittle out, then drive in, a wooden peg for this purpose.

If you want your lacing a functional quarter-inch in width, first round any square corners from the leather. Second, start the lace free-hand, beginning a strip two or three inches long.

Then tap your knife point-first into the log so that the blade, facing away from you, is approximately one-fourth inch from the projection or peg. Next, place the already started lace between this guide and the knife edge. By pulling the lace and turning the leather, you will be able to cut around and around, making as long a thong as you have material.

RAWHIDE

Rawhide is easily attained. Just dry the green skin in the shade, whenever you have a few extra minutes scraping the fleshy side as clean as possible with any dull instrument such as a bone or stone that has been flattened on one side. With care, of course, you can also use your knife, perhaps stretching the hide part by part across a knee. Or if you're lazy and have plenty of

To remove fur from an animal skin, just wet the hair and scrape it off.

time, peg the stretched skin to some smooth surface where birds such as jays will give you an assist. If there is a dog with you, however, keep it out of his reach.

When you want this rawhide to be soft, wet the fleshy side, let it dry, then rescrape it. You may have to do this a few times before the skin is satisfactorily flexible. However, caution must be exercised not to dampen the other side if you wish to retain the hair or fur.

If the fur is too long for your purposes, it can be clipped. If you want it off entirely, just wet the coat when you first get it and the outgrowth can be scraped and pulled off in huge patches.

TANNING

Tanning is simplicity itself, but like beginning a campfire with bow and drill, it takes a lot of time and patience. If you've just skinned a wolf-killed deer or caribou, if you need leather rather than rawhide, and if you're camped in one spot without much to do, here's one of the ways you can go about the job.

The animal, of course, should have been skinned carefully and not too closely. Then, working over your knee with a knife or sharp width of stone, scrape away as much flesh and fat as you can. Now you're ready to weigh down the hide, as with stones, in water for several days. As soon as whole clumps of hair slip away with a light tug, you're ready for the next step.

Lay the hide across a smooth log. Scrape one side and then the other, taking off both hair and grain. If the skin is small enough, you may be able to complete this operation before the hide dries. However, it can be redampened. A good two-handed graining tool can be made by driving the point of your longest knife into a smooth chunk of wood for a second handle.

Once hair and grain are removed, the moist skin may be diligently rubbed with a mixture of the animal's brains and fat which have been simmered together in equal proportions. Leave it like this for three or four days. Then wash and wring it as well as you can.

All stiffness must then be rubbed, pulled, and stretched from the hide while it is drying. Finally, the skin may be smoked by suspending it well away from the campfire for a few days, within the influence of smoke but not of heat. Better still will be the making of a separate smudge of green or rotten wood, again taking the same precautions regarding warmth. An especially pleasing effect is produced with the sweet black smoke of the birch, although you have to take particular pains to keep the skin away from the heat when this ardently burning wood is used.

MAKING YOUR OWN THERMO BOOTS

A functional pair of thermo boots can be fashioned with part of the rectangle of thin plastic sheeting it's recommended you always carry, plus ordinary woolen socks and leather boots. Fit the plastic to your foot by standing on a corner, bringing the whole up around your ankle, and cutting it there. You'll need four such pieces.

Envelop each foot first in plastic. Pull on your woolen socks which, to be most effective, should be quite thick. Then put on a second layer of plastic, perhaps one of the small bags in which food often arrives, and finally draw on your boots.

You'll be astonished at the amount of body moisture which accumulates within the inner vapor barrier, and in fact this may prove to be so uncomfortable that you may abandon the whole thing except in the coldest of weather.

If you are wearing rubber boots, of course, these will serve as the outer vapor barrier, making a second layer of plastic unnecessary.

A STRATAGEM WITH SOCKS

Some sourdoughs purchase or have knit for them stretchy woolen tubing, the size of elongated stocking legs. Then, not bothering with fitting, all they have to do is tie the bottoms of two such tubes and draw them on.

When what has become the heel of one tube gets a hole in it, the practice is to put on the tube so that the hole is out of the way over the instep. All in all, you can wear each tube in four different positions without darning. Nor is that all. When the bottom becomes too frayed, just cut it off, retie the string or thong, and commence the whole practice over again.

Inasmuch as this very same principle can be used with ordinary stockings, it is a good stratagem to remember for an emergency.

FEATHERS, FUR, AND HAIR

When you're short of warm clothing in the wilderness under survival conditions, the down and feathers of any birds that can be secured for food should be saved for warmth. If you have no better way of utilizing these, just shove them beneath your clothing. Birds may also be skinned and the plumage made into crude garments, preferably by basting it to some piece of clothing that can be worn beneath regular garb.

The hollow hair of the various members of the deer family has considerable insulating value. You can distribute it as comfortably as possible beneath the clothing, or a skin may be scraped as free of flesh and fat, and worn. In this regard, such vegetable substances as grass, leaves, and dry moss will provide warmth when stuffed inside the clothes.

The more fragile furs are best sandwiched within protective coverings. One way the northern Indians do this is by covering some inexpensive material such as burlap with the skins of the snowshoe rabbit, shingling them on and basting them into place. The fur is often covered with a second piece of material to make a blanket.

One other method, still used under the Aurora Borealis, is begun by slicing and sewing skins together in elongated ribbons. These bands are sometimes loosely woven in their initial form. Sometimes, too, they are given additional strength by first being wound around a leather thong. In both cases, the loosely interlaced robe is ordinarily sewn between two other covers, such as blankets.

MAKING YOUR OWN WATERPROOFS

You can even make your own emergency waterproofs. For instance, large sections of birch bark, kept in place by flattening them under the outer clothing, will turn a large amount of water.

Entire garments of bark may be put together. A thread fashioned by the Indians, especially for sewing birch bark, can be prepared by accumulating a quantity of the finest roots of the familiar spruces and simmering them in water to toughen them. This is poked through holes made by punches and fastened to itself with a cross-stitch. Spruce gum will seal the bark seams. Just chew a quantity, then press it on.

Waterproof garments might be made by drying the large intestines of animals such as moose and caribou, opening them and flattening them, and finally sewing the strips together vertically with sinew.

DRYING WET CLOTHING

Hang each piece separately. Do not suspend things directly above the stove, as they may fall. A good general rule is never to put clothing any nearer a blaze than you can hold your hand. Nylon melts very easily, and wool quickly becomes scorched. Don't hang garments over steaming pots, naturally.

Do not attempt to warm your feet in front of a fire while wearing footwear. Your boots will burn long before your feet are warm.

DAMP CLOTHING

Old frontiersmen found out long ago that damp clothing taken into the sleeping bag at night will be largely dried by the body's heat. However, there are extremely important disadvantages to this system. Heat that would otherwise serve to keep you snug will, for one thing, when your metabolism is at its lowest, be consumed by the drying process.

Even more vital, a great deal of the dissipated moisture is eventually absorbed by the bedding itself, both increasing its weight and decreasing its warmth. Of more immediate importance, it can be clammily uncomfortable in the extreme to have any amount of wet clothing in your bed with you.

CLEANLINESS

Clothing must be kept as clean as possible if it is to retain its warmth. An example is the practice of giving something like an outside stag shirt a water-repellent quality by letting it accumulate grease.

This works, after a fashion, but if intensely cold weather is imminent, it can be dangerous for two reasons. Grease directly reduces the warmth of a garment by conducting your body heat positively away. Too, it reduces the warmth indirectly by filling the fabric's dead air spaces.

MAKESHIFT REPAIRS

Buttons need be no problem, inasmuch as a bit of bone or wood, attached at the middle, will do. So will a square or circle of leather such as may be cut from the loose end of a belt.

The dogbane, which incidentally is poisonous, is among the wild plants, which you can find by experimenting, which will give you thread. The edible nettle is another. Thin strips of dry rawhide are handier for day-by-day

Fibers of the dogbane plant can be twisted together to make thread for clothing repairs.

outdoor use. Too, strong thread can be improvised by twisting and winding fibers from your clothing, as described in some detail under the subject of making fish lines. When we come by meat to eat, we'll also have available the sinews of the bird or animal.

ON THE DESERT

Here you'll wear clothing for protection against sunburn, heat, blowing sand, and insects. If you keep your head and body covered during the day, you'll survive longer on less water.

If you can, wear long trousers and shirts with the sleeves rolled down. Keep them loose and flapping to stay cooler.

Even on the desert, a light woolen shirt will not be out of place. One is really pleasant to pull on when sunset brings its abrupt coolness. Too, it will be comfortable at times during the day, knotted around the abdomen to prevent the chilling sometimes threatened by the rapid evaporation of perspiration in the dry air.

Wear a cloth neckpiece to cover the back of your neck from the sun. If you have no hat, make a headpiece like that worn by the Arabs. Too, a

Arab-style headpiece

parachute can be adapted as a light portable sunshade. During dust storms, cover mouth and nose with a kerchief or perhaps a strip of parachute cloth.

A pocket handkerchief is useful to protect against sunburn on the back of your neck, or to shield your nose and mouth during a dust storm.

Being Prepared 7

Anyone at any time may suddenly find himself dependant upon his own resources for survival. You can get ready by digesting the facts in this book, pertinent to your own possible situation, and by making reasonable preparations for a possible emergency. If you are not ready, it may mean your and others' lives.

Naturally, you'll seldom wish to cruise, drive, or fly over country that is part wilderness dressed like a lumberjack. But if a journey is going to take you into vast wilderness areas, it will be only prudent to carry a few outdoor clothing essentials, such as good warm boots and an eiderdown jacket, where you can get at them in an emergency.

And if you're in the wilderness already, perhaps on a hiking or fishing holiday, it's only sensible to be dressed so that you can take care of yourself if you are forced to remain out in bad weather.

This section, then, will amplify the clothing considerations of the preceding chapter on how to stay warm, on the premise that when you outfit in any part for the outdoors, you'll be well advised not necessarily to get the most expensive, but certainly to buy the best.

But what is best? Usually you have a choice. Let's consider a few of them.

WHAT ABOUT HIGH BOOTS?

High tops nearly always wrinkle and when they are softened, sag at the ankle. The trouble is that this can bring pressure on the Achilles tendon,

A strip of bark can help relieve pain sometimes caused by pressure of the boot top on the Achilles tendon.

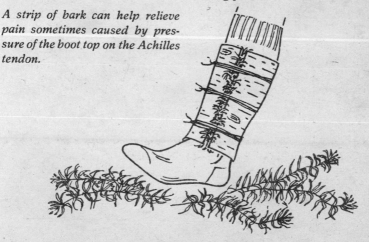

the body's largest, at the back of your ankle. This may become negligible in the case of well-broken-in boots. Too, it can be offset with even rubber tops by the insertion of some stiffener such as a strip of bark or of some pad such as a folded handkerchief.

Unless there is an important reason for high tops, however, the point remains that such unrelieved pressure can set up a painful inflammation of the sheath through which this tendon runs. This is known medically as synovitis. Although in civilization aspirin for the pain and cortisone for the inflammation help, the only remedy in the bush is ten days off the feet, although you can get some relief by splinting the ankle with birch bark and sphagnum moss.

Then there is the matter of weight. A boot with a ten-inch top will weigh some eight ounces more than one six inches high. This is an additional half-pound to be lifted three inches high and to be carried twenty-eight inches ahead about twenty-five hundred times every mile. This extra expenditure of energy really builds up on a long trek back to civilization.

LEATHER-TOPPED RUBBER BOOTS

Boots with rubber bottoms and leather tops are popular in North America, particularly where it's wet. Unless there is a valid reason to the contrary, they should be purchased with tops no more than six to eight inches high. Leather-topped rubbers should be worn with one or two pairs of woolen socks.

The better boots of this sort, and you can buy some awful dreadnaughts, are ideal for fall excursions except in the steepest terrain because they are nearly noiseless and because they can easily be kept water-repellent all the way to the top. They're a poor choice for wear in the very abrupt mountains of the West, especially on snow-covered steepnesses. However, I've worn them very comfortably in winter down to about thirty degrees below zero, when they become too cold.

When they are worn with adequate innersoles and laced loosely, the insole and socks compress with a bellows effect at every step, pumping air in and out. Leather-topped rubbers, therefore, are excellent for summer wear in country where the ground is often moist with dew even during the fairest of days, and where there are swamps.

HIKING BOOTS

The favorites among many trail veterans, particularly in the West, are the special boots for hiking, which may be imported or domestic, stocked by the big catalog-issuing sporting goods dealers. The best of rubber lug soles give these high traction and long wear. They are comfortable, quiet, and safe, but not inexpensive. With reasonable care they will be good for years, particularly as they can be successfully resoled when necessary.

SPECIAL SHOES

It is often practical to transform a well-broken-in pair of leather work or outdoor boots into excellent trail performers by the addition of the widely available neoprene rubber cleated soles that, seen on many of the best trail boots, will grip on almost everything except glare ice and ice-sheathed rock. In this case hobnails, also to be found in the stores, are still supreme.

The practice of buying such boots for the trail is not a wise one, however, as for very little more money you will be able to buy ready-made boots particularly designed for this purpose.

If your local sporting goods dealer does not have cleated rubber soles, the large catalog-issuing outfitters do. Two treads are generally available. The first of these boasts a more pronounced cleat for a longer and more functional life during general hiking. The second, a lighter sole with a shallower cleat, is designed especially for rock climbing.

THERMO BOOTS

There is a fine, recently developed method of insuring warm feet, although it makes for a heavy boot that is best suited to ice fishing and snowmobile riding rather than to extended walking. However, the better of these thermo boots are comfortable, flexible, compact, and tough. I successfully tested a boot of this sort in the Far North at temperatures sixty degrees below zero.

The principle involves the use of a unicellular material that works much as a thermos bottle does. Each small cell is completely enclosed and safe from body moisture. Since each contains trapped dead air, it acts as an insulator both against the loss of body heat and the entrance of cold air from the outside. Placed between the outside layer of the boot and the lining, this insulation in the better footwear covers the entire foot and instep, extending well above the ankle. The first time you stand around in the dry, subzero snow with them you're amazed at their warmth.

CANVAS SNEAKERS

These are light, easy to stow, and are far better than city shoes along reasonably smooth trails when the weather is not too cold. For adequate ankle protection and support, buy them with approximately six-inch tops. For woods use, the rubber soles should be cleated or roughly corrugated. Sneakers are best worn with one pair of medium-weight woolen socks.

Sneakers will soon wet through in rain, in swamps, and even in heavy morning dew. With the woolen socks this is not uncomfortable, however, and once the going improves they'll dry out rapidly without stiffening.

NORTHERN PRACTICE

It is the custom throughout much of the Far North to wear soft warm footwear, perhaps a felt boot or Indian-made high moccasins or mukluks over woolen stockings, covered with a sometimes waterproof but always snow-barring outer boot that is removed before one enters a cabin.

Snow boots and mukluks with warm linings are practical footwear for snowy country.

This outside footwear may be a larger pair of moosehide moccasins, mukluks, one of the zippered canvas shells that have become popular for snowmobiling, or even ordinary overshoes. The combination is warm, soft, and quiet.

Incidentally, if you'd like to order some by mail, mukluks are sized the same as boots.

BUYING THE RIGHT SIZE

Too many individuals wear wilderness footwear that is too tight. There's a simple formula that will keep you on the right track. For use with one pair of thin or medium-weight woolen socks, get your boots one size longer and one size wider than your correct fit in city shoes.

For heavy socks, buy them one and one-half sizes longer and wider. If half sizes are not obtainable, get the next full size larger. For the extra pair of socks you may find most comfortable in a severely cold environment, experiment to achieve the same easy fit as with boots.

BREAKING IN FOOTWEAR

The boot, where the woodsman and the wilderness meet, is of course the most important part of the clothing. What about breaking them in?

New footwear should, if at all possible, be well broken in before you take to the woods. Even with something like low rubber boots, which need no breaking in as such, there will be pressure points that you'll want to toughen and perhaps to modify temporarily in the field with a strategetically placed handkerchief or piece of birch bark.

There are two eminently practical ways of breaking in new leather boots. You can stand in four inches of water for fifteen minutes, then hike until the shoes dry on your feet, a procedure that is far less uncomfortable than it sounds. Or you can go at it more gradually by hiking two miles the first day, three the second, and so on up to five miles, by which time the process should be completed.

WATERPROOFING FOOTWEAR

Boots, particularly in this day of silicones, are usually nearly waterproof when new. After a day of hiking, some water may seep through at the seams. During continued wet travel, a bit of water will work through the leather.

If wax, preferably that containing silicone, is then worked into the seams, wrinkles, stitchings, and where the uppers meet the lowers, they will once more be fairly waterproof until the compound wears off. Leather footwear should be waxed this way about once a week when you're using it. Treating it more often than this can make the leather too soft.

In any event, the dubbin will go on more easily and satisfactorily if the leather is slightly warm.

That leather footwear is seldom entirely waterproof is usually all to the good, for otherwise the boots would make your feet more uncomfortably wet than would leather still able to breathe.

INNERSOLES

Plastic mesh insoles, which tend to ventilate the soles of the feet and which are both nonabsorbent and nonmatting, are an excellent choice.

Not liking the flat feel of the usual boot, however, I personally compromise with a multilayered leather insole with a steel arch support which can be adjusted with the fingers. In cold weather, I use the same type of insole but with a soft, closely clipped lambskin surface next to the feet.

Felt insoles are common, and before they become damp are indeed warmer than the ideal plastic mesh variety. Laden with moisture, however, they become excellent conductors of heat. You can get around this by carrying a dry pair, but at best this is a nuisance.

SOCKS

Three closely fitting pairs of good woolen socks are not as warm as two more loosely fitting pair. Aside from the fact that the feet's already poor circulation is further impeded by such a tight fit, the resulting compression of the woolen fibers cuts down on the insulative dead air space. Here again, thickness means warmth.

The simple but vital formula for the most efficient wilderness walking is heavy socks and big shoes. Regardless of cold or heat, wetness or dryness, only good woolen socks are suitable for the long hike you may have to take to get out of your predicament. Nylon stitching, augmenting the strength of heels and toes, may serve to lengthen their usefulness. These socks may vary from thin to medium during the growing seasons and from medium to heavy in the chilly months.

Throughout the year, nevertheless, try to wear only the best quality, painstakingly processed, and well-made woolens. If you can possibly avoid it, have nothing to do with shoddy products in this category especially. Poor woolens mat, soon losing much of their insulative quality. They contain impurities that irritate the all-too-vulnerable feet. As for loosely and skimpily knit socks, these are abominable from the first time you don them.

If you are one of the rare individuals whose feet seem allergic to wool, try wearing thin socks of some other material beneath the wool. These may be of well-knit cotton, but not the thin, stretchy products that frequently appear on the market. Or you may select nylon, which surely has longevity but which, for many of us, is much too slippery unless either worn too tightly or gartered in some way, neither of which fits in the outdoor routine.

Do your best to start out with well-fitting and reasonably new socks with no harsh seams or unduly rough darns. Wash both the feet and the socks, if at all possible, when you stop to camp for the night. When the going is rough and not too cold, it is refreshing to stop several times during the day and bathe the feet. At this time, if you can, change to a fresh pair of socks, hanging the damp ones on the outside of your pack or looped through your belt in back where they can dry.

THE LAYER SYSTEM

In extremely cold weather you can freeze very rapidly in wet clothing. It is therefore imperative under such circumstances to keep from sweating. This you can accomplish by shedding layers of clothing as you warm up, thereby always staying moderately cold. This ability to gauge and maintain a comfortable body temperature increases markedly with experience.

This is a major reason why for the ordinary individual, the layer system is best in the farther places. In the chill of the morning, which actually deepens at sunrise because of the breezes stirred by the lifting of the sun, many like to start with everything on. Whether you are on a winter desert or high in mountainous realms, the practice is to continue shedding layers as the sun soars higher.

There is one thing to watch out for with such a system, and that is not to carry it too far. In the thin dry air of the upper altitudes, the sun burns deeply, even through a basic low-regions tan. The shoulders and back, so vital if you are backpacking, are particularly vulnerable.

It is always best to anticipate personal warmth variations and to open clothing before you'd otherwise begin to sweat and to close it again before you actually feel chilly. This takes a certain degree of experience, to be sure, and is one of the sure signs that a cheechako is maturing into a sourdough.

No matter what you wear, the garments as a whole must be sufficient to give you an average thickness that will be adequate according to both temperature and your particular rate of metabolism. With correctly designed clothing and the proper new underwear, you can wear your maximum insulation throughout the day and ventilate any excess heat out from inside it.

The way, when you find you are wearing too much at the moment, is first to uncover that most efficient heat radiator that you have, your head. If that isn't enough, open your neck and if necessary your front to let out the heat accumulating about your torso.

The wrists and hands are next on the ventilating scale. The veins you see close to the surface on the underneaths of your wrists make these effective radiators. Not only that, but by permitting air to come in at the wrists and move up the arms, you are cooling the armpits which are one of the foremost sweat-producing regions of the human system.

The final source of ventilation is the legs. The general practice, often necessary because of deep snow, is to leave them very lightly insulated. Although this generally works, it increases the tendency toward cold feet by dropping the blood temperature as it travels down the exposed legs.

If you consult the catalogs of the big outfitters supplying mountain-climbing equipment, though, you'll find clothing with zippers that can be opened from the waist down to the snow level. I've used this system in temperatures more than thirty degrees below zero and found it an even more convenient way of cooling the whole body than exposing the chest.

CLOTHING IDEALS

Always make certain that no part of your garb is too tight or restrictive. Knees especially should work freely.

A side point is that many woodsmen choose to have their debris-collecting trouser cuffs removed and the legs stagged some three inches shorter than city garments. Otherwise, the trouser legs, particularly if they are at all full, have the dangerous tendency to catch on snags and trip you.

Picking out clothing with fast, bright colors is to be recommended for several reasons. It's much easier to spot in a wilderness terrain, especially from the air. You are less likely to break camp and leave some article behind, drying on a bush. Too, there is the very important factor of safety if you are abroad during the hunting seasons.

WHAT UNDERWEAR TO CHOOSE

The primary principle to remember is the need to prevent the always-present body moisture from entering the clothing. It will not do this if it can escape an easier way. Therefore, the basic requirement is an air space around your body so that the moisture can evaporate immediately after it is formed by insensible perspiration and perhaps a little sweating, as when you first start out in the morning before you settle down to the even pace of the trail. Then, if you leave an ample neck opening, the vapor-heavied air can move harmlessly out.

You can set the stage for all this by wearing one of the many brands of net underwear, preferably with a three eighths-inch or larger square mesh, about one-eighth inch thick and entirely open like a fishnet. Much smaller holes, as well as the familiar waffle-weave undersuits, do not permit the necessary evaporation to take place.

The neatest supplemental trick for cold country comfort lies in some of the recently developed insulative underwear. You should still don net underwear next to the skin, however. And if you begin to perspire, you should slacken your activity if possible, or remove the bottom, the top, or both parts of your insulated undergarments. These can be stowed in a pack, actual or improvised, until you stop. Then put them back on until bedtime. One of the secrets of sleeping warm is going to bed warm.

You have to be careful what you buy, however. Underwear made of some of the synthetics entrap perspiration as tightly as rubber. In weather that is at all warm, you might as well be journeying in a portable steam bath. In really cold going, much more than just discomfort is at stake. Some trapped body moisture freezes, and if you continue trying to bull it through, so may you.

The difficulty in the subzero temperatures encountered in some survival country is not so much keeping warm, but doing so without too much weight and constraint while maintaining body ventilation. One inexpensive garment that does the job is a light undersuit made with Dacron polyester insulation quilted inside a nylon shell and lining. The more expensive waterfowl down, being lighter and more compressible, is even better.

Like down, though, this crimped Dacron seems to have a built-in thermostat that adjusts it to very widely varying temperatures. The easiest way to give this an assist in ordinary cold going? Just unzip the garment as much and for as long as comfortable. Many find this underwear satisfactory in temperatures ranging from sixty degrees below to zero. When the weather becomes balmier, this undersuit generally becomes too warm.

The solution when you're trying to walk to safety and the weather gets too warm? Just take off either or both of the parts, roll and tie them together, and carry them on your back. Together, they're far lighter and more compact than one ordinary heavy sweater.

During winter in most wilderness, winds have to be combatted in addition to cold temperatures. In a twenty mile-per-hour wind, regular woolen clothing, to take an example, loses about fifty-five percent of the warmth it maintains in still air. Get a much faster wind in weather 30 degrees below and, unless you put on windproofs, you feel as if you're wearing barbwire. Dacron-insulated nylon, or better still the best quality down product, checks the wind more effectively than most other satisfactory fabrics not built particularly for the purpose.

To get the fullest benefit from insulated underwear, however, you still need a windbreaker. I like a tightly woven, white cotton parka. Another solution, which can be assembled so that it adds up to the same weight, is a wind-tight nylon parka of about two and one half-ounce material, plus a separate plastic-impregnated nylon poncho of the same weight fabric. This parka affords excellent closure and ventilative characteristics in dry cold. When the weather turns wet, the poncho gives much more ventilation than other waterproofs, thereby not condensing as badly in a cold downpour.

A fringe benefit with insulated underwear is that such a suit can be worn effectively on cold nights as a second sleeping bag inside the regular combination.

WHY DOWN?

Although insulation depends on thickness only, this does not signify that there is no material that is more practical than all others for clothing and sleeping bag insulation. There is, and for centuries it has been prime, white northern goose down.

When you need a couple inches of insulation, it is simple to see that eight layers of woolen shirts, two sheepskin coats, or even that same two inches of plastic foam wrapped around your body is going to be pretty heavy, confining, and cumbersome. Goose down, on the other hand, presents definite advantages that, when warmth may mean the difference between life and death, overweigh its cost.

It gives warmth without appreciable weight. Only one ounce of goose down, for example, will insulate some 600 cubic inches. In density, its 1.85 pounds per cubic foot is well below the 4 pounds per cubic foot of most comparable insulations.

It compresses readily. That same one ounce that insulates 600 cubic inches will wad with very little effort to 15 cubic inches. This explains why down clothing and sleeping bags will stuff in such astonishingly tiny bags for carrying or storing. It also elucidates why down is not as confining and cumbersome as the multitude of heavier insulations.

Down has the invaluable characteristic of breathing. It not only permits the body moisture to escape freely, but with the natural bellowslike action of proper clothing it keeps dry far longer than any other insulation.

It is also super resilient, withstanding innumerable and prolonged compressions and each time fluffing back to its original thickness. Kapok, on the other hand, finally turns to powder with such treatment. Many other materials steadily and too often rapidly lose their thickness.

Down is washable, and in adequately constructed garments and bags should be washed periodically to keep it fluffy and at its major-insulative degree of cleanliness. Incidentally, it is important to note that if you ever have a sleeping bag dry cleaned, you should air it very well before using it. The fumes of some of the compounds used in some dry cleaning processes can and have killed the unsuspecting occupants.

In its prime grades, white goose down is still the best garment insulation known to science. The darker goose down is nearly as good. Duck down is not quite as filling, although some manufacturers work it into their finest garments by advertising the whole as waterfowl down. The only place where down is not effective as an insulation is in the bottom of your sleeping bag directly next to the body. This is why a sleeping pad of some other substance, or even a thick layer of evergreen browse, is necessary to have in cold climes if you are to sleep warmly.

In what fabric are we going to confine this down? Fleecy wool is warm to the touch, but it mats, eventually becomes threadbare, and is unnecessarily heavy from the start. The best fabric to wear next to the body to confine down is a very thin nylon. This is both light and tough. Its slipperiness makes it easier to get into. Although initially cold to the touch, it warms quickly and actually absorbs less body heat than does, for example, cotton flannel which feels warm the moment you come in contact with it.

WOOL

For a cold or even a chilly environment, all but the underclothing and what you are wearing in the way of down or otherwise insulated garb should be lightweight wool throughout. Wool also gets wet from perspiration, but if you are dressed properly most of this moisture passes directly through it to be evaporated on the outside.

Furthermore, wet wool does not feel particularly cold. It does not chill in the same way as, for example, wet cotton unless there is a brisk wind. Under these conditions, a closely woven but still porous outside jacket of tight cotton or thin nylon should be carried for use as a windbreaker.

Wool is warm because of the insulative effect of inert air retained in the minute spaces among its innumerable fibers. A pair of light wool garments are warmer than a single heavy one of the same total weight because of the additional dead air retained between them.

COTTON

Cotton jeans are the worst things you can wear in the bush if only because of the chilly way in which they absorb water. Then there is the nationally used heat loss test. Four cans were filled with 110-degree water; three were covered, each with a different fabric, then they were left out in the wind and rain to demonstrate body heat loss through conduction and convection.

After four hours, the water temperature in the can with a wet cotton covering fell to 61 degrees, and that in the can without any covering dropped to 72 degrees. The water in the can with a wet woolen covering showed an 83-degree water temperature, and the wool-covered can protected with a plastic cover stayed at 96 degrees.

Incidentally, a sock doll test illustrates that when floating wool is partially inundated in water, it remains absolutely dry above the water line. Cotton, on the other hand, absorbs water like a wick and soon becomes soaked. If even a half-inch of a cotton sweatshirt is exposed below your raingear on a wet day, water will be soaked up through the cotton until the entire garment is sopping.

DOWN JACKET

A light, high-quality, expertly tailored down jacket, built durably enough for wilderness rigors, is a primary clothing choice in cold-weather regions. Even when you carry it in your pack because of an upward spurt of the thermometer, it is one of the most comfortable imaginable to don when you stop and kindle your small, bright campfire.

Such eiderdown jackets are far from being out of place on the desert, as in winter particularly most such sun-scoured sands become amazingly cold after sunset when the heat of the day, with little moisture in the air to beat it back, radiates out of the sand and rocks.

Almost any night in the North Woods, when you lounge in front of the crackling companionship of your campfire, an eiderdown jacket is pure pleasure against your back. And if your sleeping garments are at all cold, spread this jacket between the blankets or bag.

POCKETS

Every pocket should be zippered, buttoned, snapped, pinned, or otherwise made secure. If it has no flap, something like a handkerchief wedged above the contents before this is done will help keep them intact.

It is also smart procedure, especially when you are breasting thick brush, to check regularly to make sure that the pocket tops stay safely closed over contents whose value, if selection has been painstaking, will increase the further you are from outfitters. This is particularly true when they include such precious posessions as match case and compass.

If you go to bed in your clothes, you'll relax more fully if you first meticulously empty your pockets, keeping the contents safely together in something like a handkerchief or hat.

GLOVES OR MITTS?

If warmth is an important part of your hand protection, mittens will be more satisfactory than gloves. They should extend high enough to shield the especially vulnerable wrists, and their tops should fit sufficiently close, while still affording ventilation, to exclude snow and debris.

You may have to have these knit especially for you, but if you have to use your bare fingers on short notice, as for pressing a trigger, you'll find it worthwhile to have a slit made in the palm of one of these mittens and a generous flap added to cover that opening when it is not in use. With such a mitt on your master hand, you'll be able to free the fingers quickly whenever this may be necessary.

In very cold weather, you'll probably want to add outer mitts. These may be of some windproof material such as tightly woven cotton, light and porous enough to maintain air circulation adequate to keep perspiration from collecting. An especially handy technique in this instance, if the going is reasonably open, is to join these mitts with a cord long enough to loop around the neck. Then, with the mitts thus protected you will be able to yank either hand bare in an instant with your teeth.

Because of the paradoxical effect of curvature, the first layers of insulation you add to your hands actually increase the heat loss. This is particularly true of the fingers, and if your gloves fit tightly, you are doing more harm than good as far as warmth is concerned until you reach one-quarter inch of thickness.

Therefore, everyday gloves, even foam-insulated ski gloves, do not provide effective insulation. Most of these latter are made with straight-tailored fingers which, cramped around a ski pole, stretch so tightly over the knuckles that just where you need thick insulation you have thin spots.

Although everyone likes the unrestricted action of gloves, a thick pair of mitts where the loose fingers can warm one another will vastly prolong the comfort span, particularly if when your hands get cold, you bare and warm them next to the body, perhaps under your opposite arm pits. You will thus make every effort to keep the fingers from freezing.

Water, Water Everywhere 8

The average adult, whose body is some eighty percent water, needs about three quarts of water daily depending on such factors as activity, heat, and wind. Half of this is lost through body wastes, another third through the lungs in humidifying the air we breathe, and the final sixth in the insensible perspiration evaporated to keep the body at an even temperature.

In a pinch, you can get along with two cups a day, but what you lack now you'll have to make up for later. Dehydration of from six to ten percent of the body weight will result progressively in dizziness, headache, difficulty in breathing, and a tingling in the extremities. The body takes on a bluish hue, speech is difficult, and finally the individual finds himself unable to walk. Unless water becomes available, death follows. On the other hand, the man who has collapsed from dehydration can be restored in a very brief time by the gradual intake of water.

Fortunately, water is obtainable nearly everywhere, even on the deserts. This is all to the good, for although under favorable conditions you could get along for a month or two without food, you'd do well to stay alive much more than a week without water.

IS IT PURE?

Although you'll generally be able to get along awhile longer without a drink, just one drop of impure water may so weaken you that at the very

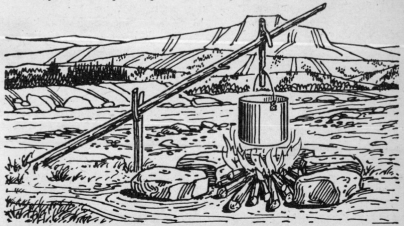

Boiling drinking water is an important wilderness precaution.

least you'll be unable to travel. It follows that you should take every reasonable care to make sure that the water you are drinking is not contaminated.

Knowing how even beaver and muskrat can infect wilderness water with tularemia, far beyond the pollution of man, I've long been cautious about what I drink in the farther places. The importance of all this care was emphasized about a dozen years ago when I was boiling the noonday kettle in a remote little canyon on the headwaters of the Peace River, where I was probably the first human within the past fifty years to set foot.

I simmered the water my usual (at that elevation) seven minutes for tea, toasted my sandwiches, and was soon continuing my explorations. A quarter mile inland, the canyon so narrowed that to proceed I had to wade the brook. Another few steps and I came upon the half-submerged, decomposing carcass of a moose which had evidently fallen in from above. Needless to say, my water-boiling precaution no longer seemed a waste of time.

The safest way to purify water before using it for drinking, cooking, dish washing, and for such intimate tasks as brushing the teeth is first to boil it for five minutes at sea level and one more minute for each additional thousand feet of elevation.

Suppose you have no receptacle? Then make one of bark or hollowed wood. A way of providing a primitive basin is by scooping a hole in soft

If you have no kettle, make a birch bark vessel for boiling water.

ground or humus, then lining it with that sheet of plastic from your pocket.

When the Indians wanted hot water, they scattered a few clean pebbles on the bottom of the inflammable receptacle for protection, then added rocks from the fire, often with the help of tongs made by bending a green stick back upon itself. In other words, no minor problem is going to puzzle you for very long in a pinch if you have the energy, resourcefulness, and enterprise to survive at all.

If you are going to use the water hot, you're well away. If you plan to carry it in a canteen for drinking later, it'll taste flat because of the driving off of the air content. This can be restored by pouring the liquid back and forth a number of times between two containers. Or, as I usually do, you may be philosophical about the whole thing. When you're thirsty, you'll scarcely notice the lack of taste.

CHEMICAL PURIFICATION

If you can't always boil water, and there are times when so treating a freshly filled canteen is a nuisance, it's a good idea to have in your pocket a small bottle of halazone tablets, obtainable at your drug store for under a dollar.

Inasmuch as the purifying action of these tablets depends upon their releasing chlorine gas when needed, they should be fresh. Don't try to save a few cents by buying surplus halazone tablets. Replace any in your survival kit about every year. The bottles should be kept tightly closed in a dry, dark place.

No purification of water by chemical means is as safe as boiling, but a couple of tiny halazone tablets will normally make a quart of water pure enough for human consumption in an hour. If the water is especially suspicious or if it is muddy, it will be a wise precaution to use four halazone tablets and to let them remain for an hour.

When you boil water, all parts of the container become hot and purify themselves. With chemical disinfectants, on the other hand, you have to take care to purify all contact points of the container so that once the water is purified it will not easily be reinfected. If you're using halazone with your canteen, for instance, replace the cap loosely and wait for five minutes while the tablets dissolve. Then shake the contents diligently, permitting some of the liquid to slosh over the top and lid of the container. Tighten the cap then and leave it that way for the desired time before using any of the water.

IODINE WATER PURIFICATION TABLETS

Chlorine-releasing compounds cannot be depended upon in semi-tropical and tropical regions. And, incidentally, it's erroneous to assume that the presence of a strong alcoholic beverage will render the water and any ice harmless. Water in these areas should either be boiled or treated with something such as iodine water purification tablets.

Containing the active ingredient tetraglycine hydroperiodide, these small tablets have proved effective against all common water-borne bacteria, as well as the cysts of *Entamoeba histolytica,* which cause dysentery; and the larvae of the parasitic fluke, *Schistosoma.* Iodine tablets are more costly than halazone, but not expensive when you take into account their capabilities. Added to water, each tablet frees eight milligrams of iodine which acts as the purification factor. One tablet will purify one quart of clear water.

These tablets are used like halazone and they, too, must be kept dry. The bottle should be immediately and tightly recapped after being opened.

USING IODINE DIRECTLY

You can use tincture of iodine from your first aid kit instead of the iodine water purification tablets. Eight drops of reasonably fresh, two and one-half percent tincture of iodine, used as the above tablets, will purify a quart of water in ten minutes. It is a good idea to let it stand twenty minutes if the water, as it may be in the mountains, is extremely cold.

POISONOUS WATER HOLES

There are no known sources of deadly poisonous water in the wilds of Canada. In the southwestern deserts of this continent, on the other hand, a very few water holes contain dissolved poisons such as arsenic. You'll generally be able to recognize such water easily, both from the presence of bones of unwary animals and from the lack of green vegetation. A good general rule, therefore, is to avoid any water holes around which green plants are not flourishing.

HARD WATER

Much more likely, both in the United States and Canada, is that water may be what we know as hard. If in the area where you are lost or stranded there is extremely hard water to which you have not become accustomed, severe digestive upsets may occur if while getting used to it you sip more than conservative portions at any one time.

Boiling may help the situation, as when lime and magnesia carbonates are held in solution by carbon dioxide. These hardening agents can be partially solidified and thus dispelled by the driving off of this gas by heat.

MAKING YOUR OWN FILTERS

You can clear water with a filter, although you should realize at the same time that this process will neither materially affect any dissolved minerals, nor will it do away with any impurities. Wilderness water is polluted, as you know, by mineral and animal substance, not by the often discoloring vegetable matter such as roots and dead leaves.

The aim of a self-contrived filter will be to clear water by straining solid foreign matter such as mud from it. Incidentally, most muddy water will clear of its own accord if you let it stand for, in some cases, up to half a day. But if you can't wait that long, dig a hole, in sand if at all possible, several feet back from the stream or pond and carefully scoop out for your use what water seeps into it.

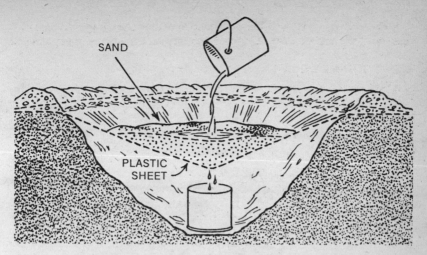

SAND

PLASTIC SHEET

Filtering water will remove vegetable matter, but not impurities.

FINDING WATER ON A SEACOAST

You may be able to locate water in sand dunes above the beach or even well back from the high-tide mark on the beach itself, particularly when there is high land above it. Look in the hollows among the dunes for visible water, or dig above the high-tide line where the sand appears to be moist.

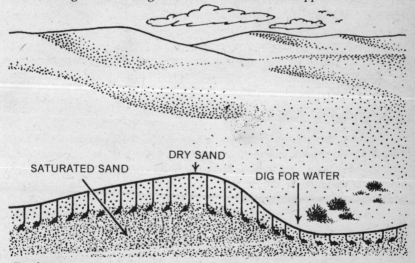

SATURATED SAND

DRY SAND

DIG FOR WATER

Fresh water may be found at a seacoast by digging in hollows among dunes.

Either that, or wait until the tide is at least part-way out and dig below the high water line, using a shell, a piece of driftwood, or anything else that is handy. Fresh water, if there is any at the spot, will lie atop the heavier salt water. The hole for this reason should not be deepened beneath the first signs of seepage, at least not until an adequate water supply has been secured. If the water is brackish, try running it through a sand filter.

The general rule for survival when water is not available, or in very short supply, is to eat nothing. The amount of food that can be eaten increases in direct proportion to the amount of drinking water available. Carbohydrates require little or no water to assimilate, while proteins require a lot of water. Fish juices contain a high amount of proteins to the point that more water is required to digest them than is derived from the juices. Obviously then, one is fighting a losing battle by consuming fish juices if water is not available.

The immersion of the body in the sea to minimize dehydration achieves nothing. The skin can not absorb water into the system, and one endangers his life by exposure to dangerous sea life such as sharks and barracuda, as well as exposing himself to contacting salt water sores. To minimize dehydration at sea it is recommended that clothing be dampened with sea water to get the effect of cooling through evaporation. This, of course, only applies to hot conditions where the intent is to eliminate loss of water through perspiration.

SALT WATER

Do not drink salt water. For one thing, it's cathartic; which action will further dehydrate the body. In large amounts, it is actually poisonous. At best, its salt concentration is so high that, far from assuaging thirst, it will require the use of already depleted body fluids to eliminate it, and eventually the kidneys will cease functioning, causing death.

Urine, in addition to containing harmful body wastes, is too salty to drink no matter how drastic may be the emergency. However, in times of dire privation, it is sometimes successfully used to wash wounds.

There is one exception with salt water. When you are afloat on the ocean and have plenty of fresh water as the result of a storm or even from dew, this will go farther and will do the human system more good if sea water is added to it. A workable proportion is a perhaps surprising one-fifth or two-fifths of sea water to fresh, or the addition of a salt tablet or one-fourth teaspoon of salt to each cup of fresh water.

WHAT ABOUT LIQUOR AND CIGARETTES?

Smoking is dehydrating and will increase the need for a drink of water. Liquor with a high alcoholic content will further dehydrate the body and should never be drunk when water is in short supply. Other beverages, such as beer and wine, with low alcoholic content can, if as is conceivable you should be shipwrecked with no water except that in a number of cases of these, and would satisfy your thirst although they might well lead you into ill-considered maneuvers. Not even soft drinks such as orangeade and ginger ale are adequate substitutes for water.

Medicines, of course, can not be substituted for drinking water. Most compass fluids are poisonous antifreezes. Radiator fluids in which there is antifreeze can not even be used in a solar still.

Sluggishness of the digestive system is a natural consequence of going without normal amounts of water and food. The condition need not cause any worry, as the body will readjust itself when regular drinking and eating habits are resumed. One should most definitely never take a laxative in such a situation; such medication, besides being weakening, will spectacularly deplete the body of much of the moisture already in it.

WATER FROM VEGETATION

There are a number of possibilities, including the finding of rain entrapped in the leaves of plants. It will be a good idea to strain this through a piece of cloth to eliminate blown and fallen debris, as well as water insects.

The sap from such trees as the birches and the maples, considered along with other similar possibilities in the section on edible wild plants, is both

Sap drawn from maple and birch trees helps satisfy thirst in an emergency.

refreshing and nutritious. The Indians used to cut V-shaped gashes in the trunks and insert, in their lower angles, spouts they made by hollowing something such as an elderberry limb.

The barrel cactus of the southwestern United States is another possible source of water, although these are becoming scarce and should be used only in a very real emergency. Cut off the top of the cactus and crush the pulp inside the remaining section as well as you can.

A barrel cactus three and one-half feet tall will yield about a quart of milky, thirst-quenching juice. Scoop this out or suck it from a hole cut low

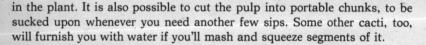

Crushed pulp from the barrel cactus yields thirst-quenching juice.

in the plant. It is also possible to cut the pulp into portable chunks, to be sucked upon whenever you need another few sips. Some other cacti, too, will furnish you with water if you'll mash and squeeze segments of it.

MUSKEG WATER

The standing water in sloughs and muskegs can be used, especially if you bail it out carefully enough not to disrupt the adjacent impurities and murkiness. In muskeg regions where the growth is in mounds of various elevations, you can often locate small pools of water around the bases of the mounds. All slough and muskeg water should be purified.

HOW TO SWEETEN WATER

Even when it has been purified, slough, muskeg, and swamp water may have an unpleasant odor and taste. It will be convenient to sweeten and purify the liquid in one operation.

Just drop several fragments of charred hardwood from the campfire into the boiling pot. Keep the water bubbling for at least fifteen minutes. Skim away the majority of the foreign matter. You can then either strain the water through a clean cloth or, if you're not short on either time or utensils, just allow it to settle.

THE IMPORTANCE OF GAME TRAILS

Game trails in dry country very often indicate the presence of water, particularly when you begin to come across them in growing numbers and when the more traveled of them become progressively wider and deeper. If you want water, just follow them.

There is an exception. In the muskeg and the burned and fallen in jackpot country of the north, where there is no shortage of water, such game trails often tell of an area ahead that is comparatively impassible except during the snowshoeing time of the year. Then if you want to make time and conserve energy, you'll do well to follow the trails around the obstruction, picking up your direction again once the obstruction is bypassed.

WHERE WATER IS

Water flows downhill, of course, eroding canyons and other declivities as it goes and encouraging a ribbon of bright vegetation, especially such telltale growth as willow and alder. You'll find water atop mountains, too, and glaciers and permanent snowbanks may also be there to refresh you.

Water also lies near the base of elevations, where it can often be distinguished by the presence of prolific vegetation. In some country, in fact, the major problem is not so much in locating water but in discovering an easy way to it.

When country is flat and open, long winding tangles of green brush tell their important stories.

In rocky areas, search for springs and seepages. Limestones and lavas have more and larger springs than any other rocks. Springs of icy water are safest, by the way. Warm water, except where there may be hot springs, has been recently at the surface and is prone to be polluted.

Limestones are soluble, and ground water erodes channels and caverns in them. Look in these caverns, both large and small, for springs, but be careful. If you venture into a large series of caves beyond the sight of the entrance, make absolutely certain that you do not become lost.

Most lava rocks are filled with billions of bubble holes through which ground water may seep. Too, look for springs along the walls of valleys that cross the rough hard flow. Some lava has no characteristic bubble holes, but, on the other hand, is marked with so-called organ-pipe joints — vertical cracks that dissect the rocks into spectacular columns a foot or more thick and often two dozen feet or more high. At the feet of such joints, you may find water bubbling out as seepage or gushing forth in springs.

Search for seepage where a dry canyon barrels through a layer of porous sandstone. As for other common rocks, like granite, water is contained only in irregular cracks. Scan hillsides for swaths where the grass is lush and green. Then scoop out your ditch at the base of the verdancy and wait for water to seep in.

Water is more abundant and easier to find in loose sediments than in rocks themselves. Look for springs along valley floor and down across their sloping sides. Even in the southwest when streams are dry, the flat benches or terraces about the meandering river valleys ordinarily yield springs and seepages about their bases. In low forests, along the seashore, and in river plains the water table is close to the surface. Very little digging generally yields an ample supply.

Percentages are so much against success, that you shouldn't waste time and energy digging in a locality where there are no favorable signs. On the other hand, you're apt to find water by digging in the floor of a valley under an abrupt slope, particularly if the bluff is cut into a terrace. Or dig out a lush green patch where there's been a spring or pocket of water during the wet season.

Water seeps slowly through clay, but a large number of clays contain sandy strips which may yield springs. Look for a wet spot on the surface of a clay bluff and try scooping it out. Try wet places at the bluff's foot.

In mud flats, during the dry season, you may be able to locate wet mud at a low point. Wring this out in a piece of cloth to get water, but do not drink it if it's salty or if it is soapy tasting.

DEW

Dew can be collected on clear nights by using your handkerchief as a sponge. During a heavy dew you may be able to collect as much as a quart an hour.

You may also scoop out a hole, line the bottom with a piece of canvas or plastic, and fill this improvised basin with cool clean pebbles taken from

Collect dew in a sheet of waterproof fabric suspended over a hole and filled with pebbles.

a foot or more beneath the surface. Dew may collect on the rocks and trickle down onto the waterproof fabric. Collect the water in the early morning.

Dew also sometimes collects on exposed metal surfaces such as aircraft parts and the covers of tin cans, as well as on stones and small desert plants such as lupine. Drain this into a cup, gently shake it onto a sheet of plastic, or mop it up with a cloth.

WATER IN THE DESERT

Water seeks the lowest levels it can reach, and on the deserts that comprise one-fifth of the world's surface these may be underground. If you're walking out instead of camping and signalling, if there seems to be no especial direction to head, and if you can see hills, start toward them, inasmuch as the likeliest spot to obtain water will be at their bottoms.

Perhaps you'll wander across the cramped, narrow bed of a stream. Even though this may be dry, water may very well be running beneath the surface. Hunt for the lowest point on the outside of a bend in the channel and dig. The same general principle may be followed if you encounter a dry lake bottom. If the presence of water is not directly indicated by damp sand, pick the lowest point and dig.

If you come across a palm, you can rely on water's being within several feet of the base of the tree. Reed grass is another good sign that moisture is near. Cattails, greasewoods, willows, elderberry bushes, rushes, and salt grass grow only where ground water is near the surface. Purify all water from any frequented pools you may discover. Incidentally, small water holes in dried-out stream channels and low places, known to the natives, are often covered. Search carefully for them.

The presence of other vegetation does not always mean that surface water is available. But the sound of birds in a semiarid brush country often means that water is near at hand. In very dry deserts, birds will circle over a water hole. Places where animals have scratched or where flies are hovering indicate recent surface water and are good indications for digging.

In the desert your life will depend on your water supply. In hot sandy wastes, for example, you'll need a minimum of a gallon of water a day. If you rest during the day in some shaded spot, even if it's only the previously suggested east-west trench, and travel only during the cool desert night, you can put some twenty miles behind you to the daily gallon. If you do your walking in the daytime sun and heat, you'll be lucky to get half that distance on the same amount of water, and you'll be in far worse shape when you stop. But whether you sit out your desert ordeal or walk back to civilization, you'll need water.

CONSERVING WATER

There are a number of ways to conserve the water you already have. Importantly, though, a major survival factor is to drink your available water until your thirst is sated, rather than to ration it in an attempt to conserve the supply. Pinpoint your energies, instead, on retaining as much as you can of the water already in your system.

By eating less, you'll cut down on the amount of water demanded by the kidneys to rid the body of waste. In any event, don't eat dehydrated foods and other dry victuals. Carbohydrates are best, one gram when assimilated by the body yielding four calories of heat energy plus water.

By doing less, you'll both reduce perspiration and also cut down on the loss of water through the otherwise exerted lungs. An important slogan might be: ration your sweat but not your water.

Breathing through your nose and holding talk to a minimum both save water. Too, keep heat out of your body by keeping your clothes on. Clothing helps control perspiration by not letting sweat evaporate so fast that you only enjoy a portion of its cooling effect. You may feel more comfortable in the desert without a shirt and trousers. This is because your sweat will evaporate faster. But it takes more sweat.

Furthermore, you risk getting sunburned even if you already have what seems to be a good basic bronze. Therefore, wear a hat, use a back cloth, and stay fully clothed. If you have any choice in the matter, light-colored garb reflects the heat of the sun better and thus keeps out more of the hot desert air. If you do not have sun glasses, make slit goggles. Stay in the shade as much as possible during the day. Sit or lie a few inches above the actual ground if this is at all possible. The reason is that it can be thirty degrees or forty degrees cooler a foot above the ground. That difference in temperature can save a lot of sweat.

Slow and steady does it on a hot desert. If you must move about in the heat, you'll last longer on less water if you take it easy.

THE SOLAR STILL

The same piece of plastic which may be folded and borne in a breast pocket for shelter and other everyday uses can save you from dying of thirst in the desert or at sea.

In the deserts of the world, with a plastic sheet six feet square, up to three pints of water a day can be extracted from a bowl-shaped cavity some twenty inches deep and forty inches across. Place a cup, can, upturned hat, or other receptacle in the center of the hole. Anchor the plastic all the way around the top of the opening with dirt or stones. Set a fist-sized rock in the center of the sheet so that the plastic will sag in a point directly over the container.

Heat from the sun shines through the plastic and is absorbed by the sand, causing the evaporation of the moisture already in the earth. The vapor is almost immediately condensed on the cooler underneath side of the plastic, the drops flowing down the underside of the steeply angled sheet and dripping into the ready container. Capillary action causes more water to be attracted to the surface of the sand to replace that which has gone, and the process will go on.

Two such stills will, when operating well, keep a man going in the desert, for even when the production lessens after a day or two, it is a simple matter to move the still. Production will even continue at night at about half the rate of the daytime flow.

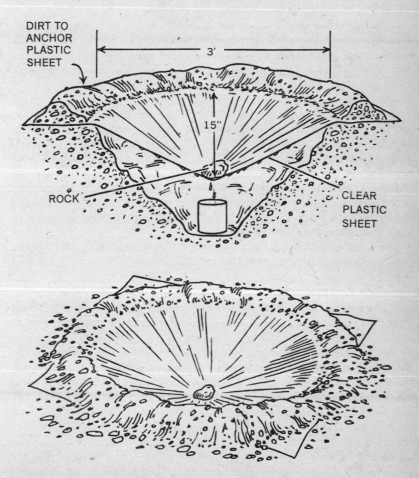

On the desert a solar still provides up to three pints of water a day.

Varying with the condition of the soil, the amount of water you can expect to extract in a twenty-four-hour day will be from somewhat less than a pint to three pints. But you can help the process along, particularly if you have selected a hollow or dry wash for your location.

You'll get even more fluid by cutting cacti and other water-holding desert plants into pieces and dropping them under the plastic. The rate of output can thus be increased up to nearly three times that of the sand alone. Too, even contaminated water such as urine, sea water, and radiator fluid not diluted with such a highly volatile substance as antifreeze can be purified if poured into the hole and allowed to vaporize and drip in the heat.

Sea water in the bottom of a boat can be vaporized and condensed in pure drinkable form by this same method. Incidentally, no matter where you conduct this operation, remove the plastic as seldom as possible, as it takes half an hour or more for the air to become resaturated and the production of water to start once more.

WATER AT SEA

Your best bets at sea, in addition to regular supplies, are solar stills and desalting kits. Desalting outfits can be used only for immediate need and during long periods of overcast when sun stills can not be utilized.

Tarpaulins can be used both to retain dew and to capture rain. Keep the tarpaulin as free of salt as possible by washing it in the sea, although a small amount won't matter. Particularly in a rough sea, it is difficult to obtain fresh rain, but mixing it with a little sea water will make it more palatable and more beneficial to the system.

Watch the clouds and be alert for any chance shower. When it does rain, drink all you can hold. At night, secure the tarpaulin as for sunshade, turning up the edges so that it will catch the dew which at sea may be considerable.

You may be out of sight of land and yet so near the influence of some great river that even far at sea the water will be fresh. If this may be the case in your situation, test the water from time to time by touching the tongue to a moistened finger.

Too, only if you already have ample water, the blood from any birds you can secure will help quench the thirst, and satisfy the appetite at the same time. These potential food sources can be caught on baited hooks, with triangular pieces of shiny metal, and by baited toggles of metal or wood. Many birds will be attracted to a raft or small boat as a possible perching place. Sit still until they settle nearby and fold their wings. Then grab them. But don't be too anxious and tip them off.

The blood of sea turtles will also, when water is available, sate thirst and hunger. Kill them by shooting them in the head, or snag them with a hook and kill them with blows on the head, avoiding their beaks and claws. The liver and fat are edible. The muscle will probably be tough but, at worst, can be advantageously chewed for awhile and then thrown away.

FRESH WATER FROM ICE

Sea ice becomes fresh during the period intervening between its formation and the end of the first summer thereafter. If you are ever in a position where you have no water but sea water, and if the weather is freezing, you will want to catch small amounts of the brine and allow ice to form in it. The slush and any remaining fluid should be discarded. You'll find the ice fresh enough to use in an emergency.

Ocean ice loses its salinity so rapidly that ice one year old is almost fresh. Sea ice two or more years old can not be distinguished, as far as taste is concerned, from river ice. The exception is when waves have been breaking over it or spray has been drenching it. If the weather is warm enough it's usually possible to find melted hollows which will contain all the fresh water you'll need.

BEFORE WATER IS SCARCE

If you have plenty of water at the moment but may have little or none later, drink as much as you possibly can, short of making yourself sick, before leaving the source of supply. You should sate your thirst, for instance, if you have the chance to do so before abandoning a ship or plane. In dry country, start drinking as soon as you reach a safe water hole and keep it up until you leave.

All efforts should be concentrated on taking what water you can, even at the cost of leaving other things behind, before quitting what may be an isolated supply. Don't ration the supply later on. In opposition to the now-outmoded ration practices of past centuries, you should drink until you have reasonably satisfied your thirst. Carrying a round, clean pebble in your mouth will help decrease the later sensation of thirst.

WHEN YOU HAVE WATER AGAIN

When meager or non-existent water supplies are finally replenished, don't make the very natural mistake of drinking a lot at once. This is apt to cause nausea and vomiting. Instead, extend the satisfaction over an hour or two, starting off with a few hearty sips.

WHAT ABOUT EATING SNOW?

Clean snow may be eaten any time you're thirsty. The only precaution you ever need take with it, aside of course from its essential purity, is not to eat too much when you're chilled or heated.

After all, snow is made up of the purest of distilled water that can be secured from the atmosphere. The only disadvantage is that it takes a lot of it to equal even a small amount of water. Hard-packed snow yields more water than light fluffy flakes. Granular snow from old storms is better yet.

You learn quickly about the low water content of snow the first time you try melting it. Hanging a snow-packed container directly over the fire often results in burning the metal and incidentally in imparting that taste to the eventual water. The trouble is, as soon as a little melts, the remaining snow blots it up.

The best procedure is to continue melting snow in small quantities until the bottom of the receptacle is safely covered with several inches of water. Or if you're in a hurry, work the snow in the initially filled container with a stick or knife until there is more water on the bottom than can be immediately absorbed by the snow above. With a fresh snowfall, the container will have to be refilled several times if a capacity amount of fluid is desired.

These drawbacks are more than made up for by the fact that snowfall makes water quickly available when you're in the wilderness. All you need do to satisfy your thirst is to scoop up clean handfuls of snow as you hike along, an invaluable advantage inasmuch as your body needs a lot more water in freezing weather than you'd suppose — at least two quarts a day — as the kidneys have to take over much of the process of eliminating waste materials otherwise handled by the sweat glands.

HOW PURE IS ICE?

It requires roughly half the fuel to obtain a given quantity of water from ice than from snow. But this water will be no purer than was the water from which it was frozen. Cold temperatures do nothing to destroy germs. They merely hold them in suspension for decades at a time.

Incidentally, it's important enough to repeat that liquor, no matter what the proof, does not purify the ice or even the water in a mixed drink.

Northern rivers continue flowing all winter, even though sheathed with ice as tall as a Cape Cod cottage. You can frequently find overflow, though, with which to fill your containers. By careful observation and repeated testing, you can also usually locate a spot where water lies not too far below the surface. This water hole, once cut or chiseled, should be covered as with a thick layer of evergreen browse to help prevent it from freezing solid again.

A pointed instrument will be best to break out ice. A number of light taps will start a crack, and then one stragetic sharp blow will break off a chunk of the size desired. On a large surface, such as a river or lake, cut toward a crack that is already there so as to avoid getting only splinters and spray.

Dining On Wild Plants 9

Experts estimate that about three hundred thousand classified plants, many of them subdivisions of the same genus, grow on the earth's surface, including many which thrive on mountain tops and conversely on the oceans' floors. Of these, no less than 120,000 varieties are edible.

Obviously, you won't be able to learn all these plants from reading this manual, but there are more than enough widely distributed edibles pictured, described, and discussed here to give you gourmet meals until you're rescued. If you read enough about these to know what to look for in the area where you find yourself stranded, can identify them, and know how to prepare them properly, you'll surprise yourself with many a delicious meal. You may even find you've put on weight during your ordeal.

Don't limit yourself to studying the illustrations and descriptions of the edible plants in this manual. Take every opportunity to see these plants in their natural habitat. Then if you are ever forced into a survival situation, you will know what the most nourishing and best tasting wild plants are.

However, don't take any chances. There are plenty of edibles covered in this volume to keep you going for years, so many in fact that there will seldom be any reason to try anything else. If you are forced to do so, however, first taste a very small amount. If this seems to be agreeable, try a spoonful. Then wait for twenty-four hours. If all seems well, eat more of the plant and wait another day. If there are no ill effects, you may safely regard the plant as edible.

Just because a plant is very familiar to you does not mean that it is edible. Clover, for one, has saved hundreds of lives during famines, but the equally familiar buttercup is poisonous. Just because an animal seems to be thriving on a particular plant does not mean that it is edible by humans. Horses relish poison ivy, for example, and squirrels eat the most poisonous of mushrooms with impunity. In short, don't eat anything unless you're sure it is edible. You have more than enough safe choices.

Adding from season to season the recognition of a few more edible wild plants can be a practical and engrossing pastime, as well as a thrifty and healthy way of pleasantly introducing new delicacies to family and friends. Such acquired knowledge can even mean, in some unforeseen emergency, the difference between eating bountifully and starving.

FAMILIAR WEEDS THAT CAN SAVE YOUR LIFE

Plantain is found all over the world, even growing up through city sidewalks. The leaves of this *Plantago* are edible raw when young and tender.

The greener they are, the richer in vitamins A and C. They are good, too, simmered; but only until just tender and still slightly crisp. For the best results, start in boiling water and keep covered so that they'll be ready as rapidly as possible.

Plantain, also called ribwort and soldiers' herb, is the short, stemless potherb whose broad, elliptic green leaves rise directly from the root about a straight central spike. This singular spike blossoms with minute greenish flowers that later turn to seeds.

In some backwoods localities fresh plantain leaves are mashed and applied to cuts, scratches, and wounds; something to remember if you ever have to do your own doctoring in the wilderness.

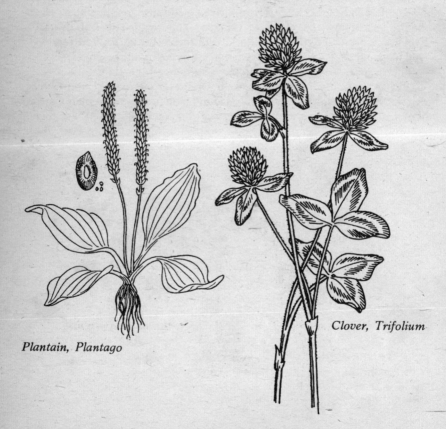

Clover, Trifolium

Plantain, Plantago

Everyone who has sucked honey from the tiny tubular florets among its yellow, white, and reddish blossoms, or who has searched among its green beds for the elusive four-leaf combination, knows the clover which grows wild throughout the world.

Bread made from the seeds and dried blossoms of clover (*Trifolium*) is extremely wholesome and nutritious and has been a mainstay in times of famine. The young leaves and flowers are also good raw. They can be boiled, too, when a little older. The sweetish roots are also delicious and nutritious.

Clover tea is one of the tastier and more sustaining wild beverages. Just gather the full-grown flowers, preferably when they are dry, and rub them into small particles between the palms. Use a teaspoon of these to each cup of boiling water and steep to taste, just as you would regular tea.

The familiar burdock, *Arctium,* thrives plentifully throughout much of the United States and southern Canada. This aggressive but delicious immigrant, brought to the New World with the early settlers, is a topnotch wild food and all the more valuable because everyone will recognize it easily, if only because of the seed-bearing burrs on some of the plants.

Burdock is cultivated throughout the Orient for the roots. The first-year roots are the ones to use. These are easy to distinguish, as the plants stemming from them are without flower or burr stalks. Just scrape these roots,

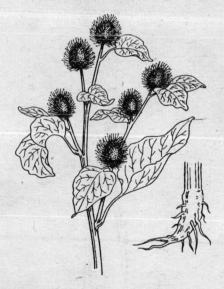

Burdock, Arctium

slice them like carrots, and simmer them until they are tender. Some like to change the water once, although when you're cooking without salt you'll likely relish the extra taste.

The youngest leaves can be boiled in two waters and enjoyed as greens. The young leaf stalks are good peeled and eaten raw. They can also be added to soups and stews, or cooked by themselves like asparagus.

The fat, rapidly growing flower stalk is one of the tastier parts of the burdock. These sprout the second year, and should be cut off just as the blossom heads are starting to appear in the late spring or early summer. Peel away the strong, bitter skin and enjoy them raw or simmered in a small amount of water for about twenty minutes.

The first-year roots, dug either in the fall or early spring, are also used to soothe burns, wounds, and skin irritations. To get the proper strength, drop a heaping tablespoon of the cleaned roots into a quart of boiling water and allow to stand until cool.

Another life-saving edible, the well-known dandelion (*Taraxacum*) is all too familiar to many because of the way it defies all but the most stringent efforts to keep it from thriving in well-manicured lawns. The whole plant and particularly the roots are famous throughout the globe for having kept many from the brink of starvation during famines.

Dandelion roots are best when peeled, sliced like carrots, and boiled until reasonably soft. When you're cooking without salt the characteristic

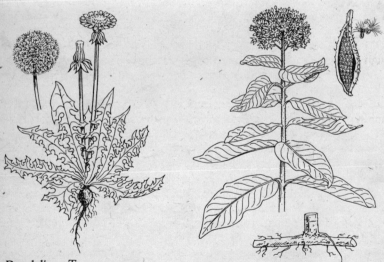

Dandelion, *Taraxacum*

Milkweed, *Asclepias*

tinge of bitterness will likely be relished. Unless it is especially distasteful to you, therefore, you'll want to eat these roots in the first water. Put the plants in whole and eat them, if you have no more civilized means, by using two peeled sticks like chopsticks and twirling the steaming green streamers around them after grasping a root.

Another wild edible with milky sap, the milkweed, thrives from the Atlantic to the Pacific and was relied upon for food by the Indians. This *Asclepias syriaca*, abundant in marshes and fields, often whitens these in the autumn when its tiny seeds with their familiar parachutes drift on the breezes. Simmered until tender, the young leaves provide fine greens. The sweet-smelling flowers, tiny and numerous, differ in color from a greenish lilac shade to an off white. The buds, by the way, provide another wilderness delicacy.

It is for its stalks, however, that milkweed is most famous as a wild edible. These are best up to about eight inches high. Cook them like asparagus, although the time required will be longer than for that garden vegetable, milkweed's being one of the tougher of the wild greens.

All parts of the plant are initially bitter and with milky juice, but this sap is readily soluble in water. So first cover your milkweed, no matter which portion you are using, with boiling water. Bring this again to a boil over a hot campfire and pour off. Some do this several times, although when you're surviving without salt you'll probably like the character of a little extra bitterness.

In the West, from British Columbia to California, Indians used the tough fibers of a mature, similar, purple-blossomed milkweed, for coarse weaving. The milky sap was applied to ringworm infestations and to warts, as well as to cuts and sores.

Because they are so positively and easily recognizable, nettles are an important emergency food. In a pinch, too, the stems of the older plants will yield a strong fiber that's useful for fish lines.

Nettles are easily identified, especially as both stem and leaf surface bristle with a fuzz of fine prickles containing the irritating formic acid. Even when delectably young, nettles, *Urtica*, should be gathered with gloves or some other protection for the hands if possible. Some of the Indian Tribes relieved the otherwise incurred stinging by rubbing the irritated skin with the dryish, rusty, feltlike growth that sheathes the likewise edible fiddleheads.

However, the dark green leaves and small entire plants quickly lose their stinging properties when dropped in boiling water. Subtly flavored, they are then nourishing sources of vitamins A and C and some of the minerals.

Another common edible plant capable of saving your life in an emergency is the sow thistle, *Sonchus*. Resembling a dandelion with prickly leaves, its clusters of yellow flowers also look like those of a dandelion except are smaller. The sow thistle also is characterized by a milky sap. This sap is bitterish, again like that of the dandelion, but when I'm cooking without

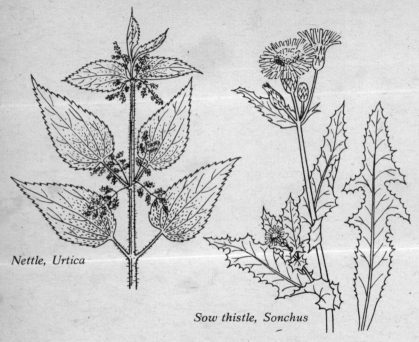

Nettle, Urtica

Sow thistle, Sonchus

salt I like even that much of a taste, although some may prefer to throw out the first water. If you catch the leaves young enough, they're tasty and even more nutritious raw.

The trailing, juicy purslane, familiar to almost everyone who has ever weeded a yard, is native to India and Persia where it has been a food for more than two thousand years. It was introduced to the New World back in colonial days and has spread throughout the United States, the warmer parts of Canada, and even to Mexico. The reason for its worldwide distribution is its tremendous production of seeds, relished by birds and rodents. Although purslane, *Portulaca,* does not become large, over fifty-two thousand seeds have been counted on a single plant.

The tender, leafy tips are delicious both raw and cooked, from late June until frost. Purslane has a mucilaginous quality, like that of okra, which will lend consistency to your soups and stews.

Shepherd's purse, *Capsella,* is another easily identified and common weed that's good to eat. The tender young leaves, like others of the mustard family, have a pleasant, peppery taste either raw or cooked. Indians even roasted the seeds for meal. Shepherd's purse, sometimes known as shepherd's heart and as pickpocket, is also used as a tea: one teaspoon to a cup of boiling water, two cups of which daily are said to be somewhat cathartic.

Purslane, Portulaca

Shepherd's purse, Capsella

Although fronds of some similar ferns are edible, it is the fiddleheads from the widely familiar and distributed pasture brake, *Pteridium aquilinum,* that are most commonly enjoyed. These young, uncoiled fronds grow luxuriently throughout the Northern Hemisphere. These are eatable, however, only while still fiddleheads and therefore young. They are then good both raw and cooked. Later, the full-grown fronds toughen and become poisonous to cattle as well as humans.

Break them off with the fingers as low as they will snap easily, remove their loose brown coating by rubbing the fiddleheads between the hands, and they're ready to eat. If you like vegetables which like okra are mucilaginous, you'll probably enjoy these raw. Cooking changes the consistency of the rather glutinous juice somewhat, but the sweetish fiddleheads are still reminiscent of okra. One way to get the nearly full food values from fiddleheads is to simmer them in a small amount of water until tender, then devour them hot. Tender young fiddleheads, raw, can add a lot to a meal of assorted wild greens. When cooked they'll provide a delectable thicken-

157

ing to stews. Too, the long rootstocks can be roasted in the campfire, peeled, and powdered between two flat stones. The nourishingly starchy insides can then be eaten as is, used to thicken soup, or employed like flour.

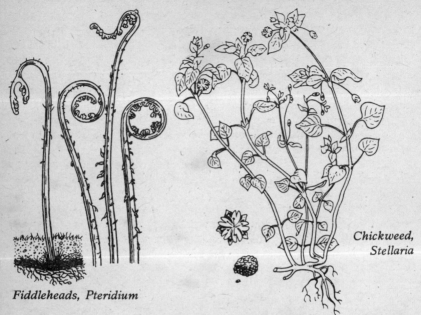

Chickweed,
Stellaria

Fiddleheads, Pteridium

Common chickweed, a member of the pink family, blooms almost everywhere in the central United States every month, although its deeply notched white flowers open only in sunshine. It grows in fields, woods, and moist places.

Easily recognized and therefore a good emergency food for stranded and hungry people, this annual, known by botanists either as *Stellaria* or *Alsine,* is unique in that it begins growing in the fall, survives the severities of cold even in the North, starts blossoming in late winter, and often finishes its life cycle and seed production in the springtime. These numberless tiny seeds in their papery capsules, as well as the plant's tender leaves, are fine eating if you can beat the game birds to them.

This abundant green has none of the disagreeable taste that many people find in spinach. If only the top stems and leaves are used, they will become tender in a very short time when boiled in a little water. The delicate taste is rather bland, and you may prefer to mix your chickweed half and half with other greens, such as dock or water cress.

MORE COMMON WILD EDIBLES

Cattails, *Typhaceae,* are found in wet places throughout the world. They're delicious both raw and cooked, from their starchy roots to their cornlike spikes, making them prime emergency foods.

Another name for this prolific wild edible — also known as rushes, bulrushes, cat-o'-nine-tails, and flags — should be wild corn. Just collect a few dozen of the greenish yellow flower spikes before they start to become tawny with pollen. Husk off the thin sheaths and, just as you would the garden vegetable, put into rapidly boiling water for a few minutes until tender. Then eat them like corn on the cob.

The thick golden pollen which later appears on the flower spikes can be collected in a cloth and made into cereal by simmering it in a small amount of water, or made into pancakes by mixing it with flour.

The tender white insides of the first foot or so of the peeled young stems are a delicacy raw or cooked, and give the cattail another occasional name: cossack asparagus.

Quantities of the nutritiously starchy roots can be dug in fall or winter, washed, peeled while still wet, dried, and then ground between two stones into a meal that can be sifted to get out any fibers.

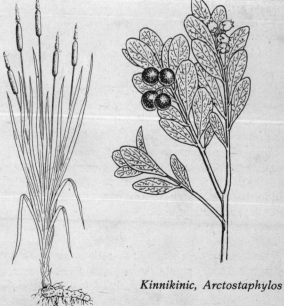

Cattail, Typhaceae

Kinnikinic, Arctostaphylos

159

Once you've staved off hunger with the rather dry and bland red berries of the kinnikinic, you can fashion yourself a smoke with the leaves. Dried and pulverized, these have been a famous frontier tobacco substitute on this continent for centuries.

Easily recognized and widely distributed across Alaska, Canada, and the tops of Europe and Asia, and in the states of California, New Mexico, and Virginia — this *Arctostaphylos* should be better known because of its potential value as an emergency food. The hard, dry berries cling to the mat-like evergreens all winter. Although they can be eaten raw, you'll likely prefer them cooked, perhaps mixed with other berries.

Because of kinnikinic, the chinook-bared hills surrounding our log cabin home in Hudson Hope, British Columbia, are green in late winter and early spring, while snow is still deep in the poplar and spruce forests. This perennial evergreen with its long fibrous roots has alternate short-stemmed leaves that are thick, small, egg-shaped, and tough. The inconspicuous little pink flowers grow like minute bells in terminal clusters. The berries, occasionally pink but more often dull red with an orange cast, ripen in the autumn.

A pleasantly bitter tea can be made of the odorless green leaves if you'll cover a teaspoonful with a cup of boiling water and allow it to steep for five minutes.

The spicy little red berries of the *Gaultheria* make this evergreen plant one of the most widely known of all the North American edibles. The some twenty-five common names accorded wintergreen, including teaberry and checkerberry, support this conclusion.

Wintergreens are diminutive members of the heath family, often thriving in the shadow of evergreens in forests and clearings from eastern Canada to the Gulf states, and as far west as the Great Lakes. Western wintergreen, less spicy than the eastern species, thrives on the other side of the continent from British Columbia to California.

The firm, berrylike fruit can be an important emergency food, especially as it clings to the stems all winter. The evergreen leaves are well worth chewing because of their characteristic flavor and are edible in a pinch, particularly when young. Freshly-gathered leaves make a very palatable tea, a teaspoonful to a cup of boiling water. Tearing them first into small pieces provides even more flavor.

Various members of the knotweed family have long provided man with fruit, vegetable, and even nuts. Some thirty species of the *Polygonum* occur in practically every part of the United States. The starchy and fleshy rootstocks of the *Polygonum bistorta* in British Columbia and the Yukon are cooked and eaten as a substitute for nuts because of their almondlike deliciousness. In the Arctic, and south to Colorado and New England, the raw roots of this edible are enjoyed for the same nutlike characteristic. Lady's thumb or heartweed, *Polygonum persicaria,* is found throughout much of this continent except in the Far North and is enjoyed raw.

It is the Japanese knotweed, *Polygonum cuspidatum,* with which many are most familiar. This is well known, although not always by name, from North Carolina to Missouri, north to southern Canada, growing in large,

Wintergreen, Gaultheria

Knotweed, Polygonum

coarse stands from about three to eight feet tall. The enlarged joints of the stalks are encased in thin, papery sheaths. When these hollow stalks die, they form bamboolike thickets which clack and rattle in the wind and which serve to identify the young edible shoots when they shoot up in the spring.

161

Knotweed shoots, before the leaves start to unfurl, are delicately delicious when about twelve to fifteen inches high. Cook them three to four minutes in boiling water, then they're good either hot or cold.

One of the knotweeds in Alaska, *Polygonum alaskanum,* is called wild rhubarb because the young stems in early spring are used the same way as domesticated rhubarb. This will work, too, with Japanese knotweed. First, carefully peel the outer skin from the thinly fleshed stalks. Then cut into segments. Simmer, preferably with some sweet fruit for flavor, until tender. This, too, is good both hot and cold, and it's replete with vitamins and minerals.

The insides of the leaves of the live-forever, or frog plant, were used by our pioneer ancestors to apply to warts. The fresh leaves also have a cooling quality and have long been used to soothe bruises, insect stings, burns, and other such irritations.

This member of the genus *Sedum,* also called Aaron's rod, is a close cousin of roseroot. As with roseroot, both the plant tops and the roots are

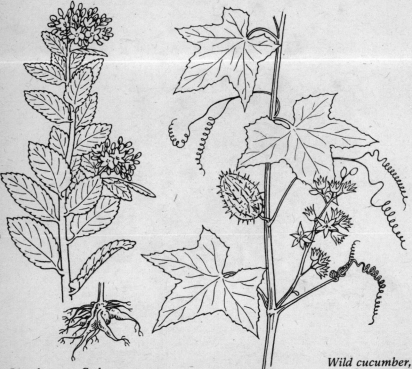

Live-forever, Sedum

Wild cucumber,
Streptopus

delicious. The ease with which this wild vegetable can be recognized makes it a prime survival food.

The stout, rounded or fingerlike, tuberous roots also are edible, but become stringy and tough when the plant blooms. In late fall large masses of newly grown, crisp white tubers can once more be located. All these are edible raw.

Both the stems and leaves when very young are tender enough to enjoy raw. Later, until the plant flowers, they may be cooked until tender by any method available to you. Even when you're safe and sound at home once again, you'll probably be back for more.

The fresh young shoots and leaves of the wild cucumber impart a taste similar to that of its namesake when mixed with raw greens. This perennial *Streptopus,* also known as liverberry and twisted stalk, has small pulpy berries that range in color from whitish yellow to orange and scarlet when they ripen. However, despite their refreshing flavor, they are cathartic and should be used sparingly. For this reason, they are known as scoot berries in some localities.

THE BEST OF THE EDIBLE GREENS

One of the most delicious of the edible greens is lamb's quarter. The tender tops of this wild spinach, *Chenopodium,* are delicious raw or cooked,

Lamb's quarter, Chenopodium

Strawberry spinach, Chenopodium

from early spring until fall. The young plant is good in its entirety. And from the older ones a quantity of tender leaves can usually be stripped. However, the pale green leaves with their mealy-appearing underneaths and slim stalks are not the only taste-tempting parts of this green, also known as goosefoot and pigweed. Indians long used the ripe seeds for cereal and for grinding into meal.

Strawberry spinach is similar to its close cousin, lamb's quarter. The major difference lies in the bright red masses of pulpy fruits which appear in early fall and make this *Chenopodium* easily recognizable. This edible, also known as Indian strawberry and strawberry blight, is common across Alaska and Canada, down into the southern states.

Its inconspicuous little flowers grow in angles between the leaves and the upper portion of the stem, as well as often in the spike at the top of the stem. They become dense, red masses, with the color and softness of straw-

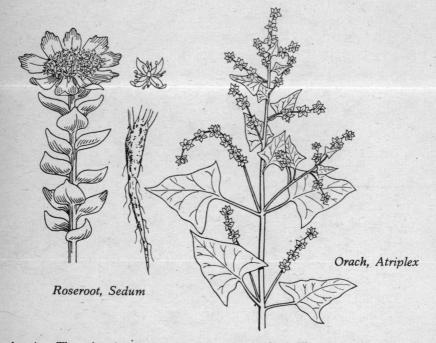

Roseroot, Sedum

Orach, Atriplex

berries. These berries are nutritious raw or cooked. The young stems and leaves, and later the young tender leaves by themselves, will ward off hunger either raw or cooked like spinach.

Roseroot, whose juicy young stems with the fleshy, pale green to pinkish leaves attached are edible either raw or cooked, is another of the wild greens known as scurvy grass because of the often life-saving amounts of vitamin C it provided early venturers on this continent's frontiers.

Easy to recognize, this *Sedum,* also sometimes known as rosewort and stonecrop, becomes unmistakable when you bruise or scrape the big, rough roots and catch the rich odor of expensive rose perfume. The perennial rose-root and some of its close cousins are prized both in North America and in Europe as a salad plant and boiled vegetable, and are good from summer until fall.

The tender tips and juicy young leaves of orach will keep you from starving, from spring to late fall. Shaped something like lance heads, the leaves of this *Atriplex* are greyish to bright green, smooth-edged, and characteristically lighter and mealy-looking underneath. The small green flowers grow in narrow, spikelike clusters. Later this is an abundance of small, starchy seeds, once ground by some of the Indian tribes for meal. Orach, also known as saltbush and as shad scale, is delicious raw and can also be used in cooking to add salt to other wild vegetables.

The more than a dozen docks thriving on this continent, from the Arctic coast to Alaska southward through Canada and the United States, provide

Dock, Rumex   *Mountain sorrel, Oxyria*

hearty greens which the Eskimos still put up in quantities for winter use. This wild edible, *Rumex,* whether eaten raw or cooked, has a more rugged flavor than some of the other wild vegetables. Overtones of both sourness and bitterness that vary with the different species often make it preferable to mix dock with other greens, especially when you're eating without salt.

Scurvy is a vitamin deficiency disease that has killed more pioneers and explorers than can ever be counted. If you have it, taking vitamin C into your system will cure you.

Eating a little vitamin C regularly will prevent scurvy in the first place. Fresh vegetables and fruits will both prevent and cure scurvy, as will lemon and lime juice. The vitamin C in these is lessened and eventually destroyed by age and oxidation, and by salt.

Scurvy grass, of which there are several species belonging to the *Cochlearia* genus, is widely distributed across the northern portions of this continent from Alaska to Newfoundland. It has a strong horseradishlike odor and the flavor of water cress. Its small white flowers, whose four petals are arranged in a cross, grow in long clusters atop branching stems, a few inches high, that rise from grouped leaves. The little blossoms produce flattish, oval pods that become filled with seeds.

Scurvy grass is delicious eaten raw or simmered briefly in a small amount of water. For the utmost in nourishment, though, eat it directly as it grows, or tear the leaves into fine pieces and use them in a salad.

Mountain sorrel, *Oxyria,* is a green that I've enjoyed in such diverse places as New Mexico, British Columbia, and the White Mountains of New Hampshire. This member of the buckwheat family, which grows from Alaska and Greenland to Southern California, is known in different parts of this country as sourgrass, scurvy grass, and Alpine sorrel.

It's interesting to note that where this wild edible grows in the Arctic, Eskimos both in North America and Asia ferment some of it as a sauerkraut. Raw or cooked, it has a flavorsome sourness that goes especially well with fish.

The importance of winter cress, *Barbarea verna* or *Barbarea vulgaris,* lies in its ability to grow during mild winter weather, so long as the ground is clear of snow.

The clusters of small, four-petaled, golden blossoms, resembling tiny Maltese crosses, show that these edible herbs belong among the numerous species of mustards. Also known as yellow rocket, Belle Island cress, scurvy grass, bitter cress, spring cress, and upland cress, winter cress is cultivated both here and abroad as winter salad green and as a potherb.

If the initial rosettes of long, dark green, smooth leaves are not gathered when they first spring directly from the roots during winter and early spring, they become overly bitter. The leaves take on too much bitterness for enjoyable eating when winter cress finally blooms, but then the buds have a broccolilike savoriness. These grow in clusters at the tops of the flowering stalks, making for quick and easy gathering. As with dandelions, the inclusion of a few open flowers does not hurt the taste. These are good raw, but particularly agreeable when simmered for about four minutes in a small amount of boiling water.

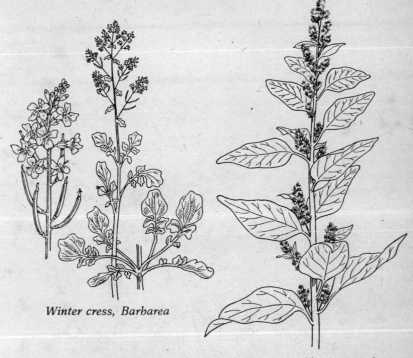

Winter cress, Barbarea

Green amaranth, Amaranthus

The nutritious green amaranth is rich in vitamins and minerals as well as being one of the most delicious of all greens. The tender tops, stalks, and leaves of this wild spinach have none of the strong taste of market varieties, and are enjoyable raw or cooked from early spring to frost-blighting fall.

Growing as a weed over much of the continent, the green amaranth, *Amaranthus,* is familiar to most individuals although not necessarily as an edible. The flowers are greenish, therefore are not usually recognized as blossoms. They grow in long, loosely branched clusters and have a pleasant taste raw. The resulting shiny black seeds were threshed by the Indians, roasted by campfires, and then used for cakes and porridge.

LETTUCE ON THE WILD SIDE

About a dozen species of the tall, white-juiced wild lettuce *Lactuca* are common in the rich, moist soil of fields and open thickets all the way across the continent.

If you like the slightly bitter taste of cooked dandelions, you'll enjoy wild lettuce as a potherb. Otherwise, you may discard the first water in which it is boiled, although without salt this is usually inadvisable. When just a few inches tall, the vitamin-teeming wild lettuce is tasty raw; and the leaves and stems are tender enough to cook until the edible is about sixteen inches high.

Wild lettuce, *Lactuca*

Prickly lettuce, *Lactuca*

One of the more succulent members of the wild lettuce family is the distinctive prickly lettuce believed by some botanists to be the forerunner of the lettuce we now buy in stores. Both the lower part of the stem and center leaf ribs bristle with prickles which, luckily, quickly lose their sharpness in boiling water. In fact, if you gather prickly lettuce young enough, it is delicately delicious raw.

In addition to providing sustenance, the prickly lettuce serves as a compass; its sharply toothed leaves twist edgewise to the sun and thus point north and south.

Also recognized as deer tongue because of the shape of its leaves and as mountain lettuce because of their edibility, lettuce saxifrage, scientifically known either as *Saxifraga* or *Micranthes,* concentrates its growth in a crisp green rosette of leaves. The members of this thick mat are up to about eleven inches long, shaped like an animal's tongue and roughened along the edges with keen, short teeth. The tender young leaves, picked before the plant flowers and eaten raw, will supply you with considerable amounts of vitamins. Lettuce saxifrage and its edible cousins grow in moist meadows and along the cool edges of brooks over most of the country.

Lettuce saxifrage, Saxifraga

Miner's lettuce, Montia

Miner's lettuce, identified by the way a pair of leaves grow together part of the way up some of the short stems and form a cup through whose middle the stalk continues, has stems and leaves which are good raw while young. When the older leaves are cooked their flavor resembles that of spinach. The plant, also known as Indian lettuce and Spanish lettuce, has been important to outdoorsmen since the days of the Forty-Niners. *Montia* grows profusely in springtime throughout the Pacific regions of the United States, Southern Canada, and into Mexico.

UNDERGROUND EDIBLES

Except in cold weather when it will take effort to scratch through the frozen ground, groundnuts can be easily uncovered, as they lie on strings of roots just beneath the surface. Often as big as eggs, they grow on long roots in series of tuberlike swellings. You can find them from Florida and the blue Gulf of Mexico north to New Brunswick and westward to Texas, Kansas, and Ontario where they are also known as Indian potatoes, bog potatoes, or wild beans.

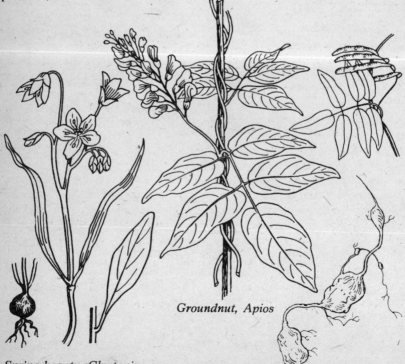

Groundnut, Apios

Spring beauty, Claytonia

The purplish or brownish flowers of this *Apios* look like those of the familiar garden peas and beans. They grow abundantly, about the time that schools are reopening, where the egg-shaped leaves lift in clumps of five to nine out of the soft vines. These blossoms give us another edible, as they develop into long slender pods resembling those of the garden green bean. Prepared like ordinary peas, they'll give you an added tidbit. The vines, incidentally, have a milky sap as do a number of the other wild edibles, disproving the often-printed statement that you should avoid all plants with whitish sap.

Although they are edible raw, groundnuts are even better cooked. They have more the character of the turnip in taste than the familiar blandness of tame potatoes. Just drop them into boiling water and simmer them until a knife or sharp twig will pass through them with little effort. If any are left over, try to warm them before the next meal as they're short on both tenderness and taste when cold.

The spring beauty, *Claytonia,* grows from small, potatolike roots that lie several inches below the surface and require a certain amount of digging. A pointed stick will do the job, though, where they're plentiful. These roundish tubers range in diameter from one-half inch to two inches, becoming more and more irregular in shape the larger they grow. Fifteen or twenty minutes of simmering the tubers in their jackets will usually cook them through. They're done when a small pointed stick shoves through them easily. Then just peel and eat them. To me, they taste like particularly choice potatoes with a hint of chestnut.

The plant's grasslike to broadly ovate leaves, depending on the species, are also edible, raw when young and briefly boiled when older. Both ways they are excellent sources of vitamins A and C.

You may know it as the oyster plant, salsify, or as goatsbeard; but no matter what the name, the three species of *Tragopogon* that grow from coast to coast in the United States and in southern Canada can save your life in time of need. Often growing two and three feet high, salsify is a perennial with an edible primary root that extends vertically downward. This becomes pithy once the tall, leafy flowering stem develops the second year, producing either purple or yellow blooms not unlike large dandelions. However, you'll generally find young roots in the same patch.

Also like dandelions, the leaves exude a milky juice when scraped or broken. Resembling wide blades of grass, they are pleasantly edible raw when young. If they are too old to enjoy this way, simmer them in water until tender.

It is for its roots, however, that salsify is most famous. Although you can eat these raw in a pinch, they're better if first scrubbed, scraped, cut lengthwise or into slices, and simmered in water until tender. To some palates they then taste something like oysters, a similarity you can enhance by browning them over the campfire on forked green sticks.

Arrowheads are sometimes cultivated along the damp rims of rice paddies in Asia, and when numerous Chinese moved into California during gold-rush days this plant was quickly adopted. It is still sold in some markets under the name "tule potato."

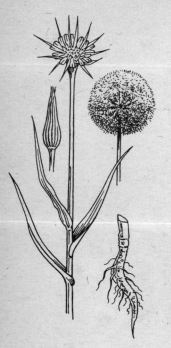

Oyster plant, Tragopogon

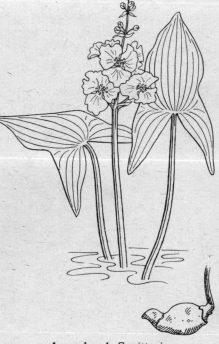

Arrowhead, Sagittaria

The leaves of this five to thirty-six-inch plant, in spite of its name, are not always arrow-shaped, but sometimes long and uniform in width, and occasionally shaped like lances.

The plant's hard tubers grow along subterranean runners and may attain the size of eggs. They're good boiled or roasted in the hot ashes of a campfire like the potatoes whose flavor they resemble. The roots mature in mid-summer and fall, and are also edible throughout the winter.

Silverweed, so named because of the white underneaths of the leaves, has roots which taste like good parsnips with overtones of sweet potato. These roots are thick and fleshy, and good both raw and when roasted in the campfire.

This common *Potentilla,* also known as wild tansy, can be found in damp places — along stream banks, amid salt meadow grasses, and on the seacoast. It is reasonable that so popular an edible should have maintained

Silverweed, Potentilla

a position in the medicine kit. The pioneers found silverweed effective in allaying diarrhea when a teaspoon of the leaves was steeped in a cup of boiling water. This beverage was drunk cold, one or two cupfuls a day, a few sips at a time.

Chufa abounds on this continent from Alaska to Mexico and from the Pacific Ocean to the Atlantic. Sweet, nutty, and milky with juice, edible *Cyperus* tubers are clustered around the base of this plant, especially when it grows in sandy or loose soil where a few tugs will release it.

Chufa, known in some localities as nut grass and as earth almond, provides one of the wilderness coffees. Just dry a few of the little tubers in front of your fire, roast them until they are a rich brown throughout, grind them between a couple of flat stones, and brew like the store-purchased beverage.

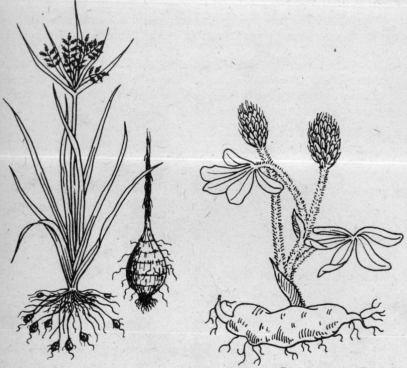

Chufa, Cyperus

Prairie turnip, Psoralea

John Colter, the mountain man who traveled with the Lewis and Clark expedition, lived for a week on prairie turnips in the area we now know as Yellowstone National Park. This notable vegetable of the plains and the West, *Psoralea,* was a mainstay of such Indians as the Sioux.

Another member of the pea family, *Psoralea* is a perennial whose large root or sometimes group of roots resembles sweet potatoes. These lie completely beneath the ground. Their bristling stalks and spikes of bluish pealike flowers, which eventually become tiny pods, mature early. They then break off and blow about the prairie.

The result is that the roots are left unmarked, and you may have to dig blindly for them if it is late in the season. Peeled, these are edible raw. Many prefer their taste, though, after they have been boiled, or perhaps sheathed with ashes and roasted in the hot embers of a campfire.

FORESTS OF FOOD

Members of the pine family — firs, hemlocks, balsams, and like coniferous trees — comprise one of the most vital groups of wild edibles in the world.

The inner bark of the pines, relished both raw and cooked, has saved actual hundreds of people from famine. Tea, made by steeping the youngest available green needles in hot water until the steaming brew is well colored, contains the invaluable vitamin C.

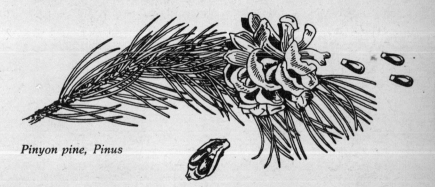

Pinyon pine, Pinus

Any of the seeds to be discovered in the cones of this great *Pinus* clan is edible. Even the young green cones themselves are good to eat. As if all that isn't enough, try chewing the new, starchy green needles. They are not only pleasantly flavored, but they'll take the edge off hunger. Even the firm, spikelike flower clusters, in which the petalless blossoms grow in circular rows on slender stalks, have a table use. Indians used to boil them to flavor their meats.

The sweetish, starchy sap layer of trees of the genus *Populus,* too, is edible both raw and cooked. This lies between the wood and the outside bark, the latter being intensely bitter. Poplar leaves, as well as the outer bark, supply salicin; used in medicine to lower fever and as a tonic.

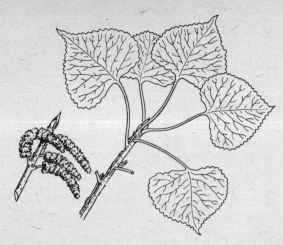

Poplar, Populus

All the birches furnish prime emergency food. Two general varieties of this *Betula* grow across the continent, the black birch family — with its tight, reddish brown, cherrylike bark which has the smell and taste of wintergreen — and the familiar white birches whose cheerful foliage and softly gleaming bark lighten the northern forests.

The inner bark of the birches, dried and then ground into flour, was frequently used by both Indians and frontiersmen for bread. It is also cut into strips and boiled like noodles. But you don't even have to go to that much trouble. Just enjoy it raw. Like the maple, all the birches have a sweet, watery, nourishing sap.

The edible maple leaf, emblem of Canada and a major reason why New England is so colorful in the fall, is known to everyone. So are the fruits, composed of a pair of brown wings with the seeds enclosed in the plump juncture. These are edible, too, as are the young leaves.

The inner bark of this tree is one of the most appetizing sap layers in the world and is eaten in emergencies, either raw or cooked. But it is for the sap that the maple, *Acer*, has been notable since Indian days. All the maples have sugar-rich sap. You can tap it with your knife in an emergency and drink the delectable juice with all its nourishing B vitamins, calcium, phosphorous, and enzymes.

The sprawling juniper grows from Labrador to Alaska, south as far as California and New Mexico. These evergreen shrubs and shrubby trees, *Juniperus*, with their compact branches, thin shreddy bark, and scalelike leaves are prolific with dark blue berries. Found year round on the shoots of the female shrubs, these are about the size of garden peas. The edible flesh cushioning the big seed is on the sweet side and is resinously aromatic. It'll keep you alive, although a large amount is apt to be irritating to the

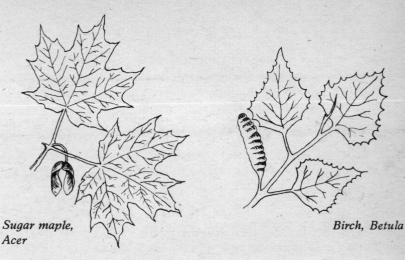

Sugar maple,
Acer

Birch, Betula

kidneys. In fact, a diuretic can be made by adding a teaspoon of the berries to a cup of boiling water. Let this cool then drink one or two cups a day, a large mouthful at a time.

Indians used to dry and grind juniper berries and boil them in water to make a thick, soft mush. The ground flour was also made into cakes.

For one of the pleasantest evergreen beverages, rich in vitamin C, drop about a dozen young, berryless sprigs into a quart of cold water. Bring this to a boil, cover, reduce the heat, and simmer for about ten minutes. Then remove from the campfire, steep for another ten minutes, and strain.

Willows are so widely distributed and so easily identified that, in an emergency, they could save your life. Between two and three hundred varieties of willow, *Salix,* grow in the world, about a third of them in this country. They vary from large, graceful trees to tiny shoots and shrubs, only a few inches high. In the Arctic and alpine regions they are often the first source of vitamin C in the spring.

Young willow shoots can be gathered at the beginning of warm weather, peeled of their outer bark, and the tender insides eaten raw. The young leaves, some of which have been found to be ten times richer in vitamin C than even oranges, are also edible raw.

So is the thin layer of inner bark which, after the outside bark has been removed, can be scraped free with a knife. This is tastiest at the start of the growing season. Bitterish in many species of willows, in others it is surprisingly sweet. Too, this inner bark is sometimes dried and ground into flour.

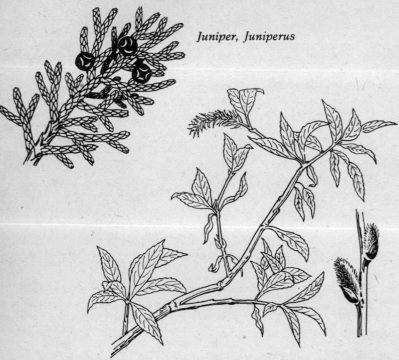

Juniper, Juniperus

Willow, Salix

The Indians used the thick, fragrant, extremely mucilaginous inner bark of the branches, trunks, and roots of the slippery elm, *Ulmus,* for food; some of the tribes boiling it with the tallow they rendered from buffalo fat. In an emergency today it will provide pleasantly life-saving nourishment, whether raw or boiled.

The inner bark and hairy twigs provide a substitute chewing gum. A pioneer tea is made by pouring a cup of boiling water over a teaspoon of shredded inner bark, covering it, and allowing it to steep until cool. When you're safely back in civilization, try this with lemon juice and sugar added.

Medically, this whitish inner bark is still sometimes used for dysentery and bronchitis. The tea suggested above will relieve coughs due to colds. For external application, the finely ground inner bark is mixed with enough

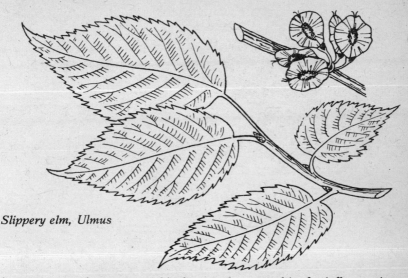

Slippery elm, Ulmus

hot water to make a paste and is then used as a poultice for inflammations and boils.

The ripe fruit of the red mulberry, *Morus,* somewhat resembles the blackberry in color as well as shape, becoming dark purple when ready to eat. Try the twigs, too; they're sweet and, particularly when tender in the spring, edible either raw or boiled.

WILD FRUITS FROM COAST TO COAST

Everyone knows the apple, *Malus.* Even though your wild find may be greenish yellow, little more than an inch in diameter, and hard and sour to boot, few wild fruits are so quickly gathered. Their very tartness and firmness lend themselves to such primitive methods of cookery as roasting in front of your campfire, perhaps impaled on a long green stick.

Hawthorns, the genus *Crataegus,* grow from one coast to the other, making them valuable when survival is a problem. The number of species in the United States is estimated to run all the way from about one hundred to as high as twelve hundred, depending on the botanist who's doing the counting. Taste varies considerably, and the only way to determine the edibility of hawthorns you've come across is by sampling. The better of them are delicious raw.

These cousins of the domestic apple are also known as thorn apples, thorn plums, thorns, mayhaws, red haws, scarlet haws, and cockspur thorns. You can readily identify a hawthorn even in winter. The long, sharp, usually straight, occasionally curved thorns, ranging in length to about five inches, are not shared by any of our other native trees and shrubs.

Wild grape, Vitis

Hawthorn, Crataegus

The rather dry fruit, which is usually red but sometimes greenish or yellowish, looks like tiny apples. Each contains one to five bony, one-seeded nutlets.

The large fox grape, the aromatic muscadine, the pleasant pigeon grape, and the notable scuppernong are a few of the familiar, broad-leaved wild grapes found throughout the continent. At least half the world's wild grapes, *Vitis,* are native to this country; some two dozen or so species being widely distributed over the United States. Fruit, leaves, and young shoots are all very much edible. Even when clusters of fruit dry like raisins on the vines, they'll still save your life during off seasons.

The widely distributed genus *Prunus* includes about fourteen native species of wild cherries, ranging in size from shrubs to large trees and all valuable to survival. Game birds and songbirds feast on their fruit when it ripens, and even before, and other animals feed on the cherries that have dropped to the ground. The rum cherry, often known as the wild black cherry, is the most important member of this group.

As you may already know, rum cherries got their name from being used by old-time New Englanders to mellow rum, brandy, and whiskey. The procedure was to sweeten the strained and simmered juice of crushed rum cherries with an equal amount of sugar, then to add it to taste to the raw liquors. The process was favored because, in addition to its soothing effect, it also thriftily stretched the available supplies of ardent spirits.

The pin cherry is a northern species, ranging from British Columbia to Labrador, south into the high country of Colorado, Tennessee, and North Carolina. It is also known as the bird cherry and the fire cherry, and is the only early, light red native wild cherry. It grows along the margins of woods, in recently burned regions, and in clearings. Despite the sourness, and the large seeds of the small fruit, the thick-fleshed berries are refreshing when you are thirsty, and they'll sustain you. In addition, gum found on the trunks can be enjoyably chewed.

Another of the *Prunus* group, the chokecherry, is perhaps the most widely distributed tree on this continent, growing from the Arctic Circle to Mexico and from the Atlantic to the Pacific. Despite their puckery quality, one handful of the small ripe berries seems to call for another when you're hot and thirsty.

The fragrant white flowers of the prolific beach plum brighten the spring-time throughout the United States and southern Canada, from Alaska and

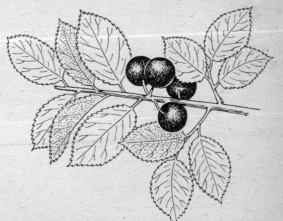

Beach plum, Prunus

California to the Great Lakes and to the eastern seaboard. Being of the *Prunus* genus, they are close cousins of the wild cherries. The fifteen or so species of wild plums themselves vary considerably, some being delicious straight off the twigs, while others are the better tasting for cooking.

Ground cherries are close relations to the tomato, but not even distant cousins of the cherry family. Also known as strawberry tomatoes and husk tomatoes, this member of the *Physalis* genus grows in all parts of the country,

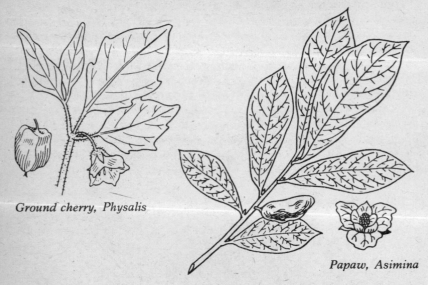

Ground cherry, Physalis

Papaw, Asimina

except Alaska, and is being raised commercially in some localities. Exceedingly refreshing when you find yourself on your own, they ripen from July through September.

This rapidly growing annual may sprawl over several feet of ground, but it seldom grows more than a foot high. The golden fruits are so well protected by their yellowish coverings that when they fall early, they still ripen on the ground.

The papaw has a wealth of bright yellow pulp whose mellow sweetness makes it really something to feast on outdoors, as any hungry raccoon or opossum knows. Also called the false banana because of its appearance, or custard apple because of its taste, this *Asimina* can be quickly gathered by a weak and starving man, often from the ground. The custardlike consistency of the ripe fruit, whose odor is also fragrant, makes it a dessert among survival foods.

This cousin of the similar tropical fruit is found from New York to Florida, west to Nebraska and Texas.

BERRIES TO SUSTAIN YOU IN STYLE

No blueberry or huckleberry is poisonous, an important fact for the starving man to remember. Other names include whortleberries and bilberries. Scientifically, blueberries are known either as *Vaccinium* or *Gaylussacia*. The pretty little bell-shaped flowers are another edible part of the plant.

Wild cranberries, also a *Vaccinium* and a close cousin of the blueberry, grow along the northern borders of the United States, and from Newfoundland to Alaska, south to Virginia and Arkansas. Three species of this prime survival food liven marshes, bogs, rocky or dry peaty and acid soil, and open coniferous woods across this continent where you may know them as lingonberries, lowbush cranberries, American cranberries, cowberries, rock cranberries, swamp cranberries, or partridgeberries.

Although they cling to the vines all winter and when kept fresh by snow are available many months as an emergency food, cranberries are at their best after the first mellowing frost. The berries, which are green before they ripen, are edible but not too appetizing raw. Cooked with enough other wild fruit to mellow their tart acidity, they're an entirely different story.

Highbush cranberry, Viburnum

Cranberry, Vaccinium

Highbush cranberries, sometimes called squashberries and moose-berries, continue to cling to their stems throughout the winter and are thus one of the most useful emergency foods in Alaska, Canada, and the northern states. Despite the name, this shrub of the genus *Viburnum,* with its red and often orange-hued berries, is not a cranberry at all.

Once you come to recognize the clean but somewhat musty odor you're never going to eat the wrong berry by mistake. Even when soft and shriveled in the spring, these berries are particularly thirst-quenching. And in fall and winter, a few of the frozen berries allowed to melt on the tongue provide a delectable fruit sherbet *au naturel.*

Although thriving under varied conditions, particularly in the West, currants and gooseberries (*Ribes*) are typical of open, moist places, and they often grow by streams, bogs, and springs across the United States and Canada. These important Indian foods were among the first adopted by the settlers and frontiersmen.

The fruit produced by these bushes with their maple-shaped leaves is edible raw, but better when cooked, although the bristliness and odor of some of the berries call for an acquired taste.

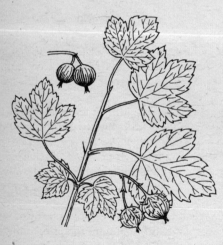

Buffalo berry, Shepherdia

Prickly gooseberry, Ribes

The three types of buffalo berries native to the continental United States, *Shepherdia,* are the only species of the sort in the world. Except in the Southeast, one or more of them flourishes in nearly every part of the country including Alaska, making them prime emergency foods.

Indians used to eat enormous quantities of these berries. They used them as we do the currants they resemble, often making a pudding of them with the flour of the prairie turnip. Tremendous amounts, dried for winter use, were cooked with buffalo meat; hence the name.

Serviceberry, Amelanchier

Partridgeberry, Mitchella

Also known as juneberries, the numerous members of the serviceberry group, the genus *Amelanchier,* are used like blueberries. Millions were once gathered by the Indians to flavor their pemmican, the most nourishing of all survival foods.

Around twenty-five species of serviceberries, or juneberries, bearing delectable fruit from Alaska and Newfoundland and south to California and the Gulf of Mexico. They thrive in such habitats as open woods, rocky banks and slopes, and swamps. Various other common names include saskatoon, shadbush, shadblow, shadberry, sugar pear, and Indian pear. Incidentally, some frontiersmen still make and use an eyewash from the boiled green inner bark; something to remember when you are on your own.

Partridgeberries, *Mitchella,* are easily recognizable and thus are an excellent emergency food. They are available from autumn to spring, clinging conspicuously to the trailing evergreen shrubs through the winter.

We have a single species of partridgeberry sometimes called checkerberry or twinberry, on this continent, a slender six to twelve-inch vine that puts down new roots along its prostrate stem. The fruit has a distinctive Siamese-twin aspect; and although dry and somewhat seedy, it will take the edge off hunger.

Barberries, which grow from one coast to the other, become fragrant masses of yellow flowers in the spring, glossy rich green expanses in the

Barberry, Berberis

summer, and brilliant crimsons and bronzes during the crisp weather of autumn. The tart, edible berries range in color from orange and scarlet to the fine blue of the so-called Oregon grape which is also of the genus *Berberis*.

The wild strawberry, smaller and much sweeter than its domestic counterpart, is familiar to everyone. Some four species of this *Fragaria* sweeten the air from the Arctic Circle to California and Florida, growing wild nearly everywhere except in arid country, often so abundantly that just a few square feet will provide a meal.

The stems and stalks of this perennial member of the edible rose family are also tasty, so strawberries are valuable emergency food throughout the year. Fresh wild strawberries have additional value by being a rich source of vitamin C.

And if you ever feel the need to offset the delicate sweetness of these most delicious of wild berries, you can brew a substantial wilderness tea by dropping a full handful of the saw-toothed leaves into two cups of boiling water and allowing them to steep for five minutes.

Even expert botanists have trouble trying to tell the numerous members of the raspberry and blackberry genus, *Rubus,* apart. Estimates as to the number of varieties in the United States vary from about forty to four hundred, including the raspberries, the hordes of true blackberries, cloudberries, baked-apple berries, salmonberries, dewberries, thimbleberries, and a lot more.

All members of the rose family, these produce closely and deliciously related fruits in commonly varying shades of red, yellow, and black. Size and softness differ, too, but they are all berries that are made up of many small, generally juicy, pulp-filled ovals, each of which contains a hard seed. They grow over most of the continent, even in the Arctic where their high vitamin C content is of especial importance.

The tender young, peeled shoots and twigs of raspberries and blackberries are also pleasantly edible. The leaves provide another of the wilderness teas.

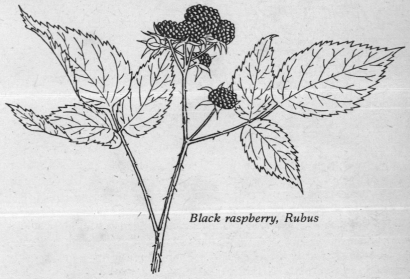

Black raspberry, Rubus

FLOWERS THAT WILL FEED YOU

Wild foods that will freely sustain you in times of need grow everywhere. There is a familiar berry easy to recognize by anyone with a respect for brambles and a modicum of outdoor knowledge that, although perhaps you've never sampled it, has the flavor of fresh apples. Throughout much of the continent you can pick all you want the greater part of the year, even when temperatures fall to sixty degrees below zero.

It is the rose hip, the ordinary seed pod of roses, *Rosa,* everywhere. Thirty-five or more varieties of wild roses thrive throughout the United States, especially along streams and in open woods and meadows, often forming briary thickets. The hips or haws are somewhat roundly smooth and contracted to a neck on top. These remain on the shrubs throughout the winter and into the following spring, and are available for food when other sources of nourishment are covered with snow.

These rose hips have a delicate flavor that's delectable. They're strong medicine, to boot. Studies show the vitamin C content of the raw pulp to be four thousand to nearly seven thousand milligrams per pound. Daily human requirements, estimated at about sixty milligrams, provide a yardstick for this astonishing abundance. Three rose hips, the food experts say, have as much vitamin C as an orange. In addition, they are more abundant than oranges in iron, calcium, and phosphorus. Rose hips are nutritious whether eaten off the bushes, cut up in a wild salad, or cooked. As a matter of fact, plain dried rose hips are well worth carrying in a pocket for lunching

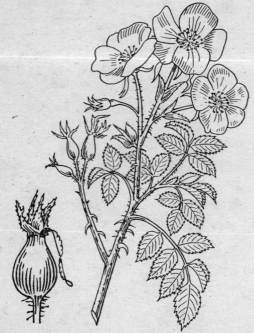

Wild rose, Rosa

on like raisins. They're most nutritious, however, when red and slightly underripe. But even after frost or later in the winter when they are shriveled and dry, rose hips are still very much worth the picking.

Earlier in the season, the petals themselves, varying in flavor like different species of apples, are delicious if you discard the bitterish green or white bases. Dark red roses are strong-tasting, the flavors becoming more delicate as colors diminish through the light pinks. These flowers make a tasty tea if two heaping teaspoons of fresh petals are covered with a cup of boiling water, then steeped for five minutes.

Leaves, roots, and the rose hips themselves are also used to make wild rose tea. Even the seeds are valuable, being rich in vitamin E. A trick in obtaining this is to boil a quantity of seeds in a small amount of water, strain this through a cloth, and drink the clear liquid. The best things in life aren't free?

The easily recognizable sunflowers, *Helianthus,* provide coffee, medicine, dye, liniment, cosmetics, and even thread in addition to food from their delectable nuts and roots, making them especially valuable in an emergency.

Also useful to remember, a strong extract made from wild sunflower roots was one of the first baths used to allay the severe inflammations that plague most of us who come in contact with poison ivy and poison oak. As if all that were not sufficient, the stalks can be used in an emergency like those of the tall, widely cultivated hemp to give delicate, silky threads.

One variety, the Jerusalem artichoke, is notable for its distinctively flavored tubers which are so nutritious and easily digested that they are a

Jerusalem artichoke, Helianthus

favored food for invalids. Just wash them, simmer them in their skins in enough water to cover until just tender, then peel and eat like potatoes. They even offer a hungry man a delicious extra. The water in which they were boiled becomes jellylike when cool, providing a flavorful and substantial basis for soup. Or you can enjoy in raw slices the crisp sweetness of the peeled tubers, which have somewhat the same texture as that of cabbage stalks.

The large meaty seeds of many of the sunflowers are nutritious and highly edible, particularly when roasted in front of a campfire.

Thousands of square miles of burned woodlands from the Aleutians and Greenland to Mexico exhibit fireweed's magenta cover every year as these tall perennials, known as *Epilobium* or *Chamaenerion,* flame into spikelike clusters of flowers.

Young fireweed stems, cut into sections and boiled until tender, are recognized by the French Canadians as *asperge* — wild asparagus. Older stalks can be peeled and their sweetish insides either eaten raw or cooked into thick soup. Young fireweed leaves cook up into satisfactory greens. But even if you don't get to these easily identifiable plants until fall, all is not lost. Steep the leaves for tea.

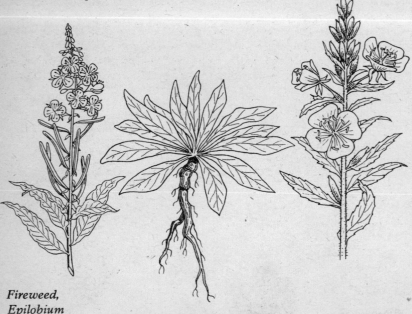

Fireweed,
Epilobium

Evening primrose, Oenothera

The familiar evening primrose, *Oenothera*, whose fragrant blossoms open at dusk, is common to wastelands and dry fields all across the continent.

The abundant, fleshy roots are sweet and nutritious only the first year, before the particular plant flowers. Their growth varies with the climate, and so do the times of year when they are at their mildest and best, so if you have a little personal experience with them, that's all to the good. To use them, just boil in two changes of water, to remove the excessive pepperiness, until tender.

One of the names it has gained through the centuries is king's cure-all, partly because its somewhat astringent qualities have caused it to be used for coughs resulting from colds. The dose is a teaspoonful of the plant, cut small, to a cup of boiling water, drunk cold during the day, a large mouthful at a time. Too, an ointment made from it is said to be beneficial in treating minor skin irritations.

A-NUTTING WE WILL GO

Half of the world's dozen species of *Juglans*, the walnuts and their kin, are native to the United States. In addition to the common black walnut, whose range extends throughout most of the East and partway into the prairies, there are two species of black walnut in the Southwest and two more in California.

The hulls which enclose the nuts dyed the homespuns of many of the first settlers. In fact, when you don't purchase your walnuts at the store, the hardest part about gathering and using them is getting off the husks with their indelible brownish dye. Under survival conditions you'll likely

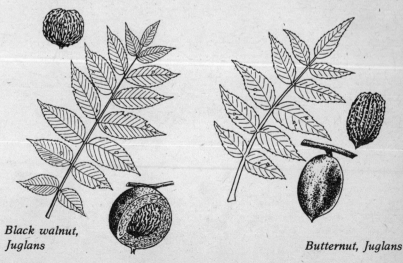

Black walnut,
Juglans

Butternut, Juglans

not care and can just stamp on the husks and break them off with the bare fingers, leaving the easily recognizable sculptured bony shells surrounding the deeply corrugated, furrowed, sweet meats. The oil in these makes them particularly nourishing.

Butternuts, which are also of the *Juglans* genus, are oblong rather than round, blunt, two or so inches long, and somewhat more than half as thick. Husks, notably sticky and coated with a mat of rusty hair, surround the nuts whose bony shells are roughly ridged, deeply furrowed, and hard. These nuts, too, are highly sustaining, and just a few handfuls a day will keep you going.

As far back as the American Revolution, a common laxative was made of the inner butternut bark, a spoonful of finely cut pieces to a cup of boiling water, drunk cold. Indians preceded the colonials in boiling down the sap of this tree, as well as that of the black walnut, to make syrup and sugar, something to remember if you're ever in want.

The three American and Canadian varieties of the low, spreading, multi-branched hazelnut (*Corylus*) are much alike, although the nuts differ some. All three can save your life.

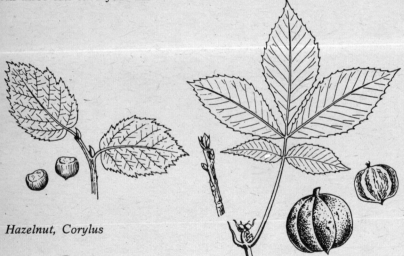

Hazelnut, Corylus

Hickory, Carya

Hickories are probably the most important native nuts. The Indians used these members of the genus *Carya* in huge quantities for food, and the settlers quickly followed suit, even in tapping the sweet sap in the spring for syrup and sugar.

Beechnuts, *Fagus,* are small and so delicious that you'll likely eat the larger part of them raw, although they're also good roasted in the campfire. You can then grind them between two stones, for brewing a wilderness coffee. More important, young beechnut leaves may be cooked as a green in the

Beechnut, Fagus

spring. The inner bark, dried and pulverized for bread flour in times of famine in Europe, can also be relished raw and is an emergency food to remember.

All acorns are good to eat, a reason why they probably occupied the primary position on the long list of free wild foods relied upon by the Indians. The only difference is that some are less sweet than others. But the bitterness that occurs in different strengths is due merely to tannin, the same ingredient that flavors tea. Although it is not readily digestible in large amounts, tannin is soluble in water. It follows, therefore, that even the bitterest acorns can be made edible in an emergency.

Many tribes ground bitterish acorns between two stones, then ran water through the resulting meal by one means or another, often for the greater part of a day, until it was sweet. The meal, for instance, might just be buried in the sandy bottom of a stream. To make the somewhat sweetish soup or gruel of the results, all you have to do is heat the ground acorns in water.

If you have or can contrive some sort of a utensil, you'll encounter no difficulty in leaching your acorns if this should be necessary. Just shell the nuts and boil them whole in water, changing the liquid whenever it becomes yellowish. The acorns can then be dried by spreading them along the fringes of your campfire, then either eaten as is or ground between two rocks into coarse bits or a fine meal.

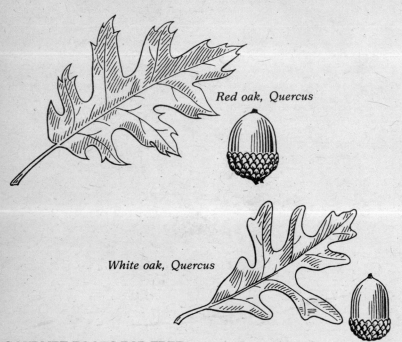

Red oak, Quercus

White oak, Quercus

GOURMET FOODS FOR FREE

The coarse, plume-topped wild rice, *Zizania,* grows on silty bottoms in shallow fresh water where there is enough circulation to prevent stagnation. Standing from four to ten feet tall, with a stout stem almost half an inch thick at the base, it will hardly be mistaken for anything else.

The slender seeds become dark and rodlike when mature, expanding in husks that are tipped with a stiff hairlike growth. These husks are loose, however, and not difficult to remove. Just rub the seeds between the palms, then gently blow away the chaff.

The purple-black seeds with their smoky sweetness are highly nutritious. To cook, stir the wild rice with some one and one-half times its volume of boiling water and simmer, without further stirring, for about thirty minutes or until you can bite smoothly through a kernel. If you have plenty of raw rice, try popping some on a hot stone on the fringes of your campfire.

Wild rice, Zizania

Water cress, *Nasturtium,* grows wild over much of North America. It is available the year around except when the clean, cold waters in which it flourishes are frozen. If you're not sure that the water in which you find it is not contaminated, soak the well-washed and tender shoots in water in which halazone tablets have been dissolved, using two of the pills to a quart of water and letting it stand half an hour.

Be sure that you are gathering just water cress. The poisonous water hemlocks, which somewhat resemble the carrot plant but with taller stems whose lower leaf stalks have three primary branchings, often grow nearby. The familiar water cress, rooting at its stem joints, usually sways and floats in the water. However, it is sometimes found creeping at the edges of cold brooks and springs.

The glossy green leaves of water cress grow with three to nine segments, the biggest of which is at the base. The minute white flowers blossom on tiny stems attached to a longish stalk. They produce needlelike pods up to about an inch long which, if tender to the bite, are tasty, too.

Water cress, Nasturtium

The whole plant has the characteristic peppery flavor of mustard, to which family it belongs. It is good both raw and cooked. As if that weren't enough, you can make a nutritious tea, rich in minerals, by steeping a teaspoonful of the leaves or roots in a cup of boiling water until it's strong enough for your particular taste.

JUST FOR FLAVOR

Because of its brilliant yellow flowers the common mustard is easy to distinguish in the fields where it grows. Most important of the five species distributed over the United States is black mustard. This annual, *Brassica,* ordinarily grows from two to six feet or taller. The leaves on the young plants, which are the ones to pick, are rather fuzzy and feel hairy.

Mustard is most agreeable when it first appears. The young stalks are not hard to identify, particularly as older mustard is often standing in the same patch. The slightly peppery young leaves are enjoyable raw. So are the young flowers with their subtle pungency. The entire young plant goes well with any fish or meat you are able to obtain. The seeds of wild mustard are easy to gather and are hard to equal for flavoring blander greens. If you wish, you can make your own table mustard by finely grinding wild mustard seeds between two stones, then adding enough water to make a paste.

Wild onion, including the leeks, the chives, and the garlics, grow all over North America except in the Far North. For the most part the wild onions (*Allium*) have slender, quill-like leaves similar to those of domestic varieties. They grow from bulbs, and flowers appear on the otherwise naked shafts. The one property on which to depend is the characteristic odor. Have nothing whatsoever to do with any plants, wild or otherwise, that resemble the onion but do not have its familiar smell! Some bulbs whose appearance is superficially like that of onions are among the most concentrated of poisons. Your nose will be your best protection.

Although you probably won't like every member of the breed, especially not the strong-tasting field garlic, *Allium vineale,* wild onions are all good to eat. The best way to find out your likes and dislikes is by trying them. Often you can use the entire plant. It'll do much to flavor wild stews and soups. Eating wild garlic, by the way, will help keep away mosquitoes.

A BEVY OF WILD BEVERAGES

Indians depended largely on edible wild plants for their beverages. When the first settlers arrived, and for centuries afterward as they were

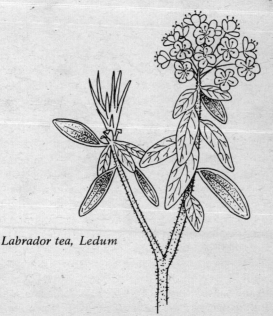

Labrador tea, Ledum

pushing their way westward, they followed suit. If these wild drinks had not been rich in vitamin C, many pioneers would not have lived to open our frontiers.

At the time of the American Revolution, even in communities where stores were well stocked, many chose wild drinks rather than continuing to use oriental tea tinged with an English tax. When the Civil War tore the country apart, many southerners and northerners alike had to turn again to the wilds for their teas and coffees.

The juices of the earlier described wild fruits are all refreshing. So are the wild teas brewed from roses, strawberry leaves, raspberry leaves, blackberry leaves, kinnikinic, wintergreen, fireweed, plantain, clover, shepherd's purse, and water cress. This holds true, too, for the coffee substitute made from such edibles as dandelion roots, chicory roots, and beechnuts.

Then there is Labrador tea (*Ledum*), also known as Hudson's Bay tea across much of the North where the Hudson's Bay Company still maintains its red-roofed white trading posts. This is a pretty evergreen shrub whose robustly aromatic leaves continue to make it one of the most famous teas of the north country.

It is found growing densely in woods, muskegs, bogs, swamps, damp mountain meadows, and across the tundras of Alaska and Canada south to New England, Pennsylvania, New Jersey, and the Great Lakes states where it is seen mainly in mountain bogs and swamps. Its leaves were among those gathered for tea during the American Revolution.

Labrador tea, a member of the heath family, is easy to distinguish. It's a resinous evergreen shrub, ranging from one to four feet tall, which is so attractive that two centuries ago the English brought it back to embellish their gardens. The telltale features are the alternate, dryly leathery, fragrant leaves whose smooth edges roll inward toward woolly undersides. These darken from greyish to reddish brown as the otherwise green leaves age.

Available in winter as well as during the warm months, the spicy leaves of Labrador tea make a palatable and refreshing tea. About one tablespoon of these per cup will make a pleasant brew. Drop them into bubbling water and immediately set this away from the campfire to steep for five minutes.

Old sourdoughs have warned me that drunk in too large quantities, this tea may have a cathartic effect. But, using it sparingly over the years, I've never experienced any ill effects. As a matter of fact, I often find it both refreshing and thirst-quenching to chew on a few leaves while hunting or getting in wood. And they're all free.

DINNER ON THE DESERT

In the deserts and dry country there is the prickly pear, or Indian fig. These are the little spiny knobs, ranging from the size of apricots to that of lemons, which bulge from the padlike joints of cactus. This fruit of the cactus, *Opuntia,* is so easy to identify, but more difficult to pick. It's best to go at this as carefully as possible with a knife and any other protection you can find.

Depending on the kind of cactus, the colors of ripened prickly pears vary from tawny green and purplish black to the choicest of them all, the big red fruits of the large *Opuntia megacantha* of the Southwest. To eat them, slice off the ends, slit the hide lengthwise, and scoop out the pulp.

Prickly pear, Opuntia

When the early Spanish conquistadores marched through the New World's Southwest, they found the natives eating the tiny little white, brown, and grey seeds of the chia, *Salvia.* Just a teaspoonful of these members of the mint family was regarded as sufficient to sustain an Indian for a day on a forced march. Too, when added to a cup of water and soaked for several minutes, the same teaspoon of chia seeds makes a nearly tasteless but extremely refreshing drink, especially on the desert, not only for its thirst-relieving qualities but also because it offsets the harshness of alkaline springs.

The easiest way to gather chia is to take some sort of a receptacle in one hand and a stick in the other, then to knock the seeds into the container by striking the dry flower tops. All a starving man has to do to get all the vitamins, minerals, and other nutriments is to eat a pinch of the seeds dry, or dilute them to a drink in which each will become separately suspended in its own whitish mucilaginous coat, or mix them with water to make a highly digestible gruel.

Chia, still eaten in the back country of Mexico and served as a beverage in some of its swankiest restaurants, continues to be highly regarded medically in some circles. For instance, several seeds placed under the eyelids when you go to bed will help clear the eyes of minor inflammation. A paste made by soaking a few seeds in a little water is used for soothing inflamed membranes and as a poultice for gunshot wounds. A drink made by stirring a teaspoonful of the seeds into a glass of cold water, then letting it stand for several minutes, is good for a disturbed stomach. And it'll nourish you at the same time.

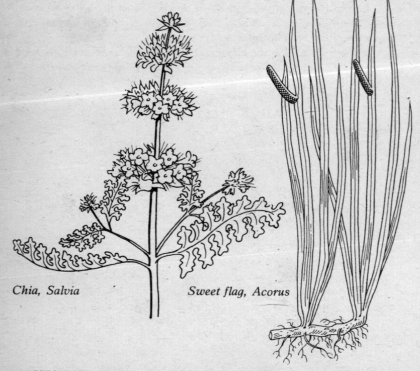

Chia, Salvia   Sweet flag, Acorus

SURVIVAL SUSTENANCE OF THE SWAMPS

Sweet flag, *Acorus,* offers prime emergency food in the spring when its partially grown flower stalks are edible raw and when the interiors of the

200

young leaf stalks, crammed with half-formed leaves, are also sweet and tasty. There is also the spicy pungency of the sweet flag's rootstock, a little of which is sometimes eaten raw as a remedy for indigestion. You'll find this cousin of the jack-in-the-pulpit in marshes and swamps across southern Canada and the northern states.

SEASHORE SPECIALTIES

If you're searching for food along the Eastern shores of this continent, look for the familiar Irish moss, *Chondrus,* attached by small disks to submerged rocks. The green, purple, red, brown, or black algae can be gathered at low tide all year long.

Although it has a pleasant, mucilaginous, salty taste, Irish moss is really too tough to enjoy raw. Too, drying makes it almost bonelike. But just a small amount of cooking will tenderize it. Hot soup made from Irish moss and fresh water alone, or the jelly it becomes upon cooling, is a palatable and nourishing emergency food. Or a handful can be cut up and cooked with any soup or stew to thicken it.

Irish moss, in addition to being nutritious, is also soothing to the digestive tract, and it used to be considered useful in stopping diarrhea. The

Glasswort, Salicornia

dose was a teaspoon of the dried plant in a cup of boiling water, drunk cold, one or two cupfuls a day, several sips at a time.

At least four species of the easy-to-identify glasswort, *Salicornia,* grow in salty country from Alaska and Labrador southward along the Pacific and Atlantic Coasts and around the Gulf of Mexico. Typical of shores, brackish marshes, and glistening tidal flats, these members of the beet and spinach family also pop up on the alkaline mud flats rimming western lakes. All in all, they thrive in salty surroundings, taste salty, and appropriately are also called saltworts. Besides being eaten raw, they can be cooked as a potherb or added to soups and stews for flavor.

Also called beach asparagus, chicken claws, and pickle plant, this plant can be a life-saving food in an emergency. Its tops, which may be eaten raw, remain tasty and tender from spring until fall.

Dulse, prolific along our Atlantic and Pacific coasts, is rich in vital minerals including iodine. These sea plants have brief stems that rapidly widen into thin, elastic fronds. They vary in color from purplish to reddish, and have smooth, flat surfaces that are frequently lobed and cleft. The whole seaweed may grow from a few inches to about a foot in length.

This seaweed, *Rhodymenia,* is edible fresh; but directly from the sea, it is tough and rubbery. The trick is to hang it or spread it out until it is partially dry. Or if you don't want to wait that long, just singe the fresh dulse on a hot campfire rock.

A premium you sometimes come by when harvesting dulse in Alaska during the midsummer herring runs is herring roe. For some delicious eating all you then have to do is drain this roe and cook it by the campfire, perhaps on a handy flat rock, until brown on both sides. As for the dulse itself, besides being eaten raw it can be used to add character to otherwise tasteless soups and stews.

Another common edible found along the seashore is laver, *Porphyra.* This seaweed furnishes a regular food crop in the Orient, and exactly the same delicacy can be harvested here. In a tight spot it may save your life.

Laver is the thin frond spied at low tide growing from rock ledges and boulders beneath the ocean's surface. Wavy edges characterize these long, narrow seaweeds. They grow up to about a foot long and from one to two inches wide, their fronds exhibiting filmy green, red, purple, and purplish brown.

Laver is perfectly edible raw, although it is better dried. A laver soup, embellished with other edible finds, can be made easily by simmering two cups of laver in a quart of water, stirring occasionally, until everything is tender.

Wild celery, also known as seacoast angelica, is even tastier than the common domestic variety. It grows in damp fields, beside moist game trails, and along rocky and sandy coastlines from eastern Canada and New England to British Columbia and Alaska.

Both the stems and leaf stalks are gathered when young and tender — in late spring and early summer — then peeled, and their juicy interiors eaten with relish. They are often boiled, and this way impart a pleasant flavor to fish. You'll probably like it, too, in soup.

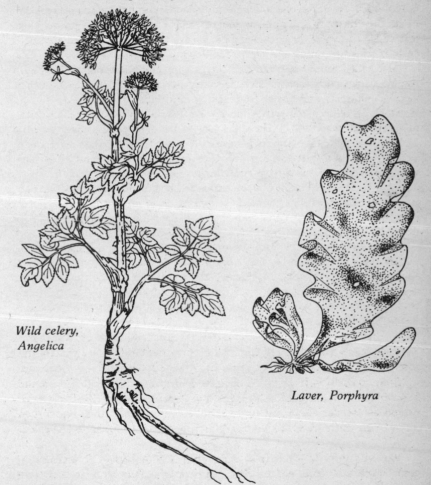

Wild celery, *Angelica*

Laver, Porphyra

Scotch or sea lovage, *Ligusticum,* another of the wild celeries, grows in wind-swept, sandy stretches along the northern coasts of both oceans. Named for its popularity among Scots as a green and cooked vegetable,

Scotch lovage, Ligusticum

it was discovered here during their early excursions to the New World. It is rich in vitamins A and C, and adds flavor as well as nourishment to your catch. The fresh young stalks and leaves are best, whether eaten raw or cooked, before the plant blossoms.

EDIBLES IN THE ARCTIC

Except for one mushroom, all plants that grow in the Arctic, north of the tree line, are edible. Some of the lichens have to be soaked first to rid them of irritating acids. But water will do, and the palatable results are so nutritious that some of them are sold in drugstores as nourishment for convalescents.

Northern explorers have lived for months almost entirely on the lichen known as rock tripe — *Umbiliceria* — the Far North's most famous edible wild plant, whose growth reaches down into our southern states. Rock tripe resembles a leathery, dry lettuce leaf, up to about three inches across, attached at its center to a stony surface. It can be eaten raw in small amounts, but you'll likely prefer it boiled to thicken soups and stews.

Because rock tripe is one of the lichens that make soil by decomposing rock, it is apt to be gritty. So wash it as well as possible, preferably soaking it in water for several hours to rid it of its bitter purgative quality. The flavor will then be improved if you roast it before the campfire until it is dry and crisp.

Then simmer it slowly for an hour or so, or until tender, whereupon it will give a gumbolike thickness to stew or soup. Depending on the other ingredients, rock tripe may be short on taste, but it will be surpassingly long on nourishment.

A favorite wildlife browse, Iceland moss is a ground-hugging, mosslike plant with branching stems instead of leaves. It grows in tufts and tangled masses, forking and branching freely, from two to four inches tall. It forms odorless mats that are brownish and greyish white to reddish. Many stalks arise from this lichen, most of them being thin, flat, and extremely narrow.

Icelanders vow that by giving them Iceland moss, a beneficent God has provided them with bread from the very rocks. *Cetraria* has prevented starvation for literally thousands. It can do the same thing for you in an emergency, and it grows across Canada and the northern states, down into New Jersey, Pennsylvania, and the mountains of North Carolina.

Like most other edible lichens, Iceland moss must be soaked before you eat it. Its unpleasantly bitter acids may otherwise cause severe digestive upset. The acids are taken away easily enough, however, by soaking the Iceland moss in two changes of water, then draining, drying and eventually pounding and crushing it into a powder.

When it is simmered with water, this powder forms a jellylike gruel that firms upon cooling. The powder is also added to thicken soups and stews. You can use it, too, to make cakes or bread.

Rock cress, of the genus *Arabis,* grows in Alaska, on the islands of the Bering Sea and the Aleutians, and in the Yukon. The similar Alpine cress thrives in the eastern Arctic, south to Newfoundland and the Gaspe Peninsula. Both are seen on ledges, cliffs, gravelly shores, cool rocks, and along the banks of trails and streams. Their rosettes, gathered while tender, have a somewhat radishlike flavor which is agreeable raw. These rosettes will also cook up into tasty greens. The flowers, too, are edible; but the stem leaves are apt to be bitter.

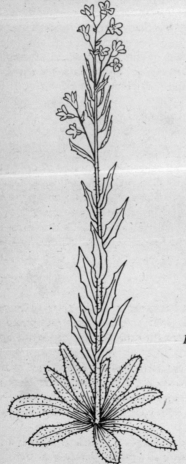

Rock cress, Arabis

THE FACTS ABOUT MUSHROOMS

Unless you are already an expert, I strongly suggest that you avoid mushrooms entirely. They have very little food value, and the risk in eating them is way out of proportion to the possible gain.

There is no single, practical test by which all poisonous mushrooms can be detected. Many such tests of edibility — such as the one claiming that silver boiled with mushrooms without its turning black indicates a nonpoisonous fungus — have proved, sometimes fatally, unreliable.

Another dangerous fallacy is the presumption that those mushrooms gathered by animals and birds are safe, too, for human consumption. Squirrels, as an example to the contrary, routinely harvest fungi of the deadly amanita group.

It cannot be overemphasized that no single test, short of eating, can distinguish between a poisonous mushroom and a safe variety. Because they contribute almost nothing to the nourishment of the survivor, they're best left alone altogether.

COOKING YOUR CATCH

A convenient way to prepare wild tubers is to cook them in the ashes of your campfire. Just rake embers and ashes from a heated piece of ground. Lay the vegetables here. Cover them with ashes, then hot coals. Timing, as is the case with the majority of such cooking, is a matter of experimenting.

Breads can also be cooked cleanly in ashes after being rolled a bit more lavishly than usual in flour. When you realize that the white of hardwood ashes can be substituted part for part for baking soda, sodium bicarbonate, in making dough, this type of cooking may not appear to be so unusual.

BAKING IN A BURROW

There's a handy way to make an oven when you're going to be camped in one place for any length of time. Start by pounding a sharpened stake, with about a four-inch diameter, straight down into a clay bank approximately a yard back from the edge.

Then some two feet down the side of the bank, far enough to make a rugged ceiling, scoop out the size oven you'd like. Dig as far back as the pole which you'll then withdraw to make the chimney. Harden the interior by smoothing it for several minutes with your wet hands. Then light a small fire inside to glaze it.

You can often find an old burrow to form the nucleus of such an oven. In any event, baking in it Indian-style is simple. Merely heat the oven by making a fire inside it. Rake out fire, embers, and ashes. Lay the food inside, perhaps on clean grass or leaves. Close both chimney and front holes. Then go about your usual activities. The food, which you can briefly check from time to time, will bake without any more attention.

BAKING ON A STICK

You'll want a peeled green stick of hardwood, about three inches thick, with several branch stubs left on it if possible. Make a stiff dough, perhaps with one of the many flours that you can make from wild plants and with sea water in the absence of salt.

Fashion this into a wide ribbon and wind it on the stick. The stubs will help to keep it in place. Lean, hold, or lay this in green crotches above a bed of coals, turning it occasionally so as to bake all sides. Once a clean sliver can be inserted and withdrawn without dough sticking to it, the bread will be done. You owe it to yourself to try this sometime hot, along with kabobs that have been charred on another green stick, biting off the latter while they are still sizzling.

Bread can also be cooked by spreading the dough in thin sheets on a hot clean rock. A little leaven, perhaps sourdough made by allowing the dough to sour and bubble, will improve the end product.

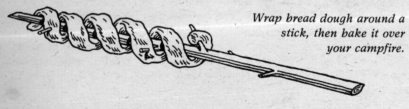

Wrap bread dough around a stick, then bake it over your campfire.

PARCHING AND DRYING

The Indians used to parch many of their grains and nuts. Just place the food in a metal container, or on a hot flat rock, and heat slowly until the seeds or such are thoroughly scorched.

Berries, other wild fruits, and edible leaves can be dried by air, sun, wind, or fire, with or without smoke. Cut the fruit in thin slices and place these in the sun or before a fire. Delicious!

PINOLE

Pinole is one of the best of the primitive concentrated foods. It is made by parching wild corn grains or wild seeds in hot ashes, atop heated stones, or in a makeshift oven. Pinole keeps indefinitely, contains a maximum of calories for its weight, is easy to prepare, and can be enjoyed either raw or cooked.

A small handful of pinole in a cup of cold water has an appealing flavor and is highly nutritious.

Getting Your Game 10

All mammals and birds are edible. Furthermore, you can keep in vigorous good health for months at a time with nothing but meat. All talk of balanced diets to the contrary, fresh rare meat, as long as sufficient fat is included, will furnish you with the necessary vitamins and minerals. You don't even have to eat all parts of the animals to stay robustly nourished, although you'll be passing up some of the most delectable portions if you do not enjoy such parts as the heart, liver, and kidneys.

Animal food will give you the most food value per pound. Anything that creeps, swims, crawls, walks, or flies is a possible source of food, although you should avoid toads. You've doubtless already eaten insects — as contaminants of the flour, corn meal, rice, beans, fruit, and greens of your daily diet.

There is, however, a qualification to this rule. An exclusive diet of any lean meat, of which rabbit is a prime example, will cause digestive upset, diarrhea, and in a surprisingly brief time — sometimes as little as a week or ten days — nephritis and death. Eating more and more rabbit, as one is apt to do when confronted with increasing weakness and the uneasiness of unsatisfied hunger, will only hasten matters. This so-called rabbit starvation is especially well known in the Far North, where, in peak years, rabbits and hares are everywhere.

The solution? Eat a little fat along with the lean meat. Fat provides twice as many calories per weight unit than do either proteins or carbohydrates. Never eat entirely lean meat, such as rabbit, for even a few days at a time. It is better to avoid such actual poisoning by existing on water alone during that period.

LUXURIES

The luxury that many of us esteem most highly is the liberty to humor our taste prejudices. These taste prejudices, that at a decisive time have more than once meant the difference between life and death, are for the most part based on two factors.

First, it is a human trait to look down upon certain foods as being beneath one's social station. When grouse have been at their peak years in Canada's eastern provinces, I've seen them disdained as a "poor man's dish" among people living on the fringes of the forests. The same year in British Columbia, where there happened to be a scarcity of grouse but an abundance of varying hares, the former were prized while residents excused themselves for eating rabbits. As happens everywhere in such circumstances, the lower the often self-appointed position in life, the more pronounced the complaints.

Second, it is normal to prefer the nutriments to which we've come to be familiar. The American or Canadian enjoys his wheat. The Mexican relishes his corn, the Asian his rice. We also like these other grains, but it would seem a privation if we had to eat them every day as we do our bread. Too, we perhaps feel an aversion at the thought of the Japanese's eating raw fish, although at that precise moment we may be admiring the tang a special sauce gives our raw oyster. The Eskimo likes birds which have been preserved under fat in seal skins. We have our choice, but far worse smelling, Camembert cheese.

In other words, there is a point where taste prejudices must be forgotten if we are to survive. It has been found among explorers that the better educated the individual is, the more swiftly and successfully can he accept the change.

No reasonable source of food should be scorned if you need nourishment. Too, you should start while your strength is near its maximum to look for any promising nutriments.

Nearly every part of any North American bird or mammal is good to eat. An exception is the liver of the polar bear and that of the ringed and bearded seals. These become so rich in vitamin A at certain times that they can become toxic and are best avoided.

Furthermore, when food is short, such portions as brains, stomach linings, and even eyes should be used. The bland young antlers of the deer family, when in velvet, are good roasted over the campfire. Good, too, are the stomach contents of the hooved animals; such greens mixed with the digestive acids are reminiscent of salads prepared with vinegar.

Even the craw or first stomach of birds — except the scavengers — might well be checked as the undigested contents may include nutritious berries, seeds, buds, and the like. As a matter of fact, some do not even bother to open the small animals and birds they secure, but pound them to a pulp and toss them whole into the cooking pot. And others seek moose and rabbit droppings for their soups and stews.

ANIMAL FOOD

Even ants are excellent, particularly the large black variety that are to be found in rotten logs, as any bear will agree. If they are large enough remove the head, the legs, and the thorax which is the middle of the three chief divisions of the body and which contains the heart, lungs, and esophagus. I've eaten fried ants whole, and they are excellent that way. If you can find enough of the eggs, they're edible, too, although rather dryly bland. Termites are similarly eaten.

Some natives take advantage of the ants' formic acid by crushing them in water sweetened with berries or sap to make a sort of primitive lemonade.

In the same rotting log or stump you may be able to find another bears' delight, the white wood-burrowing larvae of beetles. Roast or boil these grubs.

Grasshoppers and locusts are regarded as delicacies in some parts of the world. Remove the hard wings and legs. Roast the remainder. It has a nutlike flavor. Cicadas and crickets are similarly eaten.

The larger earthworms are eaten in some countries. As for lizards and snakes, they are often considered gourmet delicacies in this country, small cans of their meat selling for many times the cost of a similar amount of prime beef sirloin. The only time either may be poisonous is when it has incurred a poisonous bite, perhaps from its own fangs if it's a rattlesnake, water moccasin, copperhead, coral snake, Gila monster, beaded lizard, or the like. To prepare, cut off the head, skin, discard the entrails, and cook like chicken to whose dry white meat that somewhat stringy flesh is many times compared.

In sections of Mexico the natives make an extremely nourishing flour from the eggs of small insects located in swamps. Dragonflies, which we often call darning needles, are a delicacy in Japan. Moths, mayflies, and in fact most of the insects found in our woodlands are surprisingly palatable, and they'll all keep you from starving.

THE IDEAL WEAPON

The challenge of keeping going on your own will be easier to answer if you have a firearm and ammunition. It comes to the question of what weight ammunition used with how heavy a firearm can reasonably be relied upon, ounce for ounce, to give you the most food.

If you have any choice in the matter, hand guns are not worth their weight and bulk as survival weapons. Because of inadequacies in the pieces themselves, no matter how expert you may be, you can not be reasonably sure of anchoring your big game with them. Even in customarily good game country, you can hunt a month and see only one moose. Your life may depend on your securing that moose.

The best survival weapon, it follows, is a hard and flat-shooting rifle. There is no need to add that it should be rugged and accurate. Neither is it necessary to append that a shotgun is no adequate substitute, for although having about the same bulk and weight as a rifle, it shoots larger and heavier ammunition at usually much smaller and closer prey.

Something could be saved by using a carbine instead of a rifle, but the extra length and weight of the latter will be completely justified by the additional accuracy. As far as that goes, it would be difficult to argue against the extra pound of a good telescopic sight, if only for the often vital time one adds to the most productive game-getting periods of the day. You will also want to include a light sling.

When it comes to ammunition, you'll want one shot to do the job whenever possible for several self-evident reasons. Therefore, you'll likely prefer the explosive effect of a high velocity cartridge, with a bullet that will spread but hold together at the moment of impact.

Suppose several in your group have individual choices of survival weapons? Despite the tendency to seek diversification, the same objections to hand guns and shotguns would still hold. Chances of success in most country will be greater if each individual has an optimum rifle, permitting the group to spread out and hunt separately. These rifles should all be identical, so that parts of one can be used to repair the others.

The fact that a variety of different firearms are included in the survival kits amassed in quantity by various organizations does not conflict with the preceding reasoning, especially as such outfits are assembled with the realization that only a minimum of them will ever be used. Under such conditions, it's logical that such considerations as expense and weight should prevail.

The fundamental problem is different, however, in country where there is all sorts of small game but few if any big game animals. There the most functional firearm for surviving on your own would be a rifle for a load like the .22 Hornet. Then, so as to waste only a minimum of meat, you might carry a number of reduced loads with ballistics similar to those of the .22 long rifle cartridge.

MAINTENANCE OF YOUR WEAPON

Although you should start with a rugged rifle, you'll still need to accord it intelligent care if it is to function when you need it.

Keep the weapon clean, of course. If possible, cover it when it's not in use. Keep the action, receiver walls, bolt and assembly, and particularly the barrel clean and free from oil, dirt, mud, and snow. If the barrel should become obstructed with any foreign substance, perhaps as the result of a

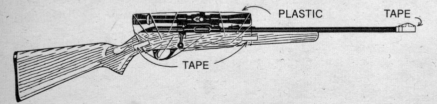

To keep your gun clean, cover it when it's not in use.

fall, be sure to clean it thoroughly before shooting. Never try to shoot out an obstruction; a burst barrel will likely be the result.

Never use your weapon as a club, hammer, or pry bar. Aside from the possible accidents that might occur, your rifle is a precision instrument on which your life may depend.

Do not over-oil your weapon. Just a few drops on the moving parts are needed, and this only in warm weather. During the winter, remove all lubricants and rust-prevention compounds from your rifle. Strip it as completely as you can and clean all parts with a quickly drying solvent such as gasoline or lighter fluid. Normal lubricants thicken in cold weather and slow the action. In subzero temperatures your weapon will function best when absolutely dry.

A piece of cloth on a string pulled through the barrel is a handy substitute for a ramrod and cleaning patch, and one often seen in the bush. If you must give a barrel a thorough cleaning and have no solvent, pour boiling water through it from the breech. Mop up the excess moisture by pulling a cloth on a string through the opening, and the hot barrel will dry itself.

A major problem will be to keep snow and ice out of the working parts, sights, and barrel. Even a small amount of snow may disable your weapon, so careful handling is particularly essential in snow. Improvise muzzle and breech covers and use them. A piece of self-adhering tape over the muzzle will keep snow out and will blast harmlessly out of the way at a shot.

Weapons sweat when they are brought from the extreme cold into a heated shelter. When they are taken out again into the cold, the film of condensation freezes. This ice may seriously affect their operation, so leave them outside or store them in unheated shelters.

The exception is when your bivouac is not greatly warmer than the outside temperature. Then bring in your weapon if you wish, but place it at or near floor level where the temperature is lowest. When you take it into a heated shelter for cleaning, remove all condensed moisture before commencing the job. It may sweat for an hour.

If a part becomes frozen, do not attempt to force it. Instead, warm it slightly, if possible, and move it gradually until thawed. If it can not be warmed, try to remove all visible ice or snow and move it carefully until action is restored. Before loading your weapon, always move the action back and forth a few times to insure that it is free.

If you are using a survival weapon with a metal stock, pad it in cold weather with tape or cloth, or pull a stocking over it, to protect your face.

THE LAW OF SURVIVAL

Modern man is the most deadly animal the world has ever known. This fact, deplorable though it may be, may save your life if you're ever thrown entirely on your own resources and forced to eat whatever you can eke from the countryside to stay alive. Procedures contrary to both the most liberal game laws and also to the most loosely observed personal ethics are vindicated in times of extreme emergency by the more ancient law of survival. But only then, it should be well noted!

Under normal circumstances many of the means of obtaining food outlined in this survival book are unlawful nearly everywhere and with the best of reasons, for a certain deep-rooted aversion accompanies even the consideration of them, while at best their success in times of exigency will not be accompanied by any satisfaction except that connected with the thus-fulfilled instinct to stay alive.

Game laws are made with good reason. So are the unwritten rules of conservation and good sportsmanship. None should ever be violated or even infringed upon in any way whatsoever unless, and only when, human lives actually are at stake.

THE ART OF HUNTING

The basic rule of surviving by hunting, continuing to follow the ounce for ounce axiom, is to depend on big game and to aim, at as short a distance as is reasonable, from the steadiest position possible at the decisive area offering the most margin for error, generally the chest cavity.

If you are new to hunting, some of the following pointers may put meat in your pot. Proceed as quietly as possible, all the time listening. Move slowly, stop frequently, and look around regularly.

Hunt preferably against the wind, or at least across it. Try to hunt uphill in the morning during normal weather, down from the middle of the afternoon onward, so as to take advantage of the thermal currents. These reverse, as you know, in stormy weather.

Always be alert, ready to get off an aimed shot at any instant. If you are an old hand, you won't become overexcited at the sight of game. Very often it may not have seen you, especially if you have been proceeding cautiously. If it has caught a glimpse of some movement — perhaps you are the first man it has ever seen! — it will be more curious than afraid. Freeze until it looks away. In any event, make your movements so slow that you will not startle the prey, and make that first shot count.

When you see a heavily and recently traveled trail, keep it in mind as a possible place for setting a snare or deadfall. Tracks, if you'll take the time to study them, will tell you whether an animal has been traveling normally, feeding, seeking a bed, and whether it has been jumped and so alerted within the past few minutes.

If the latter is the case, try to find a vantage point from which you can survey the country, or wait awhile for the animal to quiet, then maybe circle around toward it from another angle. The droppings will tell you what type of an animal has passed and often when. Too, they often reveal the favorite roosting spots of birds.

Water holes, feeding grounds, and especially licks are good places to be watching in the early morning and evening. If you have a strong flashlight and are not successful in your regular stalking, try jacking. The trails leading to such spots, too, are excellent sites for locating snares or traps.

Try standing in a smoke, first, in an attempt to obliterate your human scent. If you have a small plastic bottle of liquid buck lure in your survival kit, you'll be well away. A few drops of this on your boots when you're stalking, or scattered about your stand when you're lying concealed at a vantage point, will not only cut down on the human scent, but will actually attract game.

When you knock an animal down, hurry toward it, as closely as safety will permit, for a finishing second shot before it can regain its senses. On the other hand, if game is wounded and moves out of sight, wait at least ten minutes to allow it to lie down and stiffen up. Better still, boil the kettle and have at least some wild tea before proceeding. Then do your utmost not to lose the trail. A fatally wounded moose or deer will sometimes travel half a day before quitting, especially if you follow it too soon.

JACKING

One of the usually illegal acts is jacking — the practice of attracting and holding an animal's gaze at night by a beam of light. Deer and their ilk are among the big game animals that can be readily spotted and held in this manner long enough to be shot. Bear, in contrast, will sometimes fall backwards in their hurry to scramble away. Eyes of spiders and insects are good reflectors, so there will be frustrating times when you shine up eyes but can't find the rest of the creature.

Most warm-blooded, hairy animals are wary and hard to bag. But the majority of them move at night, and it's frequently possible to get close enough to blind them partially with a flashlight. Good places for jacking are on the downwind sides of heavily used game trails and well frequented watering places. Licks are sometimes found where the earth is so jellylike that one may sleep in the brush or tall grass until roused by the quivering provoked by the animal's weight. Well located trees are especially good, both because of the confusing way your scent will be scattered and because of the increased visibility.

Plans for all reasonable contingencies should be decided upon ahead of time, for you'll have to move and hold the flashlight so as to view both the prey and your sights. The darker the night, the better will be the opportunities for jacking. On the other hand, when the moon or aurora borealis is sufficiently bright, it's frequently possible to find and shoot large game without extra light, especially if you have a good telescopic sight.

SNARING BIG GAME

Even when you have a weapon, several judiciously placed snares on well traveled game trails will save ammunition, energy, and time. You'll need a snare of cable, heavy wire, or stout rope. Make the actual noose two feet in diameter and hang it a foot and a half above the ground at its lowest point.

Capture large animals along game trails with a snare of heavy rope.

You'll need a strong dry pole or a dead tree at least ten feet long and six inches in diameter for a drag. If the snare is well anchored, the animal will likely kill itself within a short time.

Visit any such snares at least every morning and preferably again along toward evening. Never leave a locality, perhaps in the excitement of rescue, without at least closing the loop so that the snare will be harmless.

APACHE FOOT SNARE

The Apaches devised a foot snare. It requires more work, but may be made necessary by the lack of suitable materials for the preceding noose.

A hole, about six inches deep and with a diameter the width of the well traveled path, is dug in a soft part of the game trail. Preferably, a rectangular piece of heavy paper or cardboard is laid over the hole, although you can use a grid of small, easily broken branches.

A snare made of something comparable to the nylon line found on parachutes is placed over the cover and is fastened to a heavy log. The set is then camouflaged by a light and judicious sprinkling of the removed earth, with perhaps a few leaves added to make the spot as natural as possible.

An Apache foot snare can be devised with a minimum of materials.

The cover will make it likely that the snare will remain about the animal's foot until it is drawn tight. The animal will then be tied to the log which it can drag until exhausted. Again, check such a snare once or twice a day, and never go away leaving it set.

BOWS AND ARROWS

It is suggested that you include some steel hunting arrowheads and a bowstring in your long-pull survival kit. With these you can't be expected to be as proficient on short notice as was the experienced American Indian, but an otherwise weaponless man should be able to get more meat with a bow and arrow than barehanded.

Well-seasoned wood is the best to use for the bow especially, but pick a branch or limb that is not brittle. A tree that has been killed by a forest or prairie fire, especially an ash, is particularly good bow material. Other good woods are hickory, juniper, oak, white elm, cedar, ironwood, willow, birch, hemlock, and especially yew. Anthropologist Jeanne-Nicole Ledoux, an expert on this subject, has found this latter to be superior in her tests in the field.

The proper individual fit for an Indian bow is often determined by holding the bow stave diagonally across the body, with one end of it clasped in

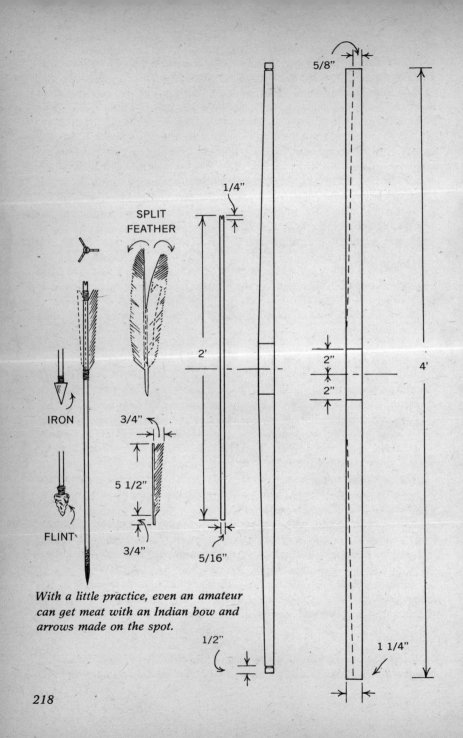

SPLIT FEATHER

IRON

FLINT

3/4"

5 1/2"

3/4"

1/4"

2'

5/16"

1/2"

5/8"

2"

2"

4'

1 1/4"

With a little practice, even an amateur can get meat with an Indian bow and arrows made on the spot.

the right hand at the hip and the other touching the fingers of the left hand when this is held straight out to the side, shoulder high.

The Sioux, Crow, and other western tribes generally used four-foot bows. In the East certain tribes carried a longer bow. Ordinarily, all these bows were perfectly flat when unstrung.

To make your survival bow on the spot, take a well seasoned yet supple branch or stick about four feet long that can be worked into a bow stave an inch and a quarter wide at the center and five-eighths inch wide at the ends. The bow can be either flat or rounded. A branch, incidentally, will be more easily worked into a rounded bow.

To fashion your bow properly, start with your one and a quarter inch branch and cut it off to the proper length. Then find the exact center of the remainder and mark off a space two inches wide on either side of this mid-mark for the hand grip.

Next, mark off five-eighths inch at either end. Draw a straight line from either extremity of the hand grip to the now-marked ends. Draw and whittle the bow.

About one-half inch in from either end of the bow, make the notches for the bowstring.

When the bow is finished, rub it all over with oil or animal fat. You'll find it will bend best the way the whittling has slightly curved it.

Although it is recommended that you carry a bowstring in your survival kit, one can be made in the field of twisted fishline or threads, nylon cord, a rawhide thong, or anything handy that is sufficiently strong.

Birch is one of the better woods to use for the arrows. To go with your Indian-type bow, these should be about two feet long. Make straight shafts of seasoned wood about five-sixteenths inch in diameter. Chip or whittle a nock about one-fourth inch deep in the center of one end.

The feathers come next, although direction-maintaining substitutes, even wood chips, can be used instead. Using a sharp knife, split the feathers down the middle. Cut the feather in the shape indicated.

The feathers are bound to the arrow in the following manner. The first feather goes on at right angles to the nock and straight down the shaft. The second and third feathers are placed equidistant from the first. Bind all, using fishline, cord, dental floss, or whatever else is handy.

Add to the other end of the arrow a tip of metal, bone, or rock — this last preferably flint which you'll find you will be able to chip into shape. Or simply whittle a point and harden this in the campfire. Then practice.

NO GUN?

If you have no rifle, or if big game is not plentiful where you are stranded, your mainstay, in addition to edible wild plants, will likely be small animals and birds. In general, these are far easier to secure than big game, and they're all good to eat; many of them in fact are gourmets' delights back in civilization. There are two major ways to bring such food to the pot, by snaring it in a wire or cord loop or by dropping something heavy on it.

DEADFALLS

These are particularly advantageous. One way to set one is by first lifting an end of a heavy slab or log. Carefully prop this up in such a way that any animal or bird moving the support will knock it loose. Encourage this by fastening some bait to the prop. Finally, arrange some sticks and

A deadfall with a figure 4 trigger is a good way to catch small game.

branches as naturally as possible so that to reach the bait the prey will place itself so as to get the full weight of the dislodged deadfall back of the shoulders.

There is another way of doing this, especially when you have roast fowl in mind. Scatter some bait, such as crumbs, in such a way that the birds will follow them beneath the deadfall. Be waiting, with a long cord tied to the prop, ready to jerk at the decisive moment.

An excellent trigger for a deadfall is the illustrated figure 4 device, long successful on this continent, that can be fashioned in a few minutes with your knife alone.

SNARING SMALL GAME

Even if you do have a rifle, you will be able to save ammunition by setting a few simple but effective snares. You'll be able to feast on roast squirrel and rabbit with nothing stronger than horsehair or a light cord such as fishline or one fashioned from your clothing.

The snare, well known by primitive man, is only a slip noose strategically placed, as on a heavily traveled game trail, so that the animal will walk into it, tightening it about him at the same time and holding himself.

The size of the snare depends, of course, on the size of the animal you are after. A rabbit snare, for example, should be about four and one-half inches in diameter and suspended, at its lowest arc, some three inches above the ground.

You'll want to make sure that the loop remains open, perhaps by running it through slight nicks in two upright sticks. These sticks, if you'll help things along by going one step further, can be the inside boundaries of a little fence, perhaps made of a fallen branch with its center limbs cut out, that will force the rabbit either to put his head into the noose or to leave the game trail entirely.

Small prey can be snared with a fishline noose.

Everything must be left looking as natural as possible so as not to alarm your prey. In the case of rabbits, you should have a dozen or so of these snares operating. Again, never leave them open when you quit a territory for any reason whatsoever.

One end of the snare can be fastened to a pole or tree. Or, especially if snow makes tracking simple, you can tie it to a drag such as a loose, heavy branch.

There is a more humane and surer method. Arrange a trigger and a weight, such as a pole, so balanced that its heavier end will pull a rabbit off its feet when the snare is tightened. Or bend a green branch or sapling and trigger it so that the food animal will be lifted off its feet and either choked or at least left unable to exert any direct pressure against the cord or wire. Ideally, it will be hoisted beyond the reach of other animals who might beat you to the meat.

SNARING SQUIRRELS

Squirrel have little or no gaminess and provide delicious tidbits, either roasted or simmered in a stew. You'll find some areas in softwood forests where dozens of them live in concentrated territories. A handy way to capitalize on their habits is to lean a bare pole against a spruce or similar tree under which there is heavy sign of squirrel activity.

Attach small nooses, two and one-half inches in diameter, on the pole in such a way that the animals will run their heads into a snare when scooting up and down the pole. As many as half a dozen snares to a pole will often produce results, as when any one squirrel is snared and falls free, the others will not be discouraged from using the same fatal route.

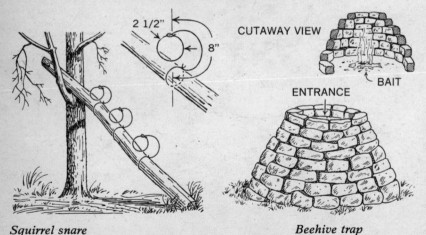

Squirrel snare   *Beehive trap*

222

BEEHIVE TRAP

One of these can be built about six feet wide and tall of piled rocks and stones. Game or fish remains left as bait on the floor inside will attract carnivores which, after satisfying their own hunger, will be unable to leave.

OTHER TRAPS

In limestone and in other rocky country there are frequently pits that can be dug out a bit more if necessary and strategically roofed with a grid of slim poles covered with browse and forest litter, baited perhaps with salt for the antlered game and entrails for bear, and used as death pits. Some natives make sure that no large game animal can escape from such a hole by implanting sharpened sticks upright along its bottom.

Another aboriginal trap that you might adapt to your conditions consists of a spring and spear. This is placed along a well traveled game trail.

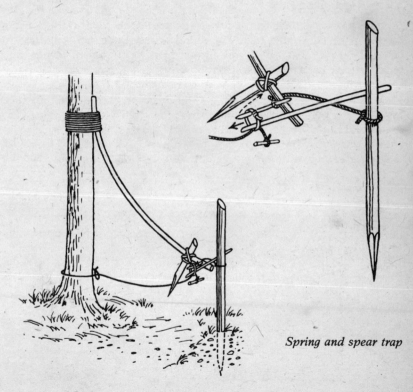

Spring and spear trap

But use such deadly contrivances only in dire necessity, beware of them yourself, and make absolutely certain that they are dismantled before you leave an area.

OJIBWA BIRD SNARE

This Indian snare will give you birds for the pot. You can make one in a few minutes with a knife. Be sure to hang the weight low enough so that the birds will not land on it instead of on the perch. The knot will keep the

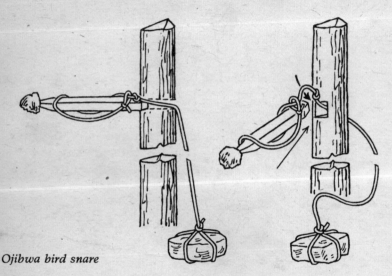

Ojibwa bird snare

baited perch in position until the landing bird depresses it, permitting the weight to yank the knot through the aperture and thus trap the bird's feet in the noose.

BOOMERANG

Then there is the boomerang. Made from pieces of hardwood with the curve of a parabola, these come principally from three different parts of a tree.

The hunting variety is cut from either a tree crotch or from near the base. The warfare type is cut near a branch. The returning kind, useful primarily for play but also for hunting, comes from the angle in which the tree branches.

The boomerang, which can secure birds and small game, is discharged by grasping it by one end, the convex edge being forward and the flat side upward. Swing it back and then sharply forward. With a little practice, you can become surprisingly accurate.

TRAPPING TURKEY

If you have a gill net or want to take the trouble of constructing a stick fence, you can bait and trap the usually cautious wild turkey. The procedure is to get the large birds eating along the ground, finally passing under a low fence. When the food is gone, they lift their long necks, and you can often catch and club them before they reason how to get away.

CATCHING SCAVENGERS

Gulls and other scavengers can be simply if distastefully caught by the starving man if he'll sharpen a bone or short stick at both ends, secure it in the middle by a line that is preferably tied to something with elasticity in it such as a small tree, and hide it in some fish entrails or similar bait. The hook will lodge in the stomach of the prey.

When you've skinned the bird and opened it up, be careful not to release the decomposing matter in the digestive system. All scavengers, mammals as well as birds, should be very well cooked because of the danger of trichinosis.

ATTACKING A BURROW

You may have to smoke a small mammal out of its burrow. Then, using a noose attached to the end of a long pole, snare the quarry as it comes out of the hole. Or if you have nothing quickly available with which to make the loop, club the animal when it emerges.

As repugnant as it may be to you, it may be necessary to impale the quarry on a barbed pole or to drag it out by twisting a forked stick in its hair and skin, keeping this taut until you have the prey within reach of a club.

SLINGSHOTS

If you have the materials, you may fashion a slingshot that will be effective on small game. These devices are too familiar to warrant further discussion, especially as you'll be severely limited in building by what material is at hand. Skill should come with practice.

THE BOLA

You may have seen gauchos using the bola on the South American pampas, and the Eskimos have a similar device of their own. This latter consists of several strings, about three feet long, with a small weight at the end of

225

each. No matter who's using the bola, it is grasped at its center, and the weights are twirled above the head. Whirled at flying birds, the spinning cords often twist about one of them, bringing it down.

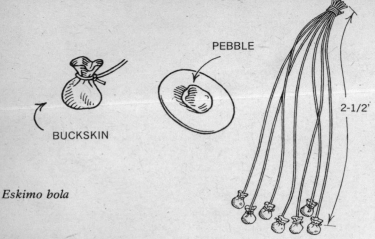

PEBBLE

2-1/2'

BUCKSKIN

Eskimo bola

DRESSING YOUR GAME

Some birds, such as grouse and ptarmigan, can be skinned by the fingers alone. Just break the skin on the breastbone and work around the body. You'll be losing a lot of flavor if you don't pluck the fowl instead of merely skinning it. However, the skinned plumage may be worn between shirt and coat to keep out the cold.

The fishy taste of water birds is lessened if they're skinned instead of plucked.

Gulls, fish-eating ducks, and other waterfowl should ordinarily be skinned to cut down on their fishy taste. The craw or first stomach of all birds except the scavengers should always be checked, both to ascertain where the bird is feeding and also because many of the undigested contents such as buds, berries, and the like are edible.

The abdominal wall of the rabbit or hare is so weak that, with a certain amount of practice, you get so that you can flip out the entrails by holding the front legs and giving the animal a sudden, strong snap. Both animals can be skinned almost as easily as pulling off gloves. The fragile fur may be comfortable in your shoes if stockings have begun to wear.

Skin game as soon as possible after it's killed.

The following is a good general pattern for skinning most animals. When the prey is too heavy to raise, skin one side to the backbone, spread out

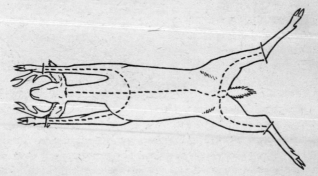

that half of the hide, roll the animal cleanly onto it, and finish skinning the other side.

All internal organs except perhaps the kidneys — and these should be taken out and used within the next few days — should be removed to prevent bloating. Prop open the body cavity so that it will cool as quickly as possible. Deer, moose, elk, and the like will be bled sufficiently by the modern high-speed bullet.

Big game is more easily handled when it has been butchered into manageable chunks. If you are staying in one place, though, the meat will keep better intact. Skin it as soon as possible, while it is still warm.

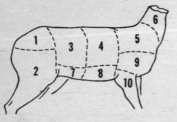

Cuts of meat from a large game animal: rump (1), round (2), loin (3), ribs (4), chuck (5), neck (6), flank (7), short ribs (8), shoulder (9), shank (10)

Keep flies off by hanging it, clear of all foliage, upwards of twelve feet in the air. Or put it in a shaded spot, covered as well as possible with evergreen boughs, until you can finish butchering it. If you down your quarry in the open, give the flesh a glaze by building a smoke beneath it and smearing the moisture as evenly as possible over the skin, both inside and out.

Heart, liver, kidneys, tongue, brains, stomach lining or tripe, and even the eyes of all game can be used with the exception, as considered elsewhere, of the liver of the polar bear and of the ringed and beaded seals.

Don't overlook the marrow. The soft vascular tissue inside the large bones of an animal that was in good condition when secured is not equalled in caloric value by any other natural food. Too, it is the most delectable part of the animal. It is wasteful to roast such bones, as is often done, until they crumble. Crack them at the start, as with two clean stones. The less the marrow is then cooked, the more nutritious it will be.

If rations are meager, use as much of the blood as you can. Blood is similar to milk and particularly rich in quickly absorbed vitamins and minerals. For example, you need iron. If you depend on eggs for this, it will take ten average-sized hen eggs to give you your daily requirements. Four tablespoons of blood will do the same thing.

One way to use blood is in broths and soups. Under survival conditions, fresh blood can be secured and carried in a bag improvised from the entrails. Use it as soon as possible.

COOLING

When the weather is warm, small quantities of meat that are to be kept for a day or so should stay as cool as possible. If a covered metal container

228

is at hand, set it in water or bury it in the damp ground, preferably where it will be shaded from the sun.

Another method of cooling is to dig a cavity horizontally in a hillside, lake shore, or stream bank. Place the food in a ventilated container within this cave, and close the hole with a chunk of sod. Even better will be to use, instead of sod, a heavy curtain of some fabric which can be saturated with water in the morning. This will then cool the chamber behind by evaporation throughout the day. If the meat molds, just scrape or cut this off, as your butcher does, and cook as usual.

If you are surviving on the tundra or in the Arctic, just dig a foot or so to the perma-frost, and you'll be in the refrigeration business.

WHICH DEER TO KILL

An elk, moose, caribou, or some other member of the deer family is what you're most apt to kill for food among this continent's big game. If you have a choice, which animal should you down?

The adult males are plumpest just before the mating season which commences in early fall. They then become steadily poorer. At the end of the rut the prime bull or buck is virtually without fat even in the usually rich marrows.

The adult cow or doe is the logical target for the survivor once the rutting season is under way, and remains the choice until early spring. About then the adult male again takes on the most fat. Usually, the older animals are plumper than the younger.

CARIBOU

Still the most numerous members of the deer family, caribou immigrate in great herds which generally afford easy shooting once they're located. Come in on them low and downwind, or hide in their path.

Even after you've downed one, the others will often flank you closely in their curiosity. When grazing in small herds, often in high valleys, they repeatedly scan the horizon for danger, so crawl to the tops of ridges and have your long searching look before exposing yourself.

Caribou meat is particularly good. When you have plenty of plump fresh meat, enough to make reasonable the sacrifices of a certain amount of nutriments in exchange for the lift of a barbeque, let a hardwood fire fall to coals in a pit. Then spread a grid of green hardwood poles over the mouth of the pit.

Lay on the chunks of meat, turning them over after the first few minutes to seal in as much of the juices as possible. These will be further protected if, instead of piercing the meat to turn it from time to time, you use sticks as tongs or spatula. The results will be optimum if when flame curls up from the sputtering of fat, these are immediately dampened with a bit of water.

A couple of hours will generally do the job, although it's easy enough to cut into a slab of meat occasionally to make sure it does not become too done for your particular liking.

MOUNTAIN SHEEP AND GOATS

In my opinion the best tasting meat in North America, domesticated or wild, is that of mountain sheep. They and the goats stay high much of the year, but you can often hide by a water hole or feeding ground, and they'll come down to you in the late afternoon. Otherwise, try to get above them, as when alarmed they climb. When skinning a goat, keep the hair from touching and tainting the meat.

GETTING YOUR MOOSE

In country where it is hunted by timber wolves, especially, the moose is a wary animal. You can often find it in midday, more easily if there is some snow on the ground, by observing when it starts to zigzag. Then it is generally seeking a bed where it can watch its tracks, while being protected at the back by the wind. It is frequently possible to circle around crosswind, however, close enough for a sure shot.

In deep snow, both moose and deer yard, — trample the snow in a small feeding area — where they can be rather easily approached, particularly if you have fashioned snowshoes for yourself.

BAKED RABBIT

Small individual ovens can be made by covering the cleaned but not skinned rabbit, the cleaned but not plucked partridge, or the cleaned but unscaled fish with moist clay. Mix this clay with water to the consistency of stiff dough. Mold a sheet an inch thick. Then shape it around the food. Or if this isn't workable with the meat you're cooking, make a looser mixture with more water and dip and redip the food in it until it is satisfactorily encased.

Lay the moist article carefully in hot ashes over which a good fire is burning. An hour of such cooking readies a rabbit to my taste, to give you an idea for best satisfying your own palate. When you break away the brick, the hair will stay attached to it, leaving you a moist, clean, morsel with all the juices intact.

Tularemia, a plaguelike disease of rodents — especially of hares, rabbits and squirrels — can be transmitted to man by ticks or by handling infected animals with the bare hands, by eating partially cooked animals that are infected, and by handling or drinking infected water. Avoid all rabbits and such that are not active and apparently healthy. If there is the slightest question, skin them with gloves and discard the hides. Cooked thoroughly, the meat itself will be harmless.

THE DAM BUILDERS

Beaver, which just chew round and around the base of a tree until it topples, are sometimes trapped by an unexpectedly falling tree. Being rich with fat, they are one of the best tasting and most nutritious animals in the North American wilderness.

Don't miss that old-time trapper's tidbit, the tail. When briefly toasted in front of the campfire, the black hide will puff and peel off in great sheets, exposing a white gelatinous meat that is delicious both by itself and, because it is so rich, especially in soups and stews.

It will usually be a waste of time to try to dig into the mound of sticks and mud that is the beaver's home, inasmuch as it has numerous escape tunnels. However, particularly when most of these underwater thoroughfares are frozen, it is frequently possible to catch a beaver on dry land and dispatch it.

THE WALKING PINCUSHION

The highly nourishing porcupine is found in most forested areas of the northern states and Canada. Be on the outlook for signs of its eating: trees with their bark chewed off fairly high above the ground.

The porcupine can be easily secured with no weapon other than a club or spear. Pick it up carefully by a front foot, turn it over, and skin from the abdomen out, peeling the hide back over the sharply pointed quills.

Do not waste any of the fat with which this animal is so richly endowed, as this will be invaluable in your diet to offset such lean animals as rabbits. The big liver is a gastronomical delight.

EVEN LEMMING

Lemming, the little stub-tailed mice that are famous for starting to swim the ocean by the hundreds during their migrations, can be valuable as an emergency food course. Winters you have to dig for them, as they nest close to the ground in deep snowdrifts. Summers you'll very often locate them by overturning flat rocks. Snares of very fine wire, looped close to the ground along their runways, are productive. Too, watch the activities of fox, weasel, shrew, and the owl. Any of these will keep you from starving.

SEAL

The common jar seal, seen along the majority of the arctic coastline, is an animal that lost and stranded men can secure and from it derive both food and fuel. This seal usually swims underwater but surfaces every minute or two to breathe. If frightened, though, it will flee several hundred yards before coming to the surface again. When unalarmed, however, it is curious and will come in to investigate a tapping or scratching noise.

You can shoot it, preferably in the head, when it is swiming from the first of September to the end of May, for it will then float. During June, July, and August, however, its lean body will sink in the decreased saltiness of inshore coastal waters.

This seal lives under the ice during the winter and maintains its air intake through open breathing holes. These are usually covered with snow, and often located in pressure cracks of small peninsulas. They are difficult to find, but if you can sneak up on one that's in use, you can shoot the seal in the head as it comes up to breathe. Or if you have hooks, lower them in the hole in such a way that the animal will catch itself upon diving.

During the springtime, you can stalk the seal as it suns itself on the edge of the ice. When it raises its head every minute or two for a look around, remain perfectly still. Then crawl, glide, and slide closer until you are within easy range. A white parka, if you have it, will aid in your camouflage.

HOW ABOUT A BEAR?

Bear will come to bait, so it's a good idea when you need more food, or its fur, to watch the entrails of a big game animal for a few days, especially when it starts to become odiferous. The bear's big appetite will bring it, too, to berry patches in the fall. I've seen as many as six adults on one serviceberry-dotted slope at the same time.

A bear, on the other hand, may dispute your right to his dinner. This is particularly true of the grizzly and the polar bear. If you have an adequate rifle, the bear itself can be your meal. If you are unarmed, you'll probably do better to avoid the scene. You especially shouldn't argue with either of the above two, or with Alaska's big brown bears.

If it is a black bear and runs at your approach, come up to the kill with caution and build a large fire beside it to diminish the chances of the bruin's return. Get your meal and quit the territory with reasonable dispatch. Even the usually philosophical black bear can be dangerous in the extreme if cornered, particularly a female separated from her cubs.

Bear are valuably fat much of the year. Throughout the twelve months a bear roast or stew will rival the choicest venison in taste, while surpassing it in nourishment. As much as forty pounds of fat can be secured from a large black bear in the fall. If you have to revert to rabbit thereafter, this stored fat can actually save your life. Because of possible trichinosis, bear meat should always be well cooked.

ALL BIRDS ARE EDIBLE

All the birds are edible. Most of them are surprisingly toothsome. It is frequently possible to catch them at night while they are roosting. One way then to take them is with a noose at the end of a pole.

This method is frequently successful, too, with ptarmigan and with spruce grouse that have flushed and are watching you from a limb. Willow ptarmigan gather in large flocks among willow clumps in bottom lands and are easily snared.

When birds are moulting, you can corner them on foot with a club. In the great nesting grounds of the Arctic, for example, they go through a flightless period of two to three weeks when you can run them down. At that time whole flocks can be driven into traps or nets.

All eggs, even those with embryos in them, are nourishing, although some, such as the robin, require an educated taste. One occasionally has access to a large congregation at nesting time, and it is then possible to provide yourself with a continuing supply of fresh eggs by marking the older ones already in the nest, possibly removing all but a few and eating those. Do not overlook the young, either.

If you're in the North, even your solitary camp will often be visited by Canada jays, also known as whiskey jacks and as camp robbers. These are very tame and will often, if coaxed with bait, take food from your fingers. A baited deadfall will take them and other small birds.

Then there are the winged hunters such as owls. You can sometimes come close enough to an owl with a fresh kill to knock it down, especially if it is having trouble in getting off the ground with its prey. An owl is as tasty as a partridge. Such predatory birds as eagles and hawks, both of which may inadvertently hunt for you, are edible in their own right.

GRILLED PHEASANT

A game bird such as a pheasant, trout or other fish, or something such as a rabbit can be cleaned and then impaled on a green hardwood stick. Or two sticks can be clamped over the meat and held together by a twisted root or vine. If you are only going to cook one side at a time, an ordinary forked green stick will be sufficient.

Sear the meat first, to retain more of the healthful juices, by thrusting it briefly into flames. Then cook it over a bed of seething coals, raking these to one side of the blaze if necessary. This way the meat will be cooked throughout without wasteful burning.

If there are other matters to which you can be attending while the grilling is going on, make a crane, thereafter pausing only to examine the meat occasionally and to turn it periodically until the repast is ready.

MAKING YOUR OWN JERKY

Cut meat across the grain in quarter-inch strips, some six inches long and two inches thick. Dry it in the sun or wind; or smoke it to produce the dry, hard, black, and incidentally sustaining and delectable jerky.

You can lay the strips of meat on a wooden grate and dry them until the meat is brittle. Use willow, elder, cottonwood, birch, or other hardwood for the fire, because the pitchy woods such as spruce and pine will blacken the meat and make it unpalatable. Never permit the heat to become great enough to cook the meat or to draw out the juices.

A teepee makes a good smokehouse when the flaps at the top are closed. Hang the meat high and build a slow, smouldering fire beneath it.

There is a quicker way of smoking meat. Start by digging a hole in the ground about three feet deep and one and one-half feet wide. Make a small fire at the bottom of the hole; when it is burning well, add green fuel for smoke. Place an improvised wooden grate slightly more than two feet up from the bottom. Use poles, boughs, leaves, or similar handy material to cover the pit.

THE BEST CONCENTRATED FOOD

The most nutritious of all concentrated foods is real pemmican, seldom obtainable commercially despite advertisements. Such true pemmican — by weight one-half well-dried lean meat and one-half rendered fat — contains nearly every necessary food ingredient with the exception of vitamin C. Eating a little fresh food, such as several rose hips daily, will supply the vitamin C necessary to prevent scurvy. It takes five pounds of fresh lean meat to make one pound of jerky suitable for pemmican.

To make pemmican, shred jerky by pounding. Cut raw animal fat into walnut-size pieces, and melt the fat from these in a pan over a slow fire, not letting the grease boil up.

When the grease is all out of the lumps, discard these and pour the hot fat over the shredded jerky, mixing the two together until you have about the consistency of ordinary sausage. Then pack the pemmican in waterproof bags. The Indians used skin bags.

SEASONING

Salt can be obtained by boiling sea water. Too, along the coast you can scrape encrustations of it into a handy container. Hickory ashes contain salt that can be dissolved out in water. When the water has evaporated, the salt will have a black tint, which is harmless.

The citric acid in wild limes and lemons can be used to pickle fish and other meat. Dilute two parts of such fruit juice with one part of salt water. Keep the fish or meat soaking for half a day or longer.

WILL YOU HAVE YOURS RARE?

When rations are limited, all food should either be eaten raw or cooked only enough to make it more palatable. The longer and hotter a food is cooked, the greater are the losses of nutritive values. Even toasting bread diminishes this food's proteins and digestibility.

If you are living on meat alone, for example, overcooking will destroy the vitamin C and make scurvy a possibility. And the overcooking of meat which is low in fat, like venison, makes the end result tough and stringy, besides wasting both flavor and nourishment.

THE MOST SATISFACTORY WAY TO COOK MEAT

When you have large amounts of meat to cook or when you're subsisting on an all-meat diet, boiling is the most satisfactory way of cooking. You tire of the animal less quickly this way, and little of the nourishment is lost if you drink the broth. Too, boiling is more saving of fuel than other methods.

When meat is tough, boiling is the best way to prepare it for later broiling, roasting, or baking. It is difficult at high altitudes, however, and impractical at heights in excess of twelve thousand feet.

Ideally, you'll have at least a large tin can for a receptacle. This can be made even more handy if you'll punch a couple of holes opposite each other just below the rim and loop a piece of light wire loosely through them. I've carried such cans with me for years whenever I'm in the bush, for the relaxation and refreshment of "boiling the kettle" at noon for tea. Other vessels can be contrived from the materials available to you.

THE SPOILED MEAT PROBLEM

Suppose you're starving and you happen upon the decomposing remains of a moose that has been killed by a fall into a canyon, or by wolves or a grizzly? Don't some natives customarily eat meat that is so ripe that its odor is repugnant? In fact, don't many gourmets in our own country follow the same practice with their game birds? Where do you draw the line?

Partially spoiled meat is not necessarily harmful, but there are some precautions which should be borne in mind. First, spoiled meat may harbor food-poisoning bacteria which could easily kill a man who was generally debilitated from starvation. The toxins or organisms like that which causes botulism are quite stable, and could easily resist any attempts to inactivate them which the wilderness dweller would have at his command. Second, there are some toxic chemicals developed in badly spoiled meat which would make a survivor very sick indeed.

The carcass of an animal which has died of some disease would be potentially more dangerous to eat than the carcass of an animal which has been shot, eviscerated, and hung.

On the positive side, if the temperature has been below forty-five degrees, there is every likelihood that the better parts of the animal — that is, any muscle which could be excised free of visibly decomposed meat — would be safe if throughly and briskly boiled, for thirty minutes at sea level. Theoretically, this should inactivate most harmful toxins.

The general rule is to eat a little of the thus prepared meat, then to wait half an hour. If you don't feel any ill effects, you can safely dig in and eat to your heart's content. Virtually all malicious toxins will manifest themselves in less than half an hour after ingestion.

CANNIBALISM

"It is rare, except in fiction, that men are killed to be eaten. There are cases where a member of a party becomes so unsocial in his conduct toward the rest that by agreement he is killed; but if his body then is eaten, it is not logically correct to say that he was killed for food," said perhaps the greatest terrestrial explorer of this century, Vilhjalmur Stefansson.

"What does happen constantly is that those who have died of hunger, or of another cause, will be eaten. But long before cannibalism develops the party has eaten whatever is edible."

SHOULD YOU EAT YOUR SHOES?

An animal's hide is as nourishing as a like quantity of its lean meat. Baking a trophy in its skin, although under some other circumstances both convenient and savory, is for that reason something we should avoid when food is limited.

Rawhide is also rich in protein. The usual practice is either to chew it raw in small bits until you tire of such mastication, then to swallow the slippery fragment, or to boil it. So cooked, it has even less flavor than roasted antlers in velvet and the look and feel of the boiled skin of a big fish.

The earlier Arctic explorers in particular tell of disputes as to whether or not leather, generally footwear or some other clothing, should be eaten by the starving men. The answer is basic. If you are so located that you'll have to walk to safety, protection of the feet comes first.

If you are cold as well as hungry, you'll stay snugger wearing the rawhide than you could by offering it to your stomach in exchange for a scant bit of extra heat through metabolism. If the article is manufactured of commercially tanned leather, the solution will be even simpler. Such leather has little if any food merit.

Seafood Stratagems 11

Freshly caught fish, as long as they're sufficiently fat and not overcooked, will sustain you in top health for an unlimited period of time. They will, that is, if you can secure all you need to eat. The trouble with fish is that, with exceptions such as salmon, they're mainly lean and short on calories.

An example is the delicious rainbow trout. The one-pound size is a toothsome one, and you'd think that half-dozen of these a day would surely nourish you, considering the fact that fish of itself provides a balanced diet. But those six one-pounders would add up to only about twelve hundred calories, whereas you'll need more like forty-five hundred calories daily under the stress of survival. But where the fishing is good, there is generally other food.

All freshwater fish in North America are good to eat. Most salt water fish that reach these shores are edible, although the odd poisonous variety may occasionally drift and swim this way. A good rule is to avoid any contact with fish, other than the delicious ling, that are strange looking.

There are no simple rules for telling undesirable fish from the nourishing ones. Often those considered edible in one locality may be unwholesome elsewhere, depending on their food, environment, and even the season. Cooking does not destroy the poison.

Almost all these dangerous fish are found in tropical waters. They usually have round or boxlike bodies with hard, shell-like skins, shielded with body plates or spines. They have small, parrotlike mouths and small gill openings. The belly fins are small or absent. Their names suggest their shapes — puffer fish, file fish, spine fish, globe fish, trigger fish, and trunk fish. Great sea eels, too, should be carefully avoided. Never eat any of the organs or eggs of any tropical fish.

Sharks are edible, their taste usually being improved if the meat is cut into chunks and soaked all day and night in salt water. Barracuda, in contrast, can cause serious digestive illness, although those less than three feet long may sometimes be eaten with impunity.

It is unwise, no matter what the circumstances, ever to risk your life with questionable sea food. Fish spoil rapidly. Never eat any with slimy gills, sunken eyes, flabby skin or flesh, or an unpleasant odor. If the flesh remains dented after you have pressed a finger against it, the fish is probably spoiled.

SUCCESSFUL FISHING

Of all the animal life in and around fresh water, fish are often the most difficult to catch. So don't expect too much from one session with hook, line, and lure. It may take hours or even days before you are successful. It can be done though, even with crude equipment, if you are patient and know when, where, and how to fish.

It is difficult to suggest the best time to fish, for different species feed at different times, both day and night. As a general rule, look for fish to feed just before dawn and directly after dusk. They also feast avidly before a storm, as the front is moving in, and often at night when the moon is full or waning. Rising fish and jumping minnows, easy to hear even when they can not be seen, may also be signs that they are feeding.

The spot you select to start fishing will depend on the type of water and time of day. During the heat of day on fast running streams, try the deep pools that lie below the riffles. Toward evening and in early morning, float your bait over the riffle itself, aiming for submerged logs, undercut banks, and overhanging bushes.

Fish deep in lakes during the heat of summer, as the prey will be seeking the coolness of deeper water. During an early summer morning or a summer evening, try the edges of the lake, for then the fish are most apt to be feeding in shallow water. Lake fishing in the spring and late fall is more productive on the edge, in shallow water, because fish are then either bedding or seeking warmer water. With some practice, you'll be able to locate the beds of a few species of fish by their strong, distinctively fishy odor.

Where the crystalline waters of streams mingle with the muddiness of a river is a fine spot to cast your lure. There will be times, however, when the most promising spot will not yield a single fish. Do not become discouraged, for there are other methods that may prove productive.

It is frequently possible to splash and flail your way up a small stream, driving the fish into a pool whose upper end you have previously dammed. Then stone up the lower end and go in with a club to secure your meal.

Small streams, also, can sometimes be momentarily shunted to another channel, leaving fish stranded. Fish in beaver country can sometimes be stranded, too, by opening a dam.

Fish can also be caught with the bare hands, especially in small streams with undercut banks and in shallow pools left by receding floods. Place your hands in the water and let them reach water temperature. Then reach slowly under the bank, keeping your hands close to the bottom if you can reach it. Move your fingers slightly until you contact a fish. Then work your hand gently along its belly until you reach the gills. Grasp the fish firmly, just behind its gills.

Small isolated pools left by the receding waters of flooded streams are often abundant with fish. Rile the mud of these puddles with your feet or a pole until the fish are forced to seek clearer water at the surface. Then throw them out with your hands or club them.

It is also possible to get a good catch of fish by feeling under the upstream edges and crevices of rocks in a fast river.

MAKING THE GILL NET

A gill net is one of the surest methods of catching fish, especially in still water near the inlet or outlet of a lake or in the backwater of a large stream which you can block with this device. It can also be effectively used beneath the ice.

Particularly if you have a parachute, a gill net can be made on the spot as from the suspension lines and the core liners pulled from the insides of these. Go about this as follows:

1. Suspend a suspension line casing—a line from which the core liner has been pulled—horizontally, at eye level, between two trees.

2. Hang an even number of core liners from this suspended line. These liners may be attached with a clove hitch or girth hitch, and spaced in accordance with the size mesh you desire. The smaller the mesh, the smaller the fish you can catch, while a small mesh will still entangle a large fish. A good standard is a mesh of two and one-half inches. The number of lines will be in accordance with the width, or length, of the net desired. If more than one person is going to work on this net, the length of the net should be stretched between the uprights. Then follow Step 8 below.

3. Start left or right. Skip the first line. Tie the second and third lines together with an overhand knot. Space according to the size mesh desired. Then tie 4 and 5, 6 and 7, and so on. One line will remain free at the end.

4. On the second row, tie 1 and 2 with the same simple overhand knot, 3 and 4, 5 and 6, and so on to the end.

5. For the third row, skip the first line and repeat Step 3 above.

6. For subsequent rows, repeat Step 4; and so on.

7. You may want to use a guideline which can be moved down for each row of knots to insure a uniform mesh. This is just another horizontal line tied to the two trees. Run this across the net on the side opposite to the one you're working on, so that it will be out of the way.

8. When you have stretched the width between the uprights and approach ground level, move the net up by rolling it on a pole and continue until the net is the desired length.

9. When the gill net is completed, string a suspension line casing along the sides to strengthen it and to make the setting of it easier.

10. Attach several wooden floats to the top of the net, and stone anchors along its bottom.

11. Set this net across a stream, at a right angle to the shore and preferably blocking the current, by using a pole. The anchor line tightens the net into place. Incidentally, you'll occasionally have the additional feast of a diving bird, caught while trying to steal a fish.

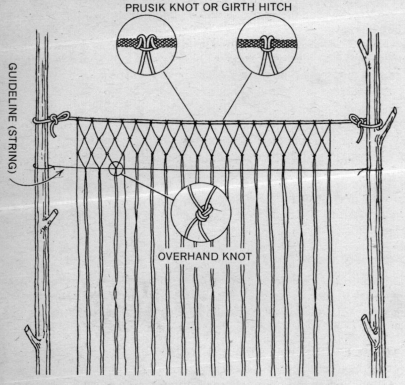

A gill net is one of the most effective methods of catching fish.

In winter, set the net by cutting holes in the ice of a lake or river. Using a pole slightly longer than the distance between the holes, attach a line to one end. Starting at the first hole, float the pole to the second hole and then on to the last hole, where it is removed from the water.

Tie the net securely to the end of the line and pull the net under the ice until it is set, several inches below the ice to keep it from freezing. Make sure the line is tied to both ends of the net to ease the work of checking and resetting.

WAYS TO FISH

The simplest way to catch fish is with a hook and line from your survival kit. Or maybe, as I do, you always carry a rolled length of line and a couple of hooks in a pocket. Use insects, shellfish, worms, or meat for your bait. Or make artificial lures with feathers, brightly colored cloth, bits of bright metal, or fuzzy seeds.

By the way, if you're short on equipment but have some light wire, a length of this from the line to the hook will prevent the fish from biting the line in two.

If you have no hooks, improvise them from wire, nails or pins; or carve them out of bone or hard wood. A thorn or sharp sliver may provide the barb. A number of primitive but deadly types are shown.

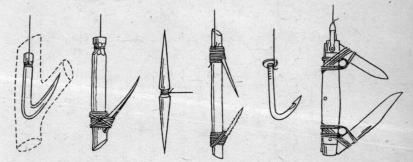

Improvised fish hooks

For a really rugged hook, lash the blade of a pocket knife partially open against a wooden wedge. A second smaller blade, so opened at the opposite angle, will provide a barb. The knife can then be concealed in a large lump of bait.

THE SCIENTIFIC WAY TO MAKE A LINE

You can make a line by unraveling a parachute suspension line or such or by twisting thread from cloth or plant fibers such as nettle. Or you can make a lace by cutting round and around a piece of rawhide or leather.

One way of making a line from the threads unraveled from clothing is to knot, at frequent intervals, lengths of a half dozen or so of the threads.

For a more scientific approach, fasten four threads at one end. Hold two threads in each hand. Roll and twist each of these double strands clockwise between thumb and forefinger. At the same time, turn those in the master hand counter-clockwise around those held in the other hand. Such twisting and winding must be done tightly, so that the completed line will not come apart easily.

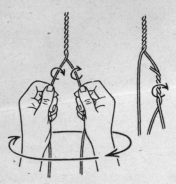

*Plant fibers or threads un-
raveled from clothing can be
twisted together to make
fishing line.*

Depending on the lengths of thread you are able to come by, end each of the four strands about two inches apart. This is to make the splicing on of the new strands more substantial. About an inch before any thread stops, twist a new thread to the one just ending.

Such an operation can be continued to make a fish line of any length. If instead of arctic grayling or rainbows your quarry is more the size of a Dolly Varden, use a dozen or more strands for your line.

IMPROVISE A LURE

A small bright button makes a good lure. So does any shiny and tiny bit of metal. The commendably thrifty Hudson's Bay Company long included in each of its survival kits a tablespoon with a hole bored in it so that a hook might be affixed for trolling or gigging.

LOCATING THE BEST BAIT

As a general rule, fish are most apt to take bait from their native habitat. Look in the water near the shore for crabs, roe, and minnows. Search the banks for worms and insects.

When you hook a fish, inspect its stomach to see what it has been feeding on, then try to duplicate this. Use its eyes, intestines, or a strip of light belly meat, if other sources are unproductive. With live minnows, pass the hook through the body of the fish under its backbone behind the dorsal fin, taking care not to kill the live bait by severing its backbone.

If you find the fish has been eating crayfish, turn over rocks in the stream until you find some of these crustaceans. If you can find enough, there's your banquet. Once these are cooked by being dropped into boiling water, the delicious lower portions are easily sucked free of the shells.

One way to catch a quantity of these fresh-water crustaceans is by herding a school into a pool, cutting off their retreat with a few judiciously placed stones, and then scooping them out with a net of tightly enlaced foliage fashioned to a loop made of a bent sapling or with a shirt or other article of clothing tied to such a frame.

A METHOD SO DEADLY IT'S ILLEGAL

Gigging, illegal in many jurisdictions, is the method of catching fish by hooking them in the body. Under emergency conditions, when the law of survival supersedes other considerations, it may get you a meal when other practices fail. It is particularly effective on Atlantic salmon and other fish that stay almost motionless in pools.

The Eskimos go about it by dangling an often barbless hook in the water, perhaps through a hole cut in the ice, with bits of shining and twisting bone two or three inches above it. When a fish's curiosity causes it to swim close enough for a smell, the line is jerked up with an odds-on chance of implanting the hook somewhere in the prey.

Another, legal, method of fishing that is known as jigging in some localities requires about a ten-foot limber cane or sapling pole, a hook, a piece of brilliant metal shaped like a commercial fishing spoon, a two to three-inch strip of white meat or fish intestine, and a piece of line about a foot long.

Attach the hook just below the spoon at the end of the short line and knot the other end of this latter to the tip of the pole. Working close to the edge of lily pads or weed beds, dabble the attention-getting bait and spoon just below the surface. Slap the water occasionally with the tip of the pole to attract large fish. This method is particularly effective at night.

THE GORGE OR SKEWER HOOK

One of the fishing methods going back to the early ages, and still used successfully if not sportingly, is the gorge or skewer hook, particularly effective when secured to the end of a set line. This is quickly and simply made by sharpening a short piece of bone or hardwood, notching or drilling the middle, and there tying the line.

Hidden in an attractive gob of bait, this skewer is swallowed whole by the fish, upon which the eventual pressure of the line turns it crosswise in the stomach. This method is similar to the Eskimo practice of bending a sharpened short length of wood and hiding it in a chunk of meat which is then put out to freeze. Eaten whole, as by a fox, it thaws at body temperature and opens in the prey's stomach, killing it.

SPEARING

This method may be difficult except when the stream is small and the fish large or numerous, as during the spawning season or when they congregate in pools.

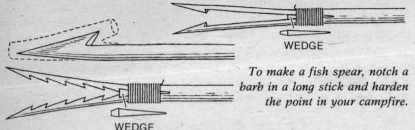

WEDGE

To make a fish spear, notch a barb in a long stick and harden the point in your campfire.

WEDGE

You can counteract the deceptive refraction to a large extent by keeping the point of the spear submerged while waiting. Too, with many fish you can approach to within a nearly sure few inches before the final jab.

You can make a spear by sharpening a long dry stick and hardening the point in the campfire after a barb has been notched in it. Or you can fashion your barbs of bones, thorns, metal, or even stone; then lash them into position.

It is frequently possible to find fish sleeping in shallow water at night around the shallow edges of lakes. These fish can be spotted with the aid of a flashlight, or a birch bark or conifer-knot torch. Aiming low to counteract refraction, bring the spear point almost to the side of the fish before making the final thrust. Light attracts fish, and so may be successfully used for other types of night angling.

SNARING

The snare is made with a loop of wire, attached to a long, light pole. The loop is passed around the fish, tightened, and the catch jerked from the water. This works when fish are spawning and when they've congregated in schools, as in a clear pool near the bottom of a waterfall.

NIGHT LINES

Set lines will fish for you while you are occupied with other tasks. Try this method when you're camping for a period of time near a lake or stream, awaiting an opportunity to continue your trip safely. Simply tie several hooks onto your line or, if you have plenty of the latter, use a separate line for each hook.

Bait them and either tie the end of the line to something stationary or, far better, to a low-hanging branch that will give with the pulls of the fish. Keep these lines in the water for as long as you are in the area, checking them periodically to remove fish and to freshen the bait. Such night lines are so effective that they are ordinarily banned by law in many localities, although not by the law of survival.

ICE FISHING

You can obtain fish in winter by angling through a hole in the ice. Keep this as open as possible when it is not in use, by covering it with brush or browse and heaping loose snow atop that lid.

Fish tend to gather in deep pools, so try to cut your ice holes over the deepest parts of the lake or river. Place an easily fashioned rig at several holes. When the bit of cloth that is serving as a signal flag moves to an upright position, pull up the fish and rebait the hook.

Gigging through the hole in the ice is another technique. You'll need a short stick, your line, and a shiny bit of metal or bone near the hook. This attention-collecting device should be kept on the move to attract the fish.

If the ice is clear, you may be able at times to see a fish swimming beneath it. Then strike the ice sharply with a rock or log directly above the fish. This will often stun it long enough for you to cut a hole and secure it.

FISH TRAPS

Fish traps are enclosures with blind openings. The fish are herded into the pen by two fencelike walls that extend out like a funnel. When they are

A fish trap is formed by a low stone wall extending out into the water.

in the restricted water, they have a difficult time in finding their way out. The time and effort you put into building such a trap depends, of course, on both your need for food and on the length of time you expect to be in one locality.

If you're on the ocean, choose the location of your trap at high tide and build at low tide. One to two hours of work should complete the project, especially if you take the location into account and save time and effort by adapting natural features.

On rocky shores, use natural rock pools. On coral islands, use natural pools on the surface of reefs by blocking openings as the tide recedes. On sandy shores, use sand bars and the ditches they may enclose. The best fishing off sandy beaches, by the way, is in the lee of offshore sand bars.

Note the swimming habits of the fish if possible. Build your simple weir as a low stone wall extending out into the water and forming an angle with the shore. If you plan a more complex brush weir, choose protected bays or inlets, using the narrowed area and extending one arm almost to the shore. Place nets across mouths of streams or at right angles to the shore.

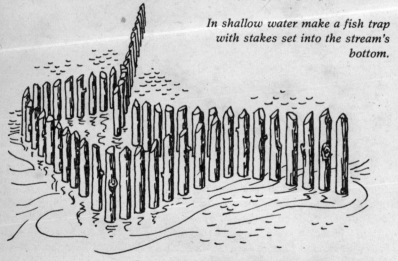

In shallow water make a fish trap with stakes set into the stream's bottom.

In small, shallow streams, make your fish traps with stakes or brush set into the stream's bottom or weighed down with stones so that the flow is almost blocked except for a small, narrow opening into a stone or brush pen in shallow water. Walk along the stream, herding the fish into your trap or clubbing them when they reach shallow water. Mud-bottomed streams can be trampled until roiled, then advantageously seined. The fish are blinded and can not avoid the nets.

Fish may be confined in properly built enclosures and kept there for days, the incoming water keeping them fed. It is a good idea to keep them alive until needed and thus assure a continuing fresh supply without danger of spoilage.

STUPEFYING FISH

Fish caught by these emergency methods are still edible and wholesome. One procedure is to crush the leaves and stalks of the mullein or fish weed, *Croton setigerus,* and drop them into a still pool or temporarily dammed brook. The fish will be momentarily narcotized and will float to the surface where they should immediately be secured. The bulbous root of the soap plant, *Chlorogalum pomeidianum,* can also be utilized in this manner, as can the seeds of the southern buckeye, *Aesculus pavia.*

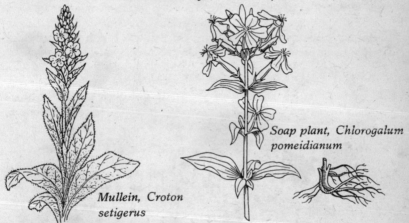

Soap plant, *Chlorogalum pomeidianum*

Mullein, *Croton setigerus*

Commercial rotenone may be used for survival fishing. However, rotenone has no effect if dusted over the surface of a pond. It must be mixed to a malted-milk consistency with a little water, then distributed in the fishing waters. If the concentration is strong, it will take effect within two minutes in warm water, while it may take up to an hour in colder water. Fish sick enough to turn over on their backs will eventually die, although the active poison is harmful only to cold-blooded life. Man can eat fish killed by this poison without any ill effects whatsoever.

An ounce of twelve percent rotenone, not a bad thing to have in your survival kit, will kill every fish for half mile down a stream that is about two dozen feet wide. After putting in the poison, follow slowly downstream and pick up the fish as they come to the surface, sink to the bottom, or swim crazily to the bank. A stick dam or other obstruction will aid you in collecting fish as they float downstream.

There are a few facts to remember about the use of rotenone. It is very swift-acting in warm water at seventy degrees and above. It works more slowly in cold water and is not practical in water below fifty degrees. It can best be applied in small ponds, streams, and tidal pools. Don't use too much, or it will be wasted. On the other hand, too little will not be effective.

Suppose you have no harmless fish poison or can find none in your vicinity. Then burn such things as coral and sea shells to obtain lime. Lime thrown into a small pond or tidal pool will kill all fish in the vicinity.

SHOOTING FISH

If you have a firearm and plenty of ammunition, you can secure fish by shooting at the larger of them when they are in no more than three feet of water. Aim low to counteract the refraction. Too, spawning fish can be successfully shot if necessary while they are writhing through shallow water.

Some explosive detonated in a school of fish will supply you with food for days. Dry or otherwise preserve those you cannot eat fresh.

MORE AQUATIC EDIBLES

The enterprising survivor can earn himself a good living along the beach by eating shellfish, snails, snakes, lobsters, sea urchins, and small octopi.

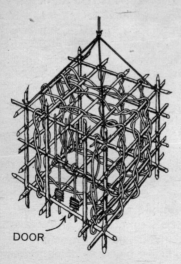

DOOR

Catch lobsters with a trap made of sticks and vines.

Fish, crabs, lobsters, crayfish, and sea urchins can be poked out of holes, crevices, and rock pools. Be ready to spear them before they can escape into deeper water. If they are already in deep water, tease them shoreward with a baited hook, piece of string, or stick. Look for fresh-water crayfish, snails, and clams under rocks, logs, overhanging bushes, and in muddy bottoms.

Shrimp and prawns lie on or near the sea bottom but may be lured to the surface by a light at night. Then catch them with a hand net which might be made of a shirt and sapling whose limber end has been curved to form a loop.

Lobsters and crayfish are creeping forms seen on the bottom in water from ten to thirty feet deep. Use a box-type lobster trap made of sticks and vines, a jig, or a baited hook. Lift your catch out of the water with a hand net.

Crabs burrow, climb, and creep and are easily caught in shallow water with a dip net or in traps baited with fish heads or animal entrails. They're all good, and it's generally possible, especially at low tide, to get all you can use by searching shore rocks and seaweed. Too, they will rapaciously attach themselves to meat that is lowered on a line.

Although land crabs are often infected with parasites and should be dropped into boiling water for at least twenty minutes, salt water varieties may be eaten raw.

The sea urchin, a marine animal that is cousin to the starfish, is a major source of food in many localities. They are safe to eat when located in the temperate and arctic waters of North America. Here they may be collected in large numbers at low tide. Sea urchins are shaped like slightly flattened balls. Their thin, easily broken shells bristle with movable spines. The lengths of eggs inside the top shell are edible raw; but better when they have been cooked.

Hunt frogs at night when you can locate them by their croaking. Club them or snag the larger ones on a hook and line. You can also frequently occupy their attention with one hand while you capture them with the other. Too, frogs have a habit of closing their mouths on a bit of bright cloth, long enough for you to jerk them ashore. Skin all frogs before using, as the skin may be toxic. Then eat the whole frog, perhaps thinking of the price you'd have to pay for just the legs in a swanky city restaurant.

The newts and salamanders found under rotten logs and beneath rocks in areas where frogs are abundant are very much edible. All lizards and alligators are also edible. Remove the scaly skin, then boil, fry, or roast the meat. Heat alligators over the campfire before skinning to loosen the plates.

You'll find flowerlike sea anemones in pools and crevices at low tide. Dropping a pebble onto them or poking them with a stick will cause them to close. Detach them with your knife. Wash well to remove slime and dirt, both inside and outside the animal. Then boil, to make a chowder.

The sluggish sea cucumber can shoot out its stomach when excited. Don't eat that, but enjoy the five strips of muscle inside the body. You can also eat the skin which is often scraped away, instead, after the insides have been discarded. These strips are good raw, boiled, fried, or turned into soup; or its flesh may be smoked or dried. The body of this easily recognizable animal is about six to eight inches long when contracted, and twice that length when expanded.

THE DELECTABLE MOLLUSKS

These include fresh and salt water invertebrates such as mussels, clams, and other bivalves; octopuses and squids; chitons; and limpets, periwinkles, and other snails. The well-known conch, actually a large snail, should be handled with caution; it has razor-sharp trap doors which it may suddenly jut out, puncturing your skin in its efforts to get away.

River snails and fresh-water periwinkles are plentiful in the rivers, streams, and lakes of the northern coniferous forests. These snails may be pencil-point or globular in shape. Both the aquatic and terrestrial snails of temperate waters are tasty sources of nourishment, but the cone snails found in the tropics should be avoided entirely.

Abalone are prizes along the Pacific Coast. Once you've pried the great mollusks from rocks at low tide, working fast before they have a chance to adhere more tightly, scoop them from their bright bowl-like shells with the same chisel-edged sticks or large knives, trim off the dark sections, slice into thin steaks, and pound between two rounded rocks until soft. Fry or roast these half a minute on each side, as further cooking toughens them.

A small heap of empty oyster shells near a hole may indicate an octopus. Drop a baited hook into the hole, wait until the octopus has entirely surrounded the hook and line, and then lift it up quickly. The meat is delicious. To kill the octopus, pierce with your fish spear. Octopuses are not scavengers like sharks but are hunters, fond of spiny lobsters and other crablike fish. They pursue their prey into shallow water at night, when they can often be easily seen and speared.

Heaps of shells beside a stream, perhaps left by a raccoon, are a clue to the presence of clams. Salt water clams, not so easily dug, can be secured at low tides along the beaches of this continent. It is important to note in regard to clams that along North America's western shores below the Aleutians, all dark portions of the meat should be discarded for the half-year starting with May and concluding with October because of possibly dangerous concentrations of toxic alkaloids taken in when they feed. Then the white meat alone should be eaten.

During the same period, mussels and oysters are poisoned by these identical alkaloids, which can not be destroyed by heat, as a result of feeding on some of the venomous organisms that drift ashore at this time. The rest of the year they're delicious. Take care not to harvest any that do not clamp their shells tightly shut when touched. You'll find these delectable little bluish-black mussels attached in dark clusters to seashore rocks at low tide.

In any event, be sure that you have a live mollusk and that you boil it. If you eat one raw, you are inviting parasites into your body.

STEAMED CLAMS

Steaming can be accomplished without a container and is especially savory with foods, like clams and other shellfish, that require little cooking. Place your food in a pit lined with rocks that have been made sizzling hot in your campfire. Cover them with live wet seaweed or, if you're not near the ocean, with wet green grass or damp green leaves. Put more seaweed, grass, or leaves over your victuals. Then force a stick down through the vegetation to the food pocket. Pack several inches of dirt over everything. Remove the stick and pour a small amount of water to the food through the remaining hole. Then block the hole.

Leave everything for four or five hours while you go about other tasks. For all its slowness, this method is delectable. All this can be accomplished most handily on a beach and is the basis of the ancient Indian clambakes.

WHAT ABOUT JELLYFISH?

Avoid jellyfish at all times, no matter what the circumstances. Do not handle or use them in any way. Even the very tiny ones are unpleasantly bitter.

CONSIDER THE TURTLE

All turtles are edible whether found in salt water, fresh water, or on land. They can often be seen sunning themselves along lake and river shores. If they waddle into shallow water, you can still get them, but watch out for their mouths and claws.

Turtles, being rich in fat from which the sun alone can render a clear flavorful oil, are especially nutritious. Their blood and juices are sometimes used at sea in an attempt to ease thirst. Kill your turtle by concussion or by getting it biting on a stick and then cutting off its head. Watch out for reflex actions after it is dead.

Then turn it over and cut the skin all around. Skin the hide down the legs to the feet which can then be easily disjointed. Now with the help of a sharp knife in the case of snappers, or with a saw or ax or edged stone with varieties such as terrapins, cut through the substance connecting the top and bottom shells and pry off the latter. The entrails can then be easily reached and discarded.

If the turtle is a small one in ratio with your appetite, simmer it in the shell until the meat has cooked free. But if you've more turtle than you can eat, settle for cutting out the four quarters.

It is occasionally possible to track a female back to a fresh nest of eggs, usually buried in sand or mud close to the water. Although these do not taste like hen's eggs, they are nourishing even when they reach the embryonic stage.

ENJOYING YOUR CATCH

Salmon and other large fish can be opened, cleaned, and then pegged flat on preheated hardwood slabs with their skin against the wood. Remove the backbone if it is in the way. Turning the slab end for end occasionally, while it leans before a bed of glowing coals, will cook it throughout. As soon as the flesh flakes beneath a testing sliver, the fish is done and ready on its own hot plate.

Don't use softwood, or the resinous spruce, pine, or such will take away from the delicate taste of the fish. Too, when cooking calls for coals, burn one of the hardwoods such as the particularly sweet-smelling birch, as softwoods burn quickly to ashes and do not make lasting beds of embers.

DRYING FISH

The methods of preserving fish and fowl are much the same as for other meats. To ready for smoking, cut off the heads and remove the backbone. Then spread the fish flat or skewer in that position. Thin willow branches with the bark removed make good skewers.

Fish can also be dried in the sun. Hang them from branches or spread them on hot rocks. When the meat has dried, splash it with salt water, if this is at hand, to salt the outside. Don't keep sea food unless it is well dried and salted. Avoid eating uncooked smoked fresh-water fish, as they may harbor parasites.

Hazards To Survival 12

Keeping healthy and fit is especially important when you're on your own. Your physical condition will have much to do with your coming out safely. Protection against cold and heat, as well as knowledge of how to find water and food, will be vital to your health. But there are more rules you should heed.

Drink enough water to avoid dehydration, an important consideration, too, in winter. If water is scarce or difficult to obtain, avoid excessive dehydration from sweating.

Save your strength, avoid fatigue, and get enough sleep. If you can't sleep at first, get a fire going if you possibly can and lie down beside it, relaxing and loosening up. If you are walking out or doing other hard work, try resting for a few minutes each hour, not long enough to stiffen up. Resting this way, you rid your body of some thirty percent of the lactic acid buildup in the first five to seven minutes. But during an additional quarter hour you'd lose only some five percent more.

Take care of your feet. These will be most important, particularly if you plan to walk out. If your feet hurt, take care of them right away. Examine your feet when you first stop to see if there are any red spots or blisters. Apply adhesive tape smoothly on your skin where shoes rub. If you have a blister, it will be better to leave it intact to decrease the possibilities of infection. But cover it with an adhesive bandage to prevent further chafing. If it is broken or punctured, do not remove the protective skin remaining over the wound. Wash with soap and water if possible and dry carefully in any event. Apply a sterile dressing.

Guard against skin infection. Your skin is the first line of defense against this trouble. Try to wash even the smallest cut or scratch, preferably with soap and water. Keep your fingernails short, especially in fly season, to prevent infection from scratching. Cuts and scratches are more apt to become seriously infected particularly in hot country, and a bad infection could hurt your chances of coming out safely. Wherever you are, make a habit of personal cleanliness. Keep your body, clothing, and camp clean.

Guard against intestinal sickness. Purify all water used for drinking, brushing the teeth, dish washing, and the like, either with water purification tablets or by boiling it for five minutes. At altitudes above sea level, boil it an additional minute for each thousand feet of elevation.

Don't worry about a slowdown of the digestive functions. This will take care of itself harmlessly in a few days if you exercise and drink plenty of water.

ARCTIC PERILS

The chief danger in winter is, of course, freezing. For protection against the cold, note the special suggestions for clothing and shelter in those sections of this book. The important thing is to keep your face, ears, nose, wrists, hands, and feet warm and dry. Good circulation is very important; don't restrict it with tight clothing. Avoid sweating. Stay out of the wind as much as possible.

Don't touch cold metal with your bare skin in temperatures much below zero. You'll be apt to freeze to the metal and tear away the skin. If necessary, thaw by gently applying heat or urine. If possible, have tool handles, gun triggers, and the metal parts of eyeglasses taped when you may have to withstand the arctic winter.

You will freeze only if the air is carrying away more heat than your body can generate. If you prevent the cold air from reaching your skin by wearing proper clothing and by keeping your body in overall heat balance, you won't freeze. Your entire body must be kept warm to maintain circulation to your feet and hands. Excessive loss of heat from any part of your body restricts circulation, leaving your extremities with little heat. With no heat coming in, your hands and feet are apt to become frostbitten.

You can get badly sunburned in the Arctic, and at high altitudes elsewhere, even on foggy or lightly overcast days. Cover up in bright sunlight, and if you have any sunburn ointment, use it.

Snowblindness is caused by the exposure of the unprotected eyes to glare from the snow. It can occur even on cloudy days and in tents. You can prevent snowblindness by wearing dark glasses whenever you are exposed to glare. Prevention is the best answer. Don't wait until your eyes hurt to wear your glasses.

A handy substitute for sun glasses is a piece of wood, bone, leather, or other material with narrow eye slits cut in it. These and similar eyeshades are fine in blizzards because the slits can be kept clean by brushing them off, whereas regular glasses may give trouble by frosting. Too, it is a good idea to blacken the area around your eyes with soot from the fire. Even though the glare may not seem to bother you, it will affect your ability to see objects at a distance and will retard your eyes' adaption to night vision. If your eyes hurt and you have boric acid ointment, apply some to the eyelids and the corners of the eyes.

Whenever there is the slightest possibility that you may become marooned in the Arctic during warm weather, have a good fly dope with you.

Mosquitoes and flies in the Arctic do not transmit diseases, but their numbers and constant activity during the long summer days are a nuisance, often preventing rest or sleep. In fact, if you have no protection against them, they can kill.

Keep your body as completely covered as possible. In the absence of protectives, use smudges, considered in the section on fire, or rest in insect-proof shelters. When traveling or relaxing, try to keep to the higher ridges or on the breezy sea coast and river and lake shores.

If you are rescued by natives, notice whether they are given to diligent scratching. If so, they may be lousy. Then diplomatically avoid all bodily contact with them. Especially try to avoid unclean bedding or quarters. Bathe and examine your body and clothes regularly.

THE VITAL FACTS ABOUT CARBON MONOXIDE

Carbon monoxide is a danger in any closed space — motor vehicle, ship, plane, cabin, hut, tent, or igloo — where there is combustion of any kind. Even a fire in a tight new stove with proper drafts can kill you, for the heat-reddened metal itself can release perilous quantities of the deadly gas.

Carbon monoxide is the common product of incomplete burning, being the ever-present carbon dioxide so necessary to life, with one part of oxygen missing. For example, there is thirty percent carbon monoxide in the fumes of an automobile and thirty to forty percent in water gas which is the gas supply of most cities. The hungry molecules of carbon monoxide take on the absent atoms of oxygen as soon as possible, and if this happens in your blood, it can be dangerous if not deadly. Carbon monoxide does not affect the tissues. The problem is to supply and get enough oxygen to the tissues.

Carbon monoxide is an especially insidious killer because of its properties of being both odorless and cumulative. This latter characteristic is particularly dangerous. The ill effects of breathing tiny amounts of the generally unsuspected poison build up gradually in the system until just one more otherwise inconsequential whiff lays the victim low, as happened to explorer Richard E. Byrd in his solitary outpost in the Antarctica. Those anemic will suffer first and more.

Carbon monoxide usually gives no recognizable warning. For example, there is no difficulty with breathing, although in a shelter you may be tipped off by the fact that a light starts to burn poorly. What ordinarily occurs is that the individual is so abruptly overcome that when he first realizes something is wrong, he already is nearly if not completely helpless.

The peril heightens as cold deepens because of the natural inclination to curb ventilation in favor of warmth. Restricted circulation of air allows the invisible and odor-free vapor to build up in an enclosed space. Furthermore, the very circumstance that the air is becoming progressively more and more stale itself adds to the formation of the deadly gas by not affording enough oxygen for complete combustion.

Carbon monoxide has killed more people in the wilderness than will ever be known. There is very real danger, even in a tent. If the spaces in the weave of the fabric are closed by waterproofing, or by rain, snow, or even frost; a small heater can and in many instances has killed all occupants. By far the best preventative is to make sure of good ventilation.

Especial danger confronts the motorist stalled by ice or snow. The inclination in such an emergency is to keep the windows snugly shut and the motor going so that the occupants can keep warm. The peril when any closed vehicle is so parked, especially if a white smother of snow is heaping around it, is that carbon monoxide can build up inside the unventilated car in killing amounts.

EMERGENCY STEPS

Symptoms of carbon monoxide poisoning, if you notice any, begin with tightness over the forehead, headache, and a slight flush. The headache becomes progressively worse with continued exposure. Then weakness, dizziness, decreased vision, nausea and vomiting make their appearance followed by collapse.

With collapse, the pulse and respiration are increased. Breathing may be labored, then alternately slower and then labored again. Eventually there is coma, convulsions, decreased respiration and pulse, and finally death.

The prescribed treatment is immediate removal to fresh air. To decrease the oxygen requirements of the tissues, the victim should be kept warm. Steady observation is necessary because improvement may be followed by reverses. Keep quiet to decrease the oxygen requirements.

If the victim is unconscious, mouth to mouth resuscitation should be commenced immediately. This is better than the Shaefer and similar methods because of the five percent carbon dioxide in the expired air.

In any event, the carbon monoxide in the system will dissipate faster if five or ten percent carbon dioxide is supplied with the air that is being breathed. This can be done by taking a deep breath, exhaling in a paper or plastic bag, and then having the patient take a deep breath of the air expired into the bag by a person not afflicted. If several people can supply such bags of air, the effects will pass more quickly, perhaps taking only thirty to forty minutes instead of several hours.

The effects are not necessarily gone when all the carbon monoxide is out of the system. Small hemorrhages in the heart muscle, brain, and other organs may persist. Depending on their location, there may be serious after-effects if these hemorrhages are in vital areas.

Again, carbon monoxide poisoning can be chronic. That is, continued exposure for four to five hours at a time, for example, can cause chronic headaches, a general feeling of sickness, digestive ailments, and so on, but never proceed to the full poisoning effect.

The diagnosis of the acute case is easy. There is the history or evidence of exposure, plus a cherry-red color to the nails, the mucous membranes of the mouth, and the tissues.

No matter what the circumstances, always maintain adequate ventilation, wherever you are, at all times.

TREATING FROSTBITE

Frostbite is the freezing of some part of the body. It is a constant hazard in subzero temperatures, especially when the wind is strong. As a rule, the first sensation of frostbite is numbness rather than pain. You can see the effect of frostbite, a greyish or yellow-whitish spot on the skin, before you feel it. Therefore, if you have someone with you, get in the habit of watching each other for visible frostbite. If you are alone, keep feeling your face and ears for stiffness.

If the freezing is only minor and local, a cupped warm hand will thaw it. Otherwise, try to get the frostbite casualty into a heated shelter if possible.

When only the surface skin is frozen and it becomes spongy to the touch, it can be rewarmed by body heat. If toes and feet are superficially frozen and you have a cooperative companion along, thaw them against his warm abdomen. Or, with a deeper frostbite, in desperate conditions kill an animal if possible, open it, and thrust your feet into the hot interior.

If deeper tissues are involved, the thawing process must take place quickly. Because the refreezing of a thawed part means the certain loss of tissue, it is often best on the trail to continue with a frozen part for a reasonable length of time rather than to thaw it when there is a strong chance of refreezing. Thawing, in any event, must be accomplished as soon as possible.

Warm the frozen part rapidly. Frozen members ideally should be thawed in warm water until soft, even though this treatment is painful. The procedure is most effective when the water is between 105 degrees and 110 degrees, that is, when it is comfortably warm to a normally protected part such as an elbow. If warm water is not available, wrap the frozen part in blankets or clothing and apply improvised heat packs, perhaps stones warmed in the fire. Thawed extremities should be immobilized.

Use body heat whenever possible to aid in thawing. Hold a bare, warm palm against frozen ears or parts of the face. Grasp a frostbitten wrist with the other warm, bare hand. Hold frostbitten fingers against the chest, under the armpits, or between the legs at the groin.

When frostbite is accompanied by breaks in the skin, apply sterile dressing. Do not use strong antiseptics such as tincture of iodine. Do not use powdered sulfa drugs in the wound.

Never forcibly remove frozen shoes and mittens. Place in lukewarm water, or thaw in front of the campfire, and then take them off gently.

Never rub frostbite. You may tear frozen tissues and cause additional damage. Never follow the old-fashioned custom of applying snow or ice, as this just increases the cold injury. Rubbing a frozen cheek with snow in very cold weather, in fact, is comparable to scrubbing a warm cheek with sand and gravel. Never make the terrible mistake of trying to thaw the frozen part in cold gasoline, oil, or alcohol at subzero temperatures, just because they are still liquid.

WHAT ABOUT SNOWBLINDNESS?

Symptoms of so-called snowblindness, when you're not actually blind, are redness, burning, watery or sandy feeling eyes, the halo one ordinarily sees when looking at lights, headaches, and poor vision. Remember, snow-blindness may not appear until four to six hours after exposure. It is often not suspected, for this reason, particularly because the symptoms may not manifest themselves until well after sunset.

Treat snowblindness by protecting the eyes from light and by relieving the pain. You can accomplish the first by staying in a dark shelter and by wearing a lightproof bandage. For the second, keep cold compresses on the eyes if there is no danger of freezing and take aspirin. Most cases recover within eighteen hours without medical treatment. However, one attack of snowblindness will make you far more susceptible to future attacks.

THE DANGERS OF IMMERSION FOOT

Immersion foot is a cold injury resulting from prolonged exposure to temperatures just above freezing. In the early stages, your feet and toes are pale and feel cold, numb, and stiff. Walking becomes difficult.

If you do not take preventive action at this stage, your foot will swell and become extremely painful. In drastic cases of immersion foot, the flesh dies, and eventual amputation of the foot or leg may be necessary. If you're then in the bush away from medical aid, you may die.

Because the early stages are not very painful, you must be constantly alert to prevent the development of immersion foot. To prevent this condition, keep your feet dry by wearing waterproof footgear and by staying as much as possible in dry bivouacs. Clean and dry your socks and shoes at every opportunity. Dry your feet as soon as reasonably feasible after getting them wet. At the same time, warm and massage them with your hands, and if possible don dry socks.

When you must wear wet socks and shoes, as is a commonplace occurence on the trail, exercise your feet continually by walking or by wriggling your toes and flexing your ankles. If you sleep in a sitting position, put on dry socks if you can, warm your feet by the fire, and elevate your legs as high as possible. Try to avoid tight footwear.

Treat immersion foot by keeping the affected part dry and warm. If possible, maintain the foot and leg in a horizontal position to increase circulation.

IF YOU EVER FALL IN

If you ever fall in water in cold weather, roll in dry snow to blot the moisture. Brush off the excess snow, then roll again until as much as possible of the water is absorbed. Don't take off your boots until you are in some warm shelter or until you have a fire crackling outdoors.

SEVERE CHILLING

If you are totally immersed in cold water for even a few minutes, your body temperature will drop. Long exposures to severe dry cold on land can also lower your body heat. The only remedy for this severe chilling is warming of the entire body. Get warm by any means available, as by kindling a brisk campfire. Ideally, the preferred treatment is warming in a hot bath, perhaps at some handy hot spring. Severe chilling may be accompanied by shock.

SHOCK

This condition is characterized by paleness, trembling, sweating, and thirst. It can accompany any injury. In fact, the more severe the wound is, the more likely it is that shock will develop.

If a companion is unconscious, lay him flat on his back. Raise his feet unless he has a head injury or breathing difficulty. Keep him comfortably warm, at the same time avoiding overheating him. Give him warm drinks if he is conscious.

If you are alone and become seriously injured, lie down in a depression in the ground, behind a tree, or any place you'll be sheltered from the wind. Try to get a good campfire going. If you can, lie with your head lower than your feet to increase the flow of blood to your head. Keep yourself as warm as possible and rest for at least a full day.

GUARD AGAINST HEAT INJURY

In hot climates develop a tan slowly by gradual exposure to the sun. Sunburn in the desert can be dangerous, so if you must be in the sun, try not to expose your head. Avoid strenuous exertion in the hot sun, as there is the danger of fatal heat stroke.

The lesser illnesses caused by heat can be prevented by consuming enough water and salt to replace the sweat. Salt tablets or table salt ideally should be taken in the proportion of two tablets or one-fourth teaspoonful to a quart of water. Treatment of heat casualties consists of cooling the body and restoring water and salt. Exposure to the desert sun can cause several types of heat collapse.

HEAT CRAMPS

The first warning of heat collapse generally is cramps in the leg or abdominal muscles. Rest. If possible, drink water in which salt has been dissolved in the proportions suggested above.

HEAT EXHAUSTION

You're first flushed, then pale. You sweat profusely, and your skin is moist and cool. You may even become light-headed or unconscious. Treat by lying in any shade, flat on your back. Take salt dissolved in water, the same two tablets or one-fourth teaspoonful to a quart.

HEAT STROKE

This may come on suddenly. Your face is red, your skin hot and dry. All perspiring ceases. You have a severe headache, and your pulse is fast and strong. Unconsciousness may result. Treat by somehow cooling yourself off. Loosen your clothing. Lie flat in the shade, preferably about a foot off the ground. If at all possible, cool by saturating your clothing with water and by fanning. Never take stimulants.

OTHER HEAT PRECAUTIONS

Avoid getting chilled at night if you possibly can. Keep your clothes buttoned and try to get under some shelter.

Use a chapstick, if you have one, on both lips and nostrils.

Keep sand and sand fleas out of your shoes. Stop often to shake them out if necessary. In some desert areas you may encounter spiders and scorpions, so shake out clothing and shoes before you put them on.

TROUBLE IN BUG COUNTRY?

The real danger in hot, swampy country especially, is the insects, many of which pass on diseases and parasites. If you are in an area where it's prevalent, malaria may be your worst enemy. It is still transmitted by mosquitoes, the Anopheles variety normally encountered from late afternoon until early morning. Too, they may bite in the shade during the day. All in all, guard against bites. Camp away from swamps, preferably on high land. If you have no mosquito netting to snooze under, smear mud on your face as protection against insects while you are asleep.

Wear full clothing, especially at night, and tuck your trouser legs into the tops of your socks or boots. Include mosquito headnet and gloves if these are available. Rub an effective fly dope on your hands and on all other exposed skin. If you have antimalaria tablets in your kit, take them according to directions for as long as the supply lasts. Then even if you are bitten by infected mosquitoes, you won't get sick for a month, by which time you should be back where you can get ample medication and care.

Ticks may be numerous, particularly in grassy places, and you may get dozens of them on your body. Strip to the skin at least once a day and inspect your hide for ticks, leeches, bed bugs, and other pests. If you have a companion, examine each other. Brush ticks off your clothing. Flick them off the skin. If ticks get attached, covering them with an irritant such as a drop of iodine will sometimes make them let go. So may heating them with a stick from the fire, but don't burn your skin. Wash the bite if possible with soap and water. Be careful when removing a tick, as the heads have a tendency to stay in and start infection.

Some ticks, especially in certain areas in and around Montana, are bearers of Rocky Mountain spotted fever which may be fatal, away from

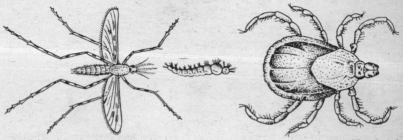

Anopheles mosquito and larva   *Hard tick*

antibiotics. Immunization with spotted fever vaccine is often recommended if you're likely to be spending much time in infected areas.

Where fleas are common, it is a good idea to keep your trousers tucked into your shoe tops or socks. Female fleas will burrow under your toenails and into your skin to lay eggs. Use a sterilized knife point to remove them, keeping the cut clean.

Mites and chiggers will burrow into the skin, often around the waist. Touch the spots with iodine, or with a drop of resin, oil, or pitch, which will kill them. Do your best to avoid scratching all bites.

If you are in an area inhabited by biting ants, never walk barefoot. Try never to camp near an ant hill or ant trail. Treat ant stings, as well as those of wasps and bees, with cold compresses or mud.

Your shoes guard against crawling mites, ticks, ants, cuts, and subsequent bacterial infections. When you are accidently dunked or forced to wade in fresh waters suspected of being infected with fluke parasites, wring out your clothes, drain and dry your shoes, and rub your body dry. Apply insect repellent over exposed areas.

SNAKEBITE

Poisonous snakes are far less abundant than most people think. There is little danger of a bite if you wear shoes, sleep off the ground, and are careful where you put your hands.

In country where there are poisonous snakes, however, it will be well to carry a small and compact snakebite remedy such as those obtainable at any drugstore. This is considered in the section on survival kits.

PLANTS POISONOUS TO TOUCH

Most of the plants that are poisonous to touch belong to either the sumac or the spurge family. The three most important poisonous plants in the United States are poison ivy, poison oak, and poison sumac. All these plants have compound leaves and small, round, white or greyish green fruits.

Poison ivy

Poison oak

Poison sumac

Poisonous plant juices are especially dangerous in the vicinity of your eyes. Danger of becoming contaminated increases with overheating and perspiring. Using the wood of any contact-poisoning plant as firewood is dangerous. The worst case of poison oak I ever incurred was a result of the inclusion of a few sticks of dead poison oak into my cooking fire.

Symptoms of plant poisoning are reddening, itching, swelling, and blistering. The best treatment after contact with these plants is an immediate and thorough wash with the strongest soap available.

WILL A WOLF GET YOU?

North American animals, except those that are so accustomed to man that they have lost most of their native timidity, are not dangerous. The polar bear is an exception. So to a lesser degree is the grizzly, which is easily provoked. A walrus can be dangerous at close quarters. Wolves are perilous only in fiction.

When in the course of ordinary events you come face to face with a large animal that, startled, shows no inclination to disappear, the best thing you can do is freeze. Then start to talk in as calm, quiet, and friendly a way as you can manage. Such a monotone has a soothing effect on any animal, large or small. Any I have so encountered in the open have, unless they fled at once, regarded me for a short time and then sifted into the shadows, usually slowly and in any event without sign of undue excitement.

If you have a rifle, you'll of course get that to your shoulder as coolly and smoothly as you can, especially if the animal is so near that any sudden motion may provoke a similar reaction. Unless absolutely necessary, it will seldom be wise to shoot under such conditions. If you must, aim an instantly anchoring shot at the brain.

If the animal shows no sign of giving ground, perhaps because it feels it is cornered or because of regard for young ones, back away as casually as you can manage, still continuing to avoid any abrupt actions and still talking quietly.

PRIMITIVE SUNBURN AID

When sunburned, besides protecting yourself from additional exposure, you can cover the affected area with ointment or with a tannin-rich substitute made by boiling the bark of a hemlock, oak, or chestnut tree. Keep the burned area covered and at rest if possible. Drink large amounts of water, partly to rid the body of wastes formerly lost through the now-blocked sweat glands.

MAKESHIFT TOOTHBRUSH

A small green twig, chewed to a pulpy consistency at one end, will serve as a toothbrush. Soap, salt, and baking soda all make good substitutes for toothpaste.

ANTIBIOTICS IN NATURE

If you ever happen to be stranded without a comprehensive first-aid kit, and if an increasingly serious infection is not responding to treatment, you may in such a grave emergency elect to eat cheese, bread, or similar rations that have become covered with green mold with the hope of introducing antibiotics into the system. In desperate circumstances, when not even this mold is at hand, it may be worthwhile as a final resort to try eating small amounts of dirt in the possibility of thus obtaining life-saving antibiotics.

MAKING YOUR OWN TORCH

An emergency torch can be fashioned in country where white birch trees are plentiful. Strip off a piece of bark about a foot wide and three feet long from one of the trees, and fold it in thirds lengthwise.

Split a three-foot pole lengthwise to within eight inches of one end. Slip the folded bark over one side of the split pole so that the split holds the bark and keeps it from unfolding. The uncut eight-inch section of pole then becomes the handle. Light the bark at the opposite end.

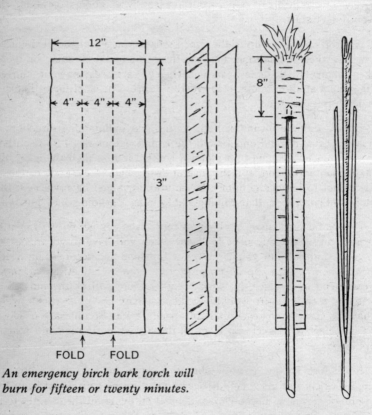

An emergency birch bark torch will burn for fifteen or twenty minutes.

For more light, turn the burning end downward so the fire will burn up on the bark. If it burns too fast, turn the flaming end upward. As the bark is consumed, pull more of it through the split in the stick handle. Such a strip will last fifteen to twenty minutes and light all the ground, trees, and bushes within about twenty feet.

Walking Out 13

Five basic requirements should be met before you try to travel out of a survival situation. If any of these can not be fulfilled in regards to your particular emergency, then camp and signal.

1. Know approximately where you are and where safety lies. If you are relatively uncertain about either your present whereabouts or about the way out, don't start.

2. Are you physically up to the trip? Perhaps you are already exhausted and in a weakened condition. Perhaps there is waist-deep snow or tough muskeg country. Be extremely cautious when you are assaying your stamina and if you are at all in doubt, stay where you are. The chief factor in exposure death is exhaustion.

3. Have a definite means of both setting and maintaining direction. If you have a compass and understand the simple essentials of its use, then you can count on keeping to a planned course. If not, then there are the stars, the sun and moon, and the several basic shadow methods of telling direction, not to forget the numerous natural signs you have learned. But if you're still hazy about determining and keeping a heading, stay put.

4. Do you have adequate clothing? Whereas you can get by with insufficient garb and especially poor footwear when you have to go no farther from your campfire than to pick up more firewood and secure food, trying to travel when you are improperly protected is an entirely different matter and could end in disaster. In warm weather there will be the masses of insects that a smudge fire would have kept at bay. Even wet socks, when you have no spares, may eventually incapacitate you. So unless your clothing is sufficient to protect you from all the hardships of the trail, remain by your bivouac.

5. Food, fuel, shelter, and the ability to signal for help at a moment's notice, as when a search plane is heard, must all be considered from the viewpoint of traveling. If you cannot depend on living off the country to at least a strength-maintaining degree, you'll do better to fit your activities more closely to your caloric intake by staying put.

Fuel may be no problem, but if you have to cross barren country, particularly in winter, then your life may depend on your carrying sufficient fire-making materials. Unless you can readily make yourself some of the bivouacs considered in this book, you'd better settle for one where you are.

And unless you know you can signal instantly from the trail as with fire or flashes, you'll do better to sit tight.

Certainly, you'll want to make up your mind in a hurry, while you're still as able as you may ever be, unless you either have this volume with you or have learned enough about the wild foods herein to keep up your strength. But if the journey is apt to be too rough a go, then you'll do much better to camp and signal.

MAKING A PACKSACK

It'll all depend, of course, on your circumstances. If you've just strayed while hunting, fishing, or hiking, you'll already have with you as much of an outfit as you're likely to amass. However, if you're stranded for some other reason, you may have a supply of essentials at hand. Then you'll need a pack of some kind, something that you'll likely be initially missing.

A so-called Alaskan back pack can often be made on the spot from materials at hand. The drawings show how. Try to arrange the pack so that the load will be comfortably supported the length of the back, rather than

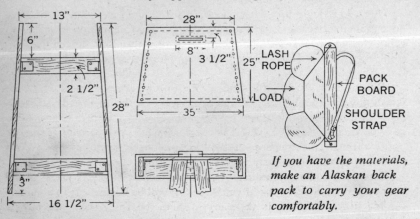

If you have the materials, make an Alaskan back pack to carry your gear comfortably.

hanging away from it, and with the center of gravity over the hips. You won't want it to be so low, of course, that it will bang your kidney region at every step.

It's even possible, if you're carrying a really heavy load, to add a tumpline across your forehead to take some of the strain off your shoulders. But try not to load on more than twenty-five to thirty-five pounds at most.

Sleeping bag and rations could make up the heavy part of the load. Ideally, you should also have as many of the following items as possible: compass, filled match case, the little four-ounce first aid kit described elsewhere, a rugged knife, watch, signal mirror, wire for snares, fishline and

266

hooks, extra socks, sun glasses, maps or at least a notebook and pencil for keeping track of your whereabouts and leaving notes, shelter fabric, binoculars if you have any, and rifle and cartridges.

MAKE YOUR OWN MAP

It's a good idea to keep a sketch map of your journey showing landmarks, distances covered, and direction. No matter where you may be, this will help to keep you on a direct course, show your progress, and enable you to get back to the starting point if necessary. And once you return to civilization, you'll know enough about keeping track of yourself that you'll never get lost in the woods again.

TRAVEL HINTS

Save your strength and minimize the possibilities of accidents by always choosing the easiest and safest way even though it may sometimes be the longest. Don't spend a morning clambering through a fallen-down burn when you can walk around it in an hour.

Don't go straight up a steep slope. Instead, climb at a slant as animals do, zigzagging back and forth to save energy. Try to maintain your height, going around the edges of gullies and canyons rather than descending and climbing up again. Don't tackle a muskeg, morass, or wet mud flat if you can proceed around it.

Take it easy. Maintain a steady, mile-eating pace which you can keep up all day if necessary. When you're traveling with others, adjust everyone's pace to that of the slowest individual. You'll go farther with a minimum of wear and tear if you occasionally rest for brief periods. Trying to bull it through at top speed, then taking prolonged breathing spells, is a good way to stiffen up early in the journey.

Especially in the exhilaration of going down a steep slope, always control your center of gravity so that if you do fall, it will be backwards in a maneuverable sitting position. In fact, anywhere in the wilderness, particularly in the stress of trying to survive, it is always wisest to expect to fall at any time, as when the bark on a dead log slips or when there is a sudden glaze of ice, and to be ready to do this in as safe a position as possible.

Fortunately, when you realize, even subconsciously, that you can not afford to have an accident, probabilities of a minor but crippling mishap shift dramatically to the safe side. For what may be only a self-punishing, responsibility-relieving, or attention-securing mishap where help is at hand can swiftly become fatal when you're on your own. The only reasonable rule in the farther places anywhere is not to take unnecessary chances, weighing always the possible loss against the potential gain and going about your affairs with as wide a safety margin as practical.

A good traveling formula that I still find myself repeating whenever I have a lot of ground to cover is: Never step on anything you can step over, and never step over anything you can step around.

MAINTAINING A STRAIGHT LINE

A good way to follow a straight course is to choose two easily visible points, such as trees or rocks, which are exactly on the line you wish to follow and as far apart as feasible. Then hike, keeping the two points in line. Before coming to the first point, select a third point in the same line ahead and continue the method.

Check your back course occasionally. Doing this will not only assure that you are traveling in a straight line, but it will also give you a back view of landscape features which will help you to recognize them if you have to backtrack.

When resting, face the direction in which you are traveling, or make a pointer of stones, twigs, or scratches on the ground.

TRAVEL ON THE DESERT

If you decide that your best chance lies in getting out of the desert on your own, travel only at night and in the coolness of early morning. Stay in the shade and rest during the hot hours. Carry all the water you can, even though this may mean leaving something else behind.

Unless you are heading for hills in the hope of discovering water, direct yourself toward a coast, a known route of travel, a definite water source, or an inhabited area. Along a coast, you can conserve perspiration by wetting your clothes in the sea.

Follow the easiest route available. This means that you should avoid loose sand and rough terrain and proceed along trails whenever possible. Among sand dunes, follow the hard valleys between the mounds or travel along the ridges.

Except in coastal areas and those regions with large rivers traversing them, avoid following streams in the hope of reaching the sea. In most deserts, valleys lead to an enclosed basin or temporary lake.

Always care for your feet. In a pinch, you can cross sand dunes barefoot in cool weather, but during the summer the sand will burn your feet.

If a sandstorm should blow up, take shelter at the earliest possible moment. Mark your direction with an arrow of stones perhaps, lie down with your back to the gale, cover your nose and mouth with a cloth, and sleep out the storm. If possible, seek shelter in the lee of a hill. Don't worry about being buried by the sand.

In fact, it's recommended that you get some protection from the sun in exposed conditions by covering your body with sand. Burrowing in the sand also reduces water loss. Some desert survivors report that the pressure of the sand affords valuable physical relief to tired muscles.

WOULD YOU RATHER RAFT?

You will save strength, time, and rations by rafting down a stream whenever possible. However, everything is relative, and raft travel is normally slow, so still don't try to hurry. Rivers are the vast highways of many great wilderness areas.

Three long logs will make, for one man, a raft that can be poled or paddled with reasonable ease. A raft for three men, on the other hand, should be about twelve feet long and six feet wide, depending of course on the size

With just a knife, hatchet, and a few sturdy logs, you can build a raft to speed your travel.

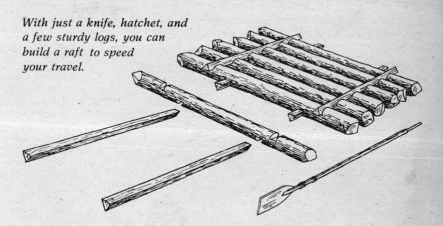

of the logs available. Ideally, the logs should be from twelve to fourteen inches in diameter and well matched in size so that the notches you make in them will be level once the crosspieces are driven into place.

A knife and hatchet will complete the job which an ax will make even easier. Build the raft on two skid logs, placed so that they slope downward to the bank. Smooth these logs so that the raft timbers will lie evenly across them.

Cut two sets of slightly offset, inverted notches one in the top and bottom of both ends of each log. Make each of these notches broader at the base than on the outer edge of the log. Use a small pole with straight edges, or a taut string, to mark the notches. A three-sided wooden crosspiece, about a foot longer than the total width of the raft, is to be driven through each of the four sets of notches.

Complete the notches on the tops of all logs. Turn the logs over and drive a three-sided crosspiece through both sets of notches on the underside of the raft. Then finish the top sets of additional notches and drive through them the two extra crosspieces.

If you have the materials, you can lash together the outjutting ends of the pair of crosspieces at each end of the raft, giving the whole contrivance added strength. When the contraption is immersed in the water the crosspieces will swell and tightly bind the raft together even without this lashing.

However, if the crosspieces are found to be fitting too loosely, wedge them with thin, boardlike pieces of wood you have split from a dry log. When the raft is in the water, these will swell, fastening the cross members tightly and staunchly.

To keep the packs, the other gear, and your feet dry, make a deck of light poles on top of the raft. Now cut yourself a sweep, or, for shallow water, a pole.

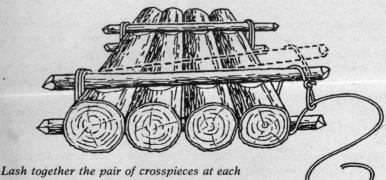

Lash together the pair of crosspieces at each end to give your raft added strength.

ICE RAFT

During subzero weather in the North, the middle parts of some rivers may be open because of the swift current. Cross such a river, if you can find no connecting ice, on an ice block raft which can be cut from the frozen shore ice, using an ax or hatchet or even sometimes a pole when there is already a crack to work on.

The size of the raft should be about two by three yards, and the ice should be at least a foot thick. A pole is used to move the ice block raft across the open part of the river.

RIVER TRAVEL

Travel strange rivers only when it is light. Take every possible precaution, keeping near enough to the shore so that you can land in a hurry if necessary. If you are on the raft alone, do not go to sleep. Be on the lookout for snags, rapids, and waterfalls.

You'll usually be able to hear rapids and waterfalls at a distance, or you may be able to see spray or mist. When the going is doubtful, hold yourself ready to go ashore and scout ahead. In any event, don't attempt to shoot rapids, and be very careful about entering sheer-walled gorges. Instead, land at a safe distance above them and reconnoiter.

Carry your gear around and either portage your raft, drift it loosely through, or build another below the bad stretch of water. In some places, of course, you may be able to save time by lining the raft through the rapids, letting it float down as slowly as possible while you walk along the bank, paying out rope. Take all vital equipment off the raft before letting it down through rapids.

AMONG THE PEAKS

Travel in mountains and other high country can be both dangerous and confusing unless you take heed of a few tricks. What looks like a single ridge from a distance may be a series of ranges and valleys.

In extremely high mountains, a snowfield or glacier that appears to be continuous and easy to travel over may cover a sheer drop of hundreds of feet.

Follow valleys or ridges in mountainous terrain. If your route leads to a hidden gorge with walls almost straight up and down, search for a bypass.

To save time and energy during mountain walking, keep the weight of your body directly over your feet by placing the soles of your shoes flat on the ground. If you take small steps and move slowly but steadily, this is not difficult.

When you ascend hard ground, lock your knees briefly at the end of each step in order to rest your leg muscles. As you zigzag up steep slopes, turn at the end of each traverse by stepping off in the new direction with your uphill foot. This will prevent crossing your feet and losing your balance.

When you descend hard ground, come straight down without traversing. Keep your back straight and your knees bent so that they take up the shock of each step. Keep your weight directly over your feet by placing the full sole on the ground at each step.

You may have to go up or down a steep slope and cliff. Before you start, do your best to pick your route carefully, making sure it has places for hand or foot holds from top to bottom. Try out every hold before you put all your weight on it, and distribute your weight.

If possible, don't climb on loose rock. Move continually, using your legs to lift your weight and your hands to keep your balance. Be sure you can go in either direction without danger at any time. In climbing down, face out from the slope as long as possible, as this is the best position from which to choose your routes and holds.

RAPPELLING

When you are traveling in mountainous country, make an effort to acquire a rope, or you may find the job of descending steep slopes difficult or even impossible. If necessary, improvise one as from parachute shroud lines. If rappelling is necessary, accomplish this as follows:

1. Loop the rope around a tree or rock, allowing the ends to hang evenly.

2. Put both ropes between your legs.

3. Wrap them around your left (right) thigh, as shown in the drawing.

4. Pass the ropes over your chest, over your left (right) shoulder, and down across the back, grasping them with your left (right) hand.

5. Take hold of the ropes in front of you with your free hand.

6. Relax your grip periodically and slowly slide down in a rhythmic manner. You must keep yourself perpendicular to the slope or cliff to keep your feet from sliding off the rock. So keep your feet spread and braced against the cliff, as shown in the picture. Slow or stop yourself by tightening your grip on the ropes and by bringing your grasping hand across your chest.

7. When you have reached the bottom, pull one strand of the doubled rope to retrieve it.

Rappelling makes the descent of steep slopes easier and safer.

A SAFER WAY OF RAPPELLING

When you have one or more companions and are looking for a safer way of descending a cliff, have one man act as belayer to give additional security to the man rappelling. Tie the rope around the waist of your companion by means of a bowline.

Get into a secure sitting position with the feet braced. The rope is passed low around the waist and is paid out as the man moves. You must remember that the man descending should have freedom of action, and you should hold him tight only when he asks for it.

WHEN THERE'S LOOSE ROCK

As you travel down a grade, be on the lookout for slopes of loose, relatively fine rock. Such slopes can aid your movement. Turn slightly sideways, keeping your body relaxed, and descend diagonally in long jumps or steps.

If the slope consists of large rocks, move slowly and carefully to prevent a boulder from rolling under your weight. Always step squarely on the top of a rock to prevent it from throwing you off balance.

THE BASIC KNOTS

When you have a rope, and even when you're working only with small lines and threads, there are a few basic knots that'll mark the difference between the success and failure of a venture. You may care to review the simpler of them, following the text while studying the illustrations.

SQUARE KNOT

The square knot will securely join two ends of the same size. If the ropes are of different diameters, it will slip, and the sheet bend should be knotted instead.

To tie the square knot, cross the two ends, pass the first under the second, reverse the directions of both ends, and then cross the first over the second and down through the bight thus formed.

To untie when the rope or cord is sufficiently stiff, grasp the standing parts of both sides of the knot. Move the hands together, forcing the loops apart. When the line is soft, the square knot can be loosened by pulling one end to as to turn the knot over, whereupon it will easily slip off the end you tugged.

SHEET BEND

No knot is more effective than the sheet bend for joining two ends of rope especially when they are wet, or frozen, or of different sizes of materials. It is simple to tie, never slips, doesn't take much line, and can be swiftly unknotted.

Make a bight in the larger rope. Then bring the end of the second rope up through the bight and around the standing parts. Finally, pass the end

Square knot

Clove hitch

Bowline

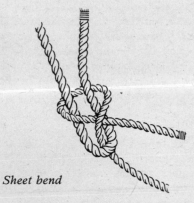

Sheet bend

Two half hitches

Timber hitch

of this second rope under itself where it comes up through the bight, in such a way that when tightened it is held against the outside of the bight.

TWO HALF HITCHES

You're always finding a use for the very simple two half hitches, an especially handy knot for tying a rope to a tree, ring, hook, or rail. The only disadvantage of this knot is its tendency to jam under heavy strain.

To make a half hitch, loop the rope around a tree at the desired height, bring the end back around the standing part, and finally down through the loop thus made. The second half hitch is made by bringing the end once more around the standing part and down through its own loop.

CLOVE HITCH

The clove hitch, which is just a pair of half hitches made in opposite directions, is useful for tying a rope so that it will remain up around a tree trunk. It will remain secure, even on a slippery pole, as the rope pulls against itself. It has the additional value of not jamming.

Loop the rope end around the tree. bring it over itself and take it around the tree once more at a slant. Slip the end under this last loop, bringing it out in a direction opposite to that of the standing part. Pressure on either end of the rope will now tighten it.

BOWLINE

The quickly tied and untied bowline provides a loop which will neither tighten or slip, nor will it jam. It's also an excellent way of tying the end of a slippery synthetic picket or mooring rope.

Make a small loop in the standing part of a rope. Bring the end up through it, leaving a working loop of the desired size. Now pass the end around the standing part of the rope and back down through the small loop.

A practical way to tie the same type of knot by feel alone, as on a pitch-black night when you want to secure a raft, is first to make a loop in the end of a rope and then to pull the standing part of the rope through it in a second loop, as illustrated.

Hold this second loop in one hand and the rope end in the other. Pass the short end into the second loop, again leaving a working loop of the desired size. Pulling the second loop back through the first, work the knot into position.

TIMBER HITCH

The timber hitch is a functional knot for hauling firewood or building logs despite the fact that it is neither a permanent knot nor one that will remain secure unless pressure is maintained on it.

To make the timber hitch, pass the end of the rope around the article to be hauled, say a log. Make a half hitch around the standing part. Then take two or more turns around the loop thus formed. Draw tight and maintain a steady pressure.

SHEEPSHANK

A sheepshank is a practical way to shorten rope that is already tied and in use. Lay three loops atop one another. Pull the nearer side of the middle loop down through the first loop, and the other side of this center loop up through the third loop. Adjust to your liking and then tighten by pulling on the standing parts.

LASHING SHEAR LEGS

When two poles are to be joined to support the ridgepole of a light bivouac, just lay them side by side on the ground. Wrap a short rope near their tops several times and then tie this off with a square knot.

Sheepshank

Shear lash

A sturdier job can be accomplished, as when more of a weight is to be supported, by first placing a wedge between the tops of the two poles to hold them a bit apart. Make a clove hitch around one pole. Take a half dozen turns around the two poles, laying these close to one another but not crossing them. Then remove the wedge and take several very tight turns around the lashings between the poles. Finish off with a clove hitch on the second pole.

HOW TO PREVENT RAVELING

Unless you take precautions, the ends of your rope will ravel. With hemp and sisal, you can just wrap the ends tightly with either medical or electrical tape. Particularly neat is dipping them into an inch of liquid glue. The ends of synthetic rope can be rapidly secured by melting them with a small flame.

Rope, too, can be spliced. One method of making such a stopper knot is begun by untwisting some six inches of the rope. Following the natural twist, turn each of the strands downward to form a loop. Then bring each adjacent strand free and up through the loop next to it. Pull the knot together evenly and tightly. To give it a finished solidity, put it on the hard ground and roll it for a minute under your shoe.

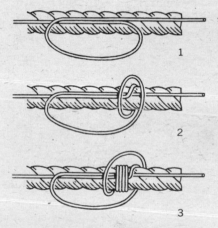

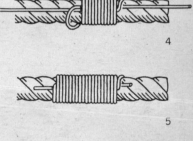

Follow these steps to prevent rope ends from raveling.

TRAVELING SNOWFIELDS AND GLACIERS

The quickest way to descend a steep snowfield is by sliding down on your feet, using a stout pole some five feet long as a brace and to dig into the snow to stop your fall if you should stumble. You can also use this pole to probe for the deadly crevasses that may extend beneath innocent-looking snow. If you must cross one of these, find the strongest part by poking with your staff, then distribute your weight by crawling.

If you are crossing a glacier, you must expect to find such cracks in the ice, usually at right angles to the direction of the flow. It is generally possible to go around them, inasmuch as they seldom extend completely across the river of ice. If snow carpets the scene, the greatest of caution must be exercised. It is a good idea when you have companions to tie yourselves together.

In any event, heavily crevassed areas should be avoided whenever possible. Unless you are already experienced in glacier travel or unless you can locate no other route, you should avoid this ice which is so dangerous for the untrained.

Travel up or across a steep slope covered with snow will be easier if you kick steps into it as you move diagonally across it. Always be on the alert for avalanches, especially during a spring thaw or after new snowfall.

If you must move where there is the peril of avalanches, stay out of the valley at the base of the incline. If you have to cross the slope, do this as high as reasonably possible. If you must climb the slope, ascend straight up.

Anyone caught in a snowslide, however, has a good chance to survive it, particularly if he can keep on top of the swirling, billowing, sweeping avalanche. One way to accomplish this is by swimming. The backstroke, especially effective if you can manage it, has saved many lives in such emergencies.

Another hazard when traveling mountainous snowfields is the cornices which will not support your weight. These often spectacular projections are formed by the snow's blowing from the windward side of a ridge. You can generally spot them from the leeward side. From windward, though, you may see only a gently rounded, snow-whitened ridge. The best practice is to follow ridges on the windward side well below the cornice line.

When crossing snow slopes in warm weather, it is less perilous to traverse them early in the morning when they have a hard crust. By the same criterion, in the spring especially, ford mountain streams in the early morning, thus avoiding the heaviest flow which takes place when the sun is melting the snow.

MAKING YOUR OWN SNOWSHOES

You'll use much less energy walking on top of the snow than struggling through it. Therefore, throughout much of the winter wilderness, you should have some sort of snowshoes even if they are but light wide evergreen boughs attached to the feet.

The oval bear-paw snowshoe will be the easiest to construct and wear and will work fine when obstructions are not too thick. When you have to go through thicker woods, a narrowed and longer web may be necessary.

For the frames, cut down substantial live saplings, let them thaw in front of your campfire if necessary, and bend them into the desired shape. Strips of rawhide will make adequate webbing. Make these heaviest beneath the foot. In hilly going, leaving on the hair and facing it outwards will help to cut down on slippage. If you have wire, string it on the frame and twist the rawhide around it.

You can also use rope in a pinch, but it has the disadvantage of stretching in cold going and shrinking in slushy travel. In the first instance, you'll likely have to stop and tighten it, whereas if you don't loosen it when it's

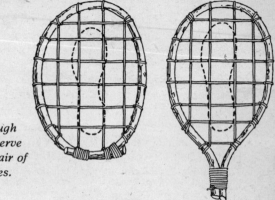

If you must walk through deep snow, you'll conserve energy by wearing a pair of simply made snowshoes.

wet, it will be apt to break the frames. Rawhide is also a nuisance when the weather warms, sagging as it does when wet. The wire nucleus will do away with this trouble.

The snowshoes should be as small and as light as you can wear and still get across the snow you have to traverse. In soft snow they'll have to be larger, with the webbing strung closer together. Naturally, you'll do the best you can, and this should be enough to get you out.

You'll want to attach the webs so that the front of the shoe will swing up and out of the way under its own weight when the foot is raised. Even with regular webs, though, some sourdoughs help themselves along in rough going by tying a rope to the end of each web and then assisting its swing with their hands.

WHAT ABOUT ARCTIC TRAVEL?

Travel in the Arctic is difficult, dangerous, and in too many instances useless. Journeys in winter or summer should ordinarily be limited to movement from an undesirable to a more advantageous place, as from an unsafe to a safe location or from a frigid valley to a less extreme position on a hillside. Energy for the most part should be expended in shelter building, in putting out highly visible signals, and in getting food.

In any event, do not travel in a blizzard or in bitterly cold wind. Make camp and conserve your strength until the gale lets up. Unless absolutely necessary, do not travel in poor visibility even when the wind is quiet.

If you must be on the move, head for a coast, a major river, or a known point of habitation. Most settlements are near the coast or close to large junctions, lake outlets, points of land, and mouths of streams. Travel downstream, and in summer use a raft if possible. In winter, the rivers generally make broad highways, but carry a long pole and beware of thin ice. Travel is sometimes easiest on the ridges, especially in summer when the low land is wet. Watch out for ice overhang.

Hindrances to summer travel are surprisingly dense vegetation, rough terrain, insects, soft ground, swamps, lakes, and unfordable large rivers. In winter, the major obstacles are soft deep snow, dangerous river ice, overflows where long stretches of fresh water from the still-flowing river are covered if at all only by a thin layer of snow or ice, severe weather, and a scarcity of food.

On all glaciers and in all snow-covered terrain in spring, travel from midnight to noon to avoid run-off streams. Surfaces are better for journeying at night, and rest periods are more comfortable during the warmer day. On valley glaciers, watch out for falling rocks early in the evening.

Cross glacier-fed streams early in the morning when the water level is scantest. When floating down a northern stream anywhere, watch out for and avoid sweepers — trees that lean out horizontally across the current and which may brush you and your outfit off the raft.

In traveling, too, remember that you will be likely to misjudge distances because of the clear polar air and the lack of familiar scale such as that furnished by trees and other landmarks. Underestimates of distances are more common than overestimates. Too, mirage is common in the Arctic.

When the sky is overcast and the ground is covered with snow, the lack of contrast makes it impossible to judge the nature of the terrain. In these conditions, men have walked over cliffs without seeing them. Do not travel in these white-out conditions, or if you must, at least keep probing ahead of you and all sides with a long, dry stick.

THE BROAD HIGHWAYS

Frozen streams and rivers are often the great highways of the North, opening country sometimes impassible during the temperate seasons. Always carry a light dry pole, long enough to bridge a gap where the ice suddenly lets go. Avoid places where such weak ice may be formed.

Stay away from rocks and partially submerged deadfall, since freezing in these areas will have been retarded by eddies. Travel on the inside of curves, inasmuch as on the outside the river current will have had an eroding effect on the underneath of the icy pavement. Travel on the bank or on the opposite side of the stream at the juncture of two streams, as the currents from both hold up, by turbulence, the formation of ice. Finally, stay on bare ice whenever possible. A deep covering of snow will insulate the water and retard freezing, perhaps leaving only a snow bridge.

IF YOU FALL THROUGH THE ICE

A lifesaving article to have where you can quickly grab it, during ice travel anywhere, is a good sheath knife. Then if you do crack through, and because of pressure holes and varying thicknesses this is possible everywhere, you can drive it into the usually solid ice nearby and with its aid roll yourself out and away.

Another way of gaining immediate traction in such an emergency is, as quick as a breath, to reach out as far as possible with your arms and to lay your wet sleeves and mitts against the remaining ice where, if temperatures are frosty enough, they will freeze nearly instantaneously.

When the weather is warmer, you may have to break away fragile ice with your hands so as to reach an expanse thick enough to support you. However, it is generally possible in the meantime to keep yourself above the surface by resting a hand or arm flatly on even thin ice. Then if there seems to be no likelier way, get as much of your shoulders as you can over the edge, bring your body as horizontal as possible with perhaps a scissoring motion with the feet, get a leg over, and roll to safety.

CANDLE ICE

Watch out in the spring for candle ice, so treacherous that you can step on an apparently solid stretch and sink through it as if it were slush. What happens is that ice up to several feet in thickness decomposes into long vertical needles, among which your pole can be driven in a single thrust.

This, then, is the way of testing ice that becomes all the more important as seasonal thawing progresses. Candle ice, which has caused the drownings of innumerable natives and sourdoughs, is best avoided completely, especially because of the difficulty in reaching safety again once you've encountered it.

A DANGEROUS COLD-WEATHER MISTAKE

A perilous error, one that has become even more widely believed than the fallacy that a frozen ear should be thawed by rubbing it with snow, is the long-held theory that you should keep on the move in extremely cold weather to avoid freezing. Particularly, you're warned, never fall asleep outdoors in subzero temperatures or you'll never awaken.

It is the opposite that is true. Why should you waste strength in, for example, walking aimlessly around a tree all night when that energy could be better conserved to keep yourself warm? Why should you risk excessive sweating that, congealing, will only make you colder and perhaps dangerously so? The best thing to do on an extremely frosty night, unless of course you can build fire and shelter, is to find as protected a spot as you can, curl up on something dry, though it may be nothing better than evergreen boughs, and go to sleep.

When you get too cold, you'll arouse, stir around just enough to get warm, and then go back to sleep if you can, or at least relax again.

This practice can be particularly vital if you are short of food, as the only way the body can of itself produce the extra warmth necessary to counterbalance the deepening cold is by burning additional calories. The supply of these internal heat units, available for this necessary compensation, will be greatly depleted if you're also burning them by hiking back and forth.

The weaker one so becomes by keeping going, the less he will be able to resist the environment. When he slumps down, spent, that is a completely different situation; there will then likely be perspiration to rob the clothing of a sizable degree of its protection. The reserve strength that would otherwise have been available for the emergency is too many times used up. From that sleep of exhaustion there is, indeed, often no awakening.

SEA ICE TRAVEL

Wind and ocean currents keep the polar ice pack in constant motion. Because of this and because you'll avoid as much rough going as possible, you'll rarely travel in a straight line.

Landmarks such as hummocks and high pressure ridges are usable only over brief distances, particularly as one or more of them may be on other floes that are shifting position. Add to this the fact that the magnetic compass is extremely unreliable so close to the magnetic pole, and the necessity for frequent directional checks on the sun and stars becomes self-evident.

The winter ice in the very high latitudes is comparatively solid. As the sun returns, however, this ice cover ebbs, and there is open water, including the famous Northwest Passage, all along the arctic coast.

Ice lies offshore along the bleak northern coast, but with strong north or west winds, floes are constantly being driven ashore. Riding one of these floes is distinctly a last-resort maneuver, especially as there is no knowing if the wind will continue until the ice grounds. These floes in the fall are less perilous, as usually they do not float too far before they freeze in once more.

The summer ice glistens with lakes and water-soaked snow. These gradually drain away, as the cover develops holes and cracks. There is virtually no dry surface anywhere. Fogs are thick, and rainy mists become frequent. All that has been said about winter journeying holds with summer travel. Survivors should quit the ice and get ashore if this is feasible. Otherwise, you should restrict your travel to a minimum, inasmuch as it will avail little and is exhausting and perilous to boot.

Cracks in stationary ice on sounds and bays do not afford any undue problems during the winter, while during the warm months they can be easily seen and must be circumnavigated by their narrow ends. Cracks in moving ice can be opened and closed with disconcerting abruptness by wind and tidal pressure, and your eyes and ears should remain continuously alert for them.

All icebergs that have become frozen in the ice are apt to attract nearby open water because of the forces of the currents on the larger mass of the berg that remains hidden. Icebergs propelled by the currents can smash through ice that is several feet thick.

Towering icebergs are always a danger in open water, too, as the mass beneath the surface is melting more rapidly than that in the air. When the berg's equilibrium changes, it topples spectacularly over. The resulting tidal waves throw the surrounding small ice cakes in every direction. For this reason, stay away from high bergs. Seek low, flat-topped icebergs for shelter and water at sea.

Even on the ice, messages should be left at every stop, setting forth especially the destination and route, as well as the date, origin, estimated length of the trip, number in party, physical condition, and any pertinent details regarding supplies.

HOW DANGEROUS ARE QUAGMIRES?

You'll sometimes come upon quagmires where mud, decomposing vegetation, and sometimes both are mixed so much with water that they won't support your weight. That's all there is to it. No suction lies within to suck you downward. Nothing operates but gravity, perhaps speeded by unwise struggling. If you attempt to withdraw one unmired foot while putting all your weight on the other, the action will force this second foot deeper.

At the worst, when you get very deep into the mire your body will likely be lighter than the semisolid it is displacing, and you'll cease sinking. You'll not become more deeply entrapped, that is, unless you writhe and twist your way downward in trying ineffectually to escape.

The thing to do is to present as much body area to the surface of the quagmire as may be necessary and to do this with the least possible delay. If when you feel the ground quiver beneath you, you run to solid ground, you'll be safe. If you cannot run, fall to your knees, for you'll usually be able to crawl out.

If you are still descending, look around speedily to see if there isn't some bush or branch you can grasp. Or you may have a pack or jacket to help support your weight. If not, flatten yourself on your stomach, with your arms and legs as far apart as feasible, and worm your way out.

You'll find quagmires in all sorts of country. Areas where water stays on the surface, and especially where water has so glittered in the immediate past, can be treacherous. You should watch out, then, for tidal flats, marshes, swamps, old game licks which tremble beneath a flooring of dried mud, and definitely for muskegs.

ABOUT QUICKSAND

Quicksand is similar to quagmire, being sand that is suspended in varying proportions of water. It may sink you considerably more rapidly, but methods of survival are alike. You do not have such a span of time, however, and unless you keep your cool you're in more potential danger.

If there is no help at hand and no support to grasp, you may succeed in throwing yourself instantly full length and either crawling or swimming to safety. You may have to duck under the surface to loosen your feet, digging them out with your hands and perhaps sacrificing your footwear. Outside of that, you'll want to avoid as far as possible all abrupt movements that will only serve to shove you deeper.

Rest, but never give up; for quagmires and quicksands often occupy a hole no bigger than a refrigerator. Another inch or two of progress may very well bring your hands either to solidness or to where you can toss over a bush a belt or a rope made of clothing.

THE BEST WAYS OF FORDING

Unless you are traveling in the desert, there is a good possibility that you will have to ford a stream or river. The water obstacle may range from a small, ankle-deep brook to a tumultuous, snow or ice-fed river. If you know how to get by such an obstacle, you can often use the roughest of waters to your advantage.

However, before you enter the water, check its temperature. If it is bitingly cold and if a shallow fording spot can not be located, it will not be advisable to cross by fording. The cold water may easily cause a severe shock which could temporarily paralyze you. In this case, try to make an improvised bridge by felling a tree across the course or build a simple raft.

Before you attempt to ford, move to high ground and examine the river for level stretches where it may break into a number of channels. Look for obstacles on the other side that might hinder your progress. Pick a spot on the opposite bank, if you can, where travel will be easier and safer. Watch out for a ledge or rocks that crosses the river, indicating the presence of rapids or other turbulence. Avoid heavy timber growths. These show where the channel is deepest.

When you select your fording site, keep the following points in mind. When possible, choose a course leading across the current at about a forty-five-degree angle downstream. Never try to ford a stream directly above or close to a deep or rapid waterfall or abrupt channel. Instead, always ford where you would be carried to a shallow bank or sandbar should you lose your footing.

Avoid rocky places, since a fall could cause serious injury at a time when you couldn't afford any such handicap. However, an occasional rock that breaks the current can be a help. Remember, except in still water the most shallow part is generally where the current is widest. Too, sheer banks are apt to continue their steepness beneath the water, while a gradual bank suggests the possibility of shoals.

A stout pole will be useful during the actual wading, both as a support against the tugging current and as an implement with which potholes can be avoided. Any pack, of course, you will want to hold loosely enough so that it can be rapidly shed if necessary.

If there is much of a flow, the most comfortable process will be to strip with the idea of holding the clothing high and thus keeping it dry. In all but the easiest going, though, you'll be wise to protect your feet by putting your boots back on. Wiped out when you're safely on the other side, they'll then be only briefly uncomfortable when put back on over dry socks.

SWIMMING OR NOT

The breast, back, and side strokes will prove less exhausting than other swimming techniques and will permit you to carry small bundles of clothing and equipment. If possible, remove clothing and gear and float it across the river. Wade out until the water is chest deep before you commence swimming. If the stream is too deep to wade, jump in feet first with your body straight, keeping your legs together and your hands at your sides. In deep, swift water, swim diagonally across the stream with the current.

If you are unable to swim, try to find a dead log or other floating aid. Test it before you set out.

If you have something like a down sleeping bag, that will be highly buoyant. Otherwise, take off your trousers in the water. Knot each leg and fasten the fly. Grasp the waistband and swing the trousers over your head, from back to front, so that the waist opening is brought down hard on the surface. Air will be trapped in each leg. Or hold the trousers in front of you and jump into the water. Either of these methods provides a serviceable pair of water wings.

Swimming in rapids or swift water is not as much of a problem as you may think. In shallow rapids, get on your back with your feet pointing downstream. Keep your body horizontal and your hands alongside your hips. Flap your hands much as a seal moves his flippers. In deep rapids, swim on your stomach and aim for shore whenever possible. Watch for converging currents whose swirls might suck you under.

In an emergency, your trousers can serve as water wings.

THE DANGERS OF SURF

You stand a better chance of surviving in surf if you know a little about it. For instance, breaking waves become higher and shorter as they move shoreward. The side facing the land curves and forms the breaker, actually moving the water toward the shore. Larger waves break farther away from shore than do the smaller ones.

In moderate surf, swim forward with the small waves and let the crests pick you up. Dive when your journey on the crest ends and just before the wave breaks.

In heavy surf, swim toward the shore while you are in a trough between the waves. As another wave froths toward you, face it, dive, and swim forward after it passes.

The backwash of incoming waves can be dangerous if the surf is heavy. If you are caught in this outbound current, don't try to swim against it. Instead, swim with it. If you are carried under, push upward from the bottom or swim to the surface and ride toward shore on the next incoming wave.

Incidentally, there is one particular precaution that you should always heed when hazarding a rocky open seacoast. This is to hold fast at the first likely place upon the nearing of a big wave. Deliberately choose a soaking instead of taking the chance of fleeing across uncertain footing and thus risking the very real danger of being hurt and even of being swept to sea and drowned.

Sitting It Out And Signalling 14

There are innumerable occasions when sitting out an emergency, as among three widely spaced signal fires on a subzero day, is preferable to trying to make it out on your own. But your chances of getting help will be markedly decreased, sometimes nearly to the point of non-existence, if you don't make adequate signals.

If people know you're lost and generally where you are, a major trouble with trying to walk out — unless you're absolutely sure of both your direction and your capabilities — is that you may hike completely out of the search area.

If food or especially water is in short quantity, to boot, you'll do well to conserve your energy by moving about as little as possible. And if the weather is excessively hot or cold, you'll be best advised to stick to an improvised shelter unless adequately clothed for the situation, and to set up signals. Exhaustion, incidentally, kills even more quickly than cold in the exposure deaths often met under survival duress.

If you're with a stranded automobile or downed plane, unless you're sure it is only a short distance to a frequented route or populated area, you should always stay with the vehicle. It's much easier to locate an airplane or automobile than an individual on foot.

Even then you'll need to signal, as is borne out by the frequency with which private planes in the United States and Canada, downed in winter usually in the mountains, are often not located until spring. An aircraft that has crashed or been forced to land will be easier to spot if highly reflecting or brightly colored objects are placed about it. Remember that any unusual sign or color contrast is visible from the air, even the tracks of one man in the snow.

SIGNALLING WITH FIRE

Three fires, or groups of three signals such as those possible with smoke, are international distress calls. As a matter of fact, if you are in one of the many forested areas where regular watches are maintained from towers and observation aircraft through most of the year, just a large fire, smoky in daylight, will bring aid in an emergency.

Otherwise, make your three signal fires at least one hundred feet apart if possible, either in a straight line or, for easier maintenance, in a rough triangle. If you are in trouble beside a pond or lake, though, it may be eminently successful to build a raft and to have a fire ready to light on it whenever the sounds of aircraft manifest themselves.

The smoke from a signal fire can be invaluable for showing wind direction to the pilot of a rescue craft.

If there is any scarcity of fuel, or if because of a dwindling food supply you are husbanding your strength, it may be preferable to keep only your

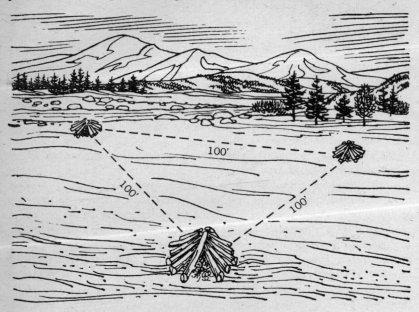

A group of three fires is an internationally recognized distress signal.

own small campfire going for warmth and companionship and to have three signal pyres, protected if necessary by bark from any rain or snow, ready for the torch.

If there is a thin cloud area, night fires will be diffused and not so readily visible from the air. But it will still be advisable to keep fires, as large as practical, burning.

SMOKE

Fire-making and the maintenance of fires have been considered at length in the section on that subject, but there is still the matter of smoke, so conspicuous during daylight hours if the weather is at all clear. If a low inversion above keeps the smoke in layers close to the ground, it is frequently possible when fuel is plentiful to get the smoke above it by kindling a larger fire than usual before adding the smoke-producing material.

Cut plenty of green boughs if they're available; when burning, they make a lot of smoke and a good signal. Evergreens are particularly efficacious in this respect, crackling readily and rapidly into black-smoking flame. A longer lasting smudge, effective against any biting insects as well, can be made by covering hot coals with wet dead leaves, damp green foliage, moist decayed wood, damp plane matting, slowly burning green wood, damp animal dung, and like materials.

Voluminous black smoke can be produced in a hurry with the oil from a disabled plane, cruiser, or even a small motorboat. This is one of the important reasons for a plane's oil to be drained in a cold environment before it congeals. It will then burn even when frozen.

Although with care oil can be thrown on a burning fire, this is not possible with gasoline, which ignites with such explosive fury that extreme caution must be exercised with it at all times. Even when it drenches an unlighted signal pyre with no live coals glowing nearby, at the moment of your tossing in a burning stick from even what seems to be a safe distance you should stand upwind and turn your face away. Gasoline will burst violently into a sheet of flame, emitting intense black smoke. Burning rubber, too, either from tires or electrical insulation, gives off heavy black smoke. When water is used with discretion it will give you a white smoke.

With an ordinary single conflagration, not one powered with gasoline, you can still send up three puffs of smoke by momentarily cutting off the column, Indian fashion, by briefly holding a wet blanket over it.

You'll always make sure, of course, that you don't unintentionally start a forest fire; or on the plains, a grass fire.

TORCH TREES

Isolated small dead trees, especially evergreens, that will make excellent signal towers are to be found in some country. Then the best idea will be to prepare to ignite them when they'll be most valuably conspicuous.

Perhaps a towering heap of inflammable materials can be laid at the base, ready for the match. Or a bird's nest of birch bark and resinous twigs can be clustered in the lower branches of such a dead, bushy landmark. If the weather is cold, make certain that the tree is shaken or hammered free of accumulated snow and frost. Then it will be ready to become a crackling torch, visible for miles around under favorable conditions.

LUMINOUS CONE

An important advantage to using a parachute-fashioned teepee for shelter when seeking help is that, with a fire inside, one stands out like a luminous cone at night. Other shelters are not so conspicuous, so you'll want to do everything you can to make searchers aware of your presence. A hearty night fire is excellent in this respect. All in all, do everything you can to disturb the natural look of the surroundings.

RESOURCEFULNESS

In some regions, as in the desert and on the polar ice, no natural fuel may seem to be available beyond what you desperately need to keep alive. But the man ingenious enough to survive in any event will usually find a way. One solution would be scratching an SOS in the sand or ice, filling this with gasoline, or gasoline and oil, and igniting it when a plane is near. Or you might get much the same flash signal by setting fire to strips of fabric soaked in gasoline, oil, or such.

A good torch can be improvised from a tin can filled with sand or ashes soaked in gasoline.

DISTRESS SIGNALS

When you are signalling for help, no matter what your predicament, the most universally recognized distress signals are based on the number three; three fires, three smokes, three flashes; even to the three dots, three dashes, and three dots of the familiar SOS.

The international Morse code, most widely used throughout the world, follows. A knowledge of it, or just the plain following of this chart, will make possible the sending and receiving of messages by mirror, flashlight, whistle, smoke, flag, radio, and innumerable other contrivances including the primitive thumping of a hollow tree.

If you undertake to learn this code, and there are less productive ways of putting in time while husbanding your strength beside a campfire and waiting for help, you'll save time by thinking directly in terms of dahs and dits; that is, longs and shorts. The other way you'll hear two dahs, for example, and have to visualize two dashes before you identify it as the letter M. You'll save this intermediate step by learning directly the sounds of the various symbols.

The familiar SOS can be scratched in ice, filled with gasoline, and ig-nited.

INTERNATIONAL MORSE CODE

Intervals	Letters	Flag
short-long	A	right-left
long-short-short-short	B	left-right-right-right
long-short-long-short	C	left-right-left-right
long-short-short	D	left-right-right
short	E	right
short-short-long-short	F	right-right-left-right
long-long-short	G	left-left-right
short-short-short-short	H	right-right-right-right
short-short	I	right-right
short-long-long-long	J	right-left-left-left
long-short-long	K	left-right-left
short-long-short-short	L	right-left-right-right
long-long	M	left-left
long-short	N	left-right
long-long-long	O	left-left-left
short-long-long-short	P	right-left-left-right
long-long-short-long	Q	left-left-right-left
short-long-short	R	right-left-right
short-short-short	S	right-right-right
long	T	left
short-short-long	U	right-right-left
short-short-short-long	V	right-right-right-left
short-long-long	W	right-left-left
long-short-short-long	X	left-right-right-left
long-short-long-short	Y	left-right-left-right
long-long-short-short	Z	left-left-right-right

WIGWAG

Such signals can be identified for miles under good conditions, especially if the sender spots himself in a clear location, preferably against a contrasting background.

Your flag may be a white or brightly colored shirt, for instance, tied to the end of a light pole about six feet long. This can be most easily maneuvered if you'll hold the heavier end of the stick in a palm at waist level, then grip it some twelve to fourteen inches higher with your master hand.

All letters begin with the flag held straight upward. The dot is made by swinging the flag down to the right, then back up again. One way to remember this is that "right" has a dot over its *i*.

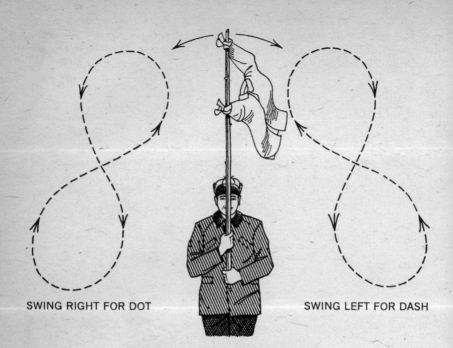

SWING RIGHT FOR DOT   SWING LEFT FOR DASH

Transmit Morse code signals with a makeshift flag.

The dash is accomplished by swinging the flag in a similar arc to the left. You'll always want to keep the flag as flat as possible for better visibility, and the simplest way of doing this is to move it in tight loops. To send the letter *A*, for example, swing right and back to upright, then left and back to upright, in what is a narrow figure 8.

Always hold the flag upright for a moment to end any letter. Lower, then raise it, in front of you to end a word. Swinging left-right, left-right several times shows that the message is concluded. Common sense, not correctness of form, is the important factor in emergency signalling, of course. Just space your letters reasonably, and the receiver will make out enough of your message at least to understand it.

MIRROR

By using contrasting long and short flashes, the international Morse code can be sent by mirror. This, however, is not the mirror's most important function in an emergency. Limited only by the curvature of the earth, its flash is visible for miles.

A substantial mirror is a valuable asset to keep on your person whenever you're in the farther places. An armed forces emergency signalling
mirror, still occasionally to be found for a few cents at surplus stores and
obtainable around air bases, is rugged enough to be especially useful to keep

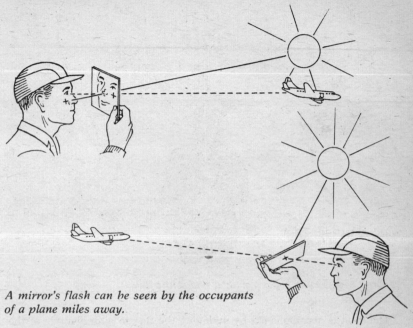

*A mirror's flash can be seen by the occupants
of a plane miles away.*

in a pocket. Instructions for its use, if you forget them, are printed on the
back. A small open cross or aperture in a screened target area facilitates
aiming.

When you're trying to get the attention of the occupants of a plane that
is no more than a right angle away from the sun, for example, hold a double-
surfaced mirror three to six inches from your face and sight at the aircraft
through the hole in the center of the mirror. Continuing to look at the plane
through the center aperture, adjust the mirror until the spot of sunlight
reflected from your face in the back mirror coincides with the mirror hole
and disappears. The reflected light will now be accurately aimed at the
plane. When the angle between aircraft and sun is more than ninety degrees,
adjust the angle of the mirror until the reflection of the light spot on your
hand behind the mirror coincides with the hole and disappears.

Stop flashing once an aircraft has definitely acknowledged your presence, except for an occasional flash if this seems necessary as a guide.
From that point on, continued flashing may blind the pilot.

On hazy days a flier and his observer can often see the flash of a mirror before the survivors can spot the plane. So signal this way in the direction of any plane you can hear even when you can not see it.

By reflecting a flashlight, such a signal can even be sent at night.

SUBSTITUTE MIRRORS

A reflecting surface of any sort whatsoever, even if it's only a peeled slab that is bright with moisture, can be used instead of a mirror. This is important, for such heliograph signals have probably effected more rescues than any other method. Some raft paddles and oars are coated with material that will reflect such a light in the darkness.

A flattened tin can, or even the shiny end of one, will provide an excellent substitute for a mirror. So will a sheet of foil. Just punch a small aiming hole in the center of either, while it's lying on a flat surface, use as instructed for a regular mirror, and you'll be well away.

THREE SHOTS

Again, the most important element is common sense. Unfortunately there is no universal agreement as to how the three signal shots should be spaced. A logical practice is to wait about five seconds between each evenly spaced shot, as this gives the listener ample opportunity to orient the signals.

The usual answer is to reply with one shot, which the man who is lost or otherwise in distress acknowledges with another single shot. Thereafter, such single shots coming from the same general direction but nearer may be regarded as questions.

The answer as to exactly where the survivor is located remains one shot unless, for example, the latter has plenty of ammunition, in which case he may wish to bring others into the act with another distress series of three shots. After calling for help and receiving a reply, do not leave your position.

In any event, a definite understanding of these points should be reached well in advance by a party operating in the bush; and, in the case of greenhorns, preferably jotted down on paper.

WHISTLE

A metal or plastic whistle, the louder the better, is especially handy for signalling in far country. Mothers can do worse than hang police whistles around the necks of the younger members of the family. Even the venerable Hudson's Bay Company includes two such whistles in their survival kits.

SOUND IN THE SNOW

Remember that sound does not carry well through snow. If your entire party is within a snow cave or igloo, you may not hear a rescue aircraft.

Keep someone on guard as spotter. Build this spotter a windbreak, but do not roof it. Especially if you are alone, always leave a conspicuous signal before going into any kind of a shelter!

RADIO

If you have battery-operated radio equipment, make every effort to keep the batteries from freezing. As you know, even an unguarded flashlight will dim and go out in subzero weather.

The international silent periods, from fifteen to eighteen minutes and from forty-five to forty-eight minutes after each hour, are the most likely times to send distress signals.

SHADOWS

Shadow signals can be extremely effective when constructed in clearings and made with sufficient contrast and size. In Canada and Alaska, for example, a cross whose arms extend northwest and southeast, and northeast and southwest, will throw the maximum sun shadow. If, instead, you were digging a single trench nearer the equator, you'd have it run east and west to throw the most shadow throughout the day.

Possibilities, varying with the terrain, are many. During the winter even a single trail will loom up dark in the snow, while the trench made by trudging back and forth in the white stuff is far better.

Best, especially if you are in Arctic regions where blocks of snow can be successfully cut, is to slice out a long trench. You could get a double shadow by piling snow on the north side of this trench.

Further south you might make signals of evergreen boughs in the snow. For major contrast, stick these up and heap a wall of brush and boughs

In a large clearing a shadow cross is an effective signal.

about them. In fact, one more way to capitalize on contrasting darkness in snow country is to floor the especially made trenches with evergreen boughs.

Stones, sand, sod, and driftwood walls will all cast their telltale shadows. Or you can dig or scratch long lines. Lengths of various material, preferably of contrasting color, will also do everywhere.

In summer in the timber make your signals of rock piles, heaps of dead wood, blocks, bark, and freshly peeled logs.

SYMBOLS

You can send actual signals by the above methods, in which case all figures should be at least forty feet long and preferably ten feet thick. Make them even larger, of course, if both terrain and time are favorable. Color contrast, again, can be vital. The code follows:

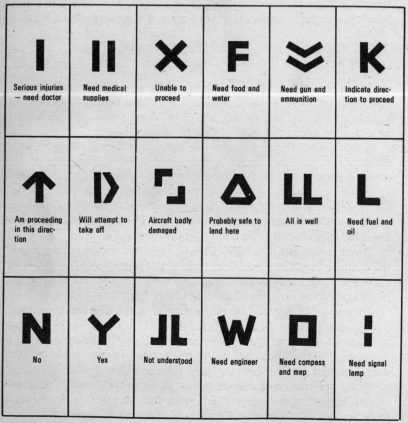

I	**II**	**X**	**F**	**≫**	**K**
Serious injuries — need doctor	Need medical supplies	Unable to proceed	Need food and water	Need gun and ammunition	Indicate direction to proceed
↑	**▷**		**△**	**LL**	**L**
Am proceeding in this direction	Will attempt to take off	Aircraft badly damaged	Probably safe to land here	All is well	Need fuel and oil
N	**Y**	**JL**	**W**	**□**	**!**
No	Yes	Not understood	Need engineer	Need compass and map	Need signal lamp

COLOR

Some survival kits have red or, better, orange strips eight inches wide by ten feet long. Such pieces can be pinned or weighed down on the open ground in an attention-getting X or in one of the symbols just considered.

Too, these fabric strips can be waved overhead from some high, preferably clear vantage point when an aircraft motor is heard. In fact, if you are able to climb a tall and isolated tree, hoist one of these strips or, better, a large flag on a pole lashed to the top.

Many survival kits also contain dye, often fluorescent, for signalling on water or snow. This should be used conservatively, particularly as a little goes a long way. Rewrap it after each use.

Use the dye only downwind, for it will quickly penetrate clothing, food, and drinking water. On a river, toss it into the current to make a quickly spreading patch. Naturally, such dye is only effective during the daylight hours, but except in a very rough sea a large spot will remain for some three hours.

COAST GUARD

If you have been drifting in continental waters, the U.S. Coast Guard may save you, as it has thousands during its long history. Certain distress signals are used by this service; and if you have a boat, it may be well to keep them in mind or at least in a handy place.

A signal consisting of a square flag having a ball or anything resembling a ball above or below, flames on the vessel as from a burning oil barrel, a rocket parachute flare or a hand flare showing a red light, a continuous sounding with any fog-signalling apparatus, rockets or shells throwing red stars fired one at a time at short intervals, a smoke signal giving off a volume of orange-colored smoke, or the slowly and repeatedly raising and lowering the arms outstretched to each side, are distress signals.

A red rocket, red light, or a flare at night, an orange smoke signal, or the combined light and sound of three single signals fired at intervals of about one minute indicates that you have been seen and that assistance will be coming at the earliest possible moment.

Haul away is signified by the waving of a red flag ashore during the daylight or by displaying at night a red light, red rocket, or red roman candle.

Slack away is indicated by the waving of a white flag ashore by day. Swinging a white light slowly to and fro, igniting a white rocket, or lighting a white roman candle means the same thing at night.

Horizontal motion of a white flag or of the arms extended horizontally by day, horizontal movement of a light or flare at night, or the firing of a red star signal any time means landing here is highly dangerous.

Waving a red and a white flag at the same time from the shore during daylight signals that it is impossible to land in your own boat. Slowly waving a red and a white light together at night means the same thing. So does a blue light at night.

The beckoning during daylight of an individual on shore, or the burning of two torches close together at night, as well as the firing of a green star signal, vertical motion of a white flag or light, and vertical motions of the arms indicate that particular place is the best spot to land.

Any of these signals can be acknowledged by the waving of a hand, shirt, flag, vertical motion of a white flag, or of the arms or a white light, or anything else that is easily visible. Response at night may be by gun, white light or flare, rocket, or by briefly showing a light over the ship's gunwale.

Negation is expressed by the horizontal motion of a white flag or white light or by the arms being extended horizontally.

BODY SIGNALS

You can also signal with your body alone. The positions understood by most airmen follow:

When you need urgent medical assistance, lie on your back with your arms stretched straight behind you. Another widely used signal signifying severe injury is indicated by lying on your back with your arms crossed over your chest.

When you stand erect with your right arm upraised and your left hand hanging at your side, you're saying, "Everything is all right. Don't wait."

Horizontal motion of a white flag followed by the carrying of another white flag in the direction indicated, or the same procedure at night with a white light or flare means, "Landing here highly dangerous. A more favorable location for landing is in the direction indicated."

If leaving your left hand at your side you extend the right arm horizontally, you're indicating you'll be able to proceed in a short time and that the plane should wait if it can.

When you continue to stand erect but lift both arms horizontally, you're signalling that you need either mechanical help or parts and that there will be a long delay on your part.

Standing and holding both arms straight above your head shows that you want to be picked up.

Standing in the same position but swinging your hands sidewise back and forth above your head means, "Don't attempt to land here."

If you wish to signal the airman where to come down, squat on your heels and point toward the recommended landing place.

If you have a radio and the receiver is working, signify this by cupping your hands conspicuously over your ears.

Pick us up

Don't attempt to land here

All is well, don't wait

Yes

No

Need mechanical help or parts — long delay

Have working radio receiver

Use drop message

Need medical assistance urgently

Can proceed shortly, wait if possible

Land here (point in direction of landing)

Body signals are understood by many airmen.

If instead you want someone in the plane to drop a message, stand erect with both hands above your head and swing the right hand down in front of you to shoulder height several times.

Waving a shirt or large handkerchief up and down in front of you means, "Yes." Waving such an article back and forth in front of you means. "No,"

Although signs vary, a plane can signify an affirmative by dipping up and down the way the head is nodded. It can show negative by a zigzag motion, comparable to shaking the head. The airplane's rocking from side to side, or green flashes at night, is an acknowledgement. A complete right hand circuit, or red flashes at night, means that the observer hasn't understood your message.

INFORMATION

Leave a written note for a search party if you leave the camp site and are on the move. Write pertinent facts: date, direction travelling, and number and condition of your party. Leave the message in a bottle or can, if possible, and suspended from a tree or tripod or under a rock cairn.

Leave a message for your search party.

A sign visible from the air should be laid out to give direction of your travel. Then blaze a trail for yourself and for those searching for you on foot.

This applies to anyone lost, strayed, stranded, or otherwise in trouble anywhere. Its importance can not be overemphasized.

It's always important in the wilderness to indicate your direction of travel.

Your Four-Ounce First Aid Kit 15

"Because I am a doctor, I am interested in having a personal first aid kit that I know to be adequate for any problem I am likely to encounter on my outings," says E. Russel Kodet, M.D. "Because I also like to backpack, I am interested in reducing weight to an absolute minimum. With these two interests in mind, I have assembled a first aid kit that can be used to treat everything from a case of dysentary to a laceration, and it weighs less than four ounces. It could save your life under survival conditions."

The story of this remarkable kit originally appeared in *Outdoor Life* from which it is used with permission. It has been minutely brought up to date for this book. The following words are Dr. Kodet's:

The items in my kit are not what the average fellow would carry. This is an important point. The average person carries a lot of worthless bulk, and nine times out of ten does the wrong thing with what he does have. I see daily evidences of this in my practice. If a fellow is going to the trouble of carrying a kit, then he should have an effective one. While the contents of the one I suggest are not so readily procurable as those of the conventional type, they are well worth the effort of getting them. You'll need some prescriptions from your doctor, and you can get the supplies from your druggist or a surgical supply house. None of them is hard to obtain.

You will note that the kit contains no liquids because of their tendency to be heavy and to spill.

TREATMENT FOR LACERATIONS AND SCRATCHES

Lacerations and scratches are probably the most common results of outdoor accidents. There is no place for the use of alcohol, Merthiolate, or similar antiseptics in these injuries, though year after year first aid books tell you to douse wounds liberally with them.

It is true that these substances kill germs, but they also kill tissue, and using them in open wounds will devitalize (kill) tissue. Because germs grow best in devitalized tissue, and some germs are always present, you can see that these preparations set the stage for a future wound infection. At the very least, they delay rather than hasten healing.

The best way to handle a cut or scrape is to wash it thoroughly with plenty of soap and water, dry it well, and apply a dressing. Since I have soap elsewhere, I do not carry it in the kit. If the wound is oozy and you feel the dressing might stick to it, a plastic-like absorbent tissue should be put over the wound first and then covered with a gauze flat. This tissue can be bought in different sizes in sterile packages in any drugstore. No dressing will ever stick when it is used. *Never use an ointment on a wound unless it is already infected.*

If the wound is gaping, it will have to be brought together. This is done most easily with a butterfly. A butterfly is a plastic tape which is applied across the laceration to pull and hold the edges together. This will suffice in most cases. For deep cuts in fingers and other places subject to much movement, a stitch may be better.

Everyone should be immunized against tetanus (lockjaw) *before* suffering an injury. Tetanus is a dreadful disease and, although it is not common, can occur from even a trivial injury.

A STITCH IN TIME

If a person is far from a doctor, it behooves him to know the rudiments for taking a stitch, or suture. This is done without Novocain. Nerves are often cut along with the skin, and the pain of the sewing needle is not so bad as one would think. I have sewed lacerations on myself and my children in this manner.

The fuss and special techniques required to handle syringes, needles, and Novocain do not justify their use in a first aid kit of this type. Sure, it hurts for just a second when a stitch is taken, but it is easier to bear this than to seek out a doctor's office when you are in a remote place.

A sterile suture package can be bought with nylon thread joined to the end of a cutting needle. I use size 3-0 for everywhere except the face. Though 5-0 is finer and has less tendency to leave a scar, either size will do.

The cut is first washed with soap and water, dried, and then sutured. The needle is held with a small mosquito clamp, also called a hemostat. This clamp is a miniature, self-locking, needle-nosed plier. It is also useful in extracting slivers, especially from under a fingernail, fishhooks, or thorns.

Once the stitch is taken, the suture is tied and cut with the scalpel blade. The ends are left a quarter-inch long to facilitate removal in seven days. The clamp can substitute as a pair of tweezers to pull out the severed stitch. Any bleeding that occurs from the wound usually stops when the stitch is taken, or with direct, steady pressure over the wound for five to ten minutes.

The suture is taken only through the skin, never deeper into the underlying fat or muscle. Anyone who has ever skinned an animal will readily visualize the thickness of skin, which is never more than a quarter inch. When one does not go any deeper, no vital structure will ever be encountered.

The only possible source of difficulty might be in hitting a blood vessel. If this happens, simply pull the suture through and out of the skin and take it in another spot a little above or below the one that caused the trouble. The bleeding will always stop with pressure for a minute or so. One word of caution: never suture close to an eyelid. The healing may pull the skin into a distorted position and cause later difficulties. I can appreciate that the taking of a stitch sounds formidable, but it is really quite simple.

In snake country I carry a set of suction cups. The scalpel blades serve as the lancets.

EYE INJURIES

The other items in my recommended kit are included because of past experiences or possible future emergencies. Don't let their jaw-breaking names discourage you. Copy them down, or perhaps take this book with you when you ask your doctor for the needed prescriptions or drugs.

I carry a tube of Butyn Opthaline Ointment, a local anesthetic for the eye. It is the thing to use if the eye is hit by a flying wood chip or anything similar. It will also give immediate relief in snow blindness. A small application to the eye each three hours suffices.

Because the Butyn anesthetizes it, the eye has lost its protective sensitivity and wink reflexes. So stay out of windy places after using it, and do not touch the eye. Better yet, wear a patch over the eye for two hours after putting in the drops; their effect is about gone by then.

I also carry a tube of Neosporin Opthaline ointment to apply two to four times daily to prevent infection after an injury to the surface of the eye.

ASPIRIN OR WHAT?

Empirin Compound is a must; it is more effective than aspirin. Many people get high-altitude headaches at elevations over six to seven thousand feet, and the caffeine in Empirin helps overcome the drowsiness that often occurs at these heights. No caffeine is present in aspirin.

Empirin is also useful in any condition involving the skin, muscles, bones, and joints. It also relieves the discomfort of sunburn, skin itching, and sprains. It has no effect on pain arising from the inner organs of the abdomen or chest.

In addition, carry six half-grain aspirin or codeine tablets for severe pain from more serious injuries.

COMBATTING MAJOR INFECTIONS

Nausea, vomiting, or intestinal cramps respond nicely to a five milligram Compazine tablet every three to four hours. If vomiting continues, however, seek help as soon as possible.

Generally sickness is a rarity on wilderness trips. But the kit contains a three-day supply of both penicillin and Ilosone for use in major infections. Because these drugs are expensive, one is usually enough. This is sufficient to handle a case of blood poisoning, pneumonia, or any other severe infection. Have your doctor prescribe them for you and tell you how to use them.

TAINTED FOOD OR WATER

There is always the possibility of consuming tainted food or water. I used to carry paregoric. It worked well, but it is a liquid and subject to spillage. A newer drug called Lomotil avoids this problem. It is supplied in two and one-half milligram tablets, and the dose is one every two to four hours for diarrhea. A dozen tablets should be enough to take along.

I also carry Sulfasuxidine in the same bottle. These sterilize the intestine of bacteria and are used in doses of two or three every four to six hours. It takes several days for them to do their job.

My kit also contains a small packet of Pyridium. Some people, women especially, are subject to bladder infections and can be miserable with them. In our family it is the basset hound that always seems to get one of these attacks far from anywhere. When he is miserable, he sees to it that we are kept miserable, too. The Pyridium tablets provide complete urinary anesthesia if one is taken every four to six hours.

HOW TO GET YOUR SUPPLY OF MEDICINES

All the drugs except the Empirin require a doctor's prescription. There are very few effective drugs available without a prescription any more because of the federal laws governing the sale of drugs over the counter.

Getting a prescription or having one called into the drugstore should present no problems if you call your doctor and explain what you want and how you want to use it. Most doctors would be happy to oblige if they knew the drugs would not be used indiscriminately.

TOTAL EXPENSE

The total cost of the kit would vary between $10.00 and $20.00, depending on whether one uses the special clamp and the Lomotil. This may seem expensive, but when you consider that a simple hunt or trip costs over several hundred dollars for travel and much more for equipment, then in its true perspective this kit is not out of line. Nothing comes cheap, least of all good equipment. Injuries and sickness are never bargained for, and one can always find better things to do with the money for drugs until they are really needed. Then they are worth much more.

All the drugs are stable and will last indefinitely, except the antibiotics. These should be replaced every two or three years. Ask your druggist when the penicillin or Ilosone should be renewed.

There you have it. Like any fisherman's tackle box, it will gradually be changed over the years or to suit certain circumstances. I have been using this kit for several years now and am well satisfied with it. When I am not traveling in remote areas from my home, I keep it in my car so it is always handy.

Your Survival Kit 16

Many find it only reasonable to carry some sort of survival kit whenever traveling in the wilderness, for men still get lost or stranded, planes continue to be forced down in uninhabited areas, watercraft both individual and imposing are still wrecked, while automobiles and even trains are stalled with alarming persistence. Today, too, there are the snowmobiles, trail bikes, and other special land vehicles by which you can travel farther in a few minutes than it would take a day to retrace by foot.

The contents of such a survival kit, added to whatever you'll likely already be carrying on your person, will be pretty much an individual matter, but let's consider some of the possibilities.

MATCHES

It will be far easier to light your campfires with matches than with any of the several primitive methods detailed earlier in this book. Therefore, a reasonable supply should be carried whenever you may need them. The long, wooden, strike-anywhere, kitchen variety is both handiest and most durable. The best way to carry an emergency supply of these is in an unbreakable waterproof container that can be fastened to the clothing as with a safety pin.

I carry two of these whenever in primitive wilderness. It's sound procedure to keep elsewhere, perhaps most safely one to a pocket, the matches you'll ordinarily be using during the day.

There are a number of plastic match cases on the market, but these should be avoided unless they are definitely unbreakable. It's too easy to take a fall in a rocky brook, as I've done, and break the ordinary plastic case, wetting the contents.

For extended trips, it's good idea to waterproof a large sealed container of matches with paraffin, thus assuring a reserve supply in case the regular box becomes wet.

METAL MATCH

One of the most important innovations of recent years for outdoorsmen everywhere is the metal match. It is a waterproof, fireproof, non-toxic, and durable stubby grey stick which will light from about one to three thousand fires, depending on its size.

It is fast and simple to use. You shave small pieces from the match with the back of your knife, a sharp rock, bit of broken glass, or any other hard sharp object. These particles are accumulated in a small area — among

305

tinder such as birch bark if you're lighting a campfire — then ignited with a spark from the match.

COMPASS

Just as there are a number of primitive but still practical ways of lighting fires, as with a bow and drill, there are numerous natural methods of telling direction, some of them more accurate than a compass.

Nevertheless, the compass can be used at any time nearly everywhere to keep you informed as to how to get back, whereas bad weather can make celestial determinations impossible for days at a stretch. Other methods — such as forest or prairie growth, wind, and the like — are only approximations at best. You should have at least one compass with you whenever in even familiar woods. In wild country I also like to carry a spare, pin-on compass attached to my clothing just in case. The philosophy of hoping for the best but always preparing for the worst is not a bad one in the woods.

Compasses are inexpensive, and they can be compact. You should have a rugged, accurate, waterproof, and durable instrument on which to depend. You may save a lot of matches some dark night if this has a luminous dial or at the very least a luminous needle.

WATCH

A substantial and reasonably accurate watch, not necessarily an expensive one by any means, comes close to being a modern-day necessity, particularly as distances in the farther places are measured less often by miles than by the time it takes to traverse them. With this watch, too, you can accurately determine direction as this book explains earlier.

GLASSES

If you need prescription lenses to get around, you'll find it only prudent to carry a spare pair in a substantial protective case. Although this book tells how to make emergency sunglasses from materials at hand, you will be wise to bring along a pair of optically correct and strongly made sunglasses if you expect to find yourself in snow, desert, or high country.

ADHESIVE BANDAGES

It's always a sound idea to have with you a few of these little gauze pads, each centered on a short strip of adhesive tape. The prompt application of one to a part of the foot that is becoming tender will often prevent perhaps otherwise crippling blisters. Too, one is frequently useful for repairs. These bandages are best carried in the sterile coverings in which they are sold.

Plain white gauze is medically superior to treated pads for general use, although you may well prefer a non-stick variety. Plastic tape will both adhere and fit better than fabric. When used on blisters, potential or actual, the dry adhesive bandage can safely be left in place until the skin toughens, as it permits healing air to reach the affected part.

MAP

Most traveled parts of North America have been mapped, which is a good thing as contour maps in particular will make journeying in remote regions far easier. These maps are, for the most part, easily and inexpensively obtained, often below actual cost and sometimes merely for the asking. A comprehensive list of sources appears elsewhere in this volume.

KNIFE

A knife comes close to being a necessity for carrying on your person or in your kit. The best one is a lastingly sharp, intrinsically rugged sheath knife that you can use for everything from butchering to building a shelter. Ideally, it has a substantial leather case with a handy carborundum sharpening stone in a separate compartment on its front.

CARBORUNDUM

If one doesn't come with your knife, you'll do well to carry a small carborundum stone, fine on one side and coarser on the other, with which to keep your edged tools sharpened. Here is a recommended method of using it:

1. Lubricate the hone with kerosene, light machine oil, or salve.

2. Place the knife diagonally on the hone.

3. Raise the side of the blade away from the surface of the hone to an angle of about twenty degrees.

4. Keeping the edge of the blade to the surface of the hone, holding both the diagonal position and the twenty-degree-angle, sweep the edge across the hone from hilt to point, always toward the edge.

5. Turn over the blade and repeat the operation.

6. Continue sharpening on alternative sides of the blade, one stroke at a time. Be sure to use even, sweeping strokes and to maintain the same angle on both sides of the blade throughout each stroke. Lessen the pressure as the edge is restored.

7. If a "wire" edge develops, hone it off by giving the blade a few light sweeps across the fine-grit hone at a high angle of about 60 degrees.

AX

Both the light belt ax and the more substantial hatchet may be useful. but for more practical survival use you may well select a good Hudson Bay ax with its cut-away butt that saves weight and its regular-sized cutting surface that will ease the job of putting up a shelter in a pinch.

Such axes are obtainable with ruggedly riveted leather sheaths. If such a covering is not included, wrap the blade safely before entrusting it to your kit.

SAW

The earliest Americans used to chip out saws of bone and stone, for Indians early learned that it's much safer and swifter to saw firewood rather than to chop it. There are a number of folding saws on the market, but those I have tested have been awkward and fragile, not suitable for the hard use you'd need to put them to when caught out in cold weather. Instead, for a long-haul kit, I'd recommend the inclusion of a lightweight saw blade of ribbonlike thin steel. It weighs little, and can be rolled into a plate-wide bundle and safely encased in canvas.

One of the two-piece, tubular-steel handles adds up to little extra weight and not a great deal of bulk. Then when everything is assembled, you'll have an efficient tool. However, you can take the blade alone, plus a couple of butterfly bolts, and bend a stout green sapling into use on the spot for your handle.

GUNS AND AMMO

A light, adequately sighted, accurate big game repeating rifle, is the most valuable survival weapon you can have with you for living off a big-game region for an indefinite period. In an area where only small game is available, the most functional caliber would be more like a .22.

PLASTIC

Two pieces of light plastic sheeting, each six feet square, can serve innumerable purposes, as mentioned throughout this book.

A sheet of plastic, eight feet long by four feet wide, is what I've carried in the North Woods for years, in a shirt pocket where it occupies no more space than a handkerchief. Although I've used it countless times, it's interesting to note that I've not yet had to replace it.

TENT OR TARP

You'd want a tent only in the most comprehensive of survival kits, perhaps an outfit carried in a private plane or boat or kept in the trunk of the car. A small, tough, flyproof, lightweight tent will be preferable to a tarp when there are insects to be excluded, when the time and energy available for erecting a shelter is limited, and where it is difficult to pitch and maintain a fabric shelter as on a mountaintop.

Otherwise, a small tarpaulin will prove more adaptable, pleasant, and efficient as at least part of a lean-to open to a companionable fire.

SLEEPING BAG

In its prime grades white goose down is the lightest and warmest insulation obtainable for the manufacture of sleeping bags. The darker goose down is nearly as good. Duck down is not quite as effective, although some manufacturers work this less expensive filler into their finest garments and advertise the whole as waterfowl down.

Cheap sleeping bags may have the bulkier, colder, and far less costly feathers of the fowl mixed in with down. You're apt to get what you pay for. A well-made sleeping bag with one of the synthetic fillers, such as Dacron, is preferable to a shoddy feather bag.

The best fabric to date in which to encase the filler is light, tough nylon. Its slipperiness makes it less confining and easier to get into. Although initially cold to the touch, it warms rapidly and actually absorbs less body heat than does, for example, cotton flannel.

A good sleeping bag is expensive, but it should last a lifetime. I bought the best obtainable ninety-by-ninety-inch robe when I first took to the big woods forty years ago, and I still use it almost every night. If you have the use for a sleeping bag, it will be shortsighted to try to save too much money in this department except on children's bags which will be soon outgrown. Shop warily; the best bags on the market are those sold and sometimes made by the large, catalog-issuing distributors.

If you have a choice, snaps are far less vulnerable than even the stoutest zipper. Most functional, too, is a robe that will open flat.

You'll want either an air or one of the newer foam mattresses to go under your bag. For air mattresses, it may be useful to note that I'm still using my original rubber, bulblike pump that works with either hands or feet. For those who need a pillow, one of the small affairs that can be inflated in a few seconds by mouth is convenient. Again, conscientiously built models of any of the above will last for years.

EXTRA CLOTHING

Care of the feet will be of primary importance if you are going to walk away from any survival situation. This may well mean the inclusion of at least two extra pairs of functional socks. For suitability of these and other articles of clothing, see the earlier section on this matter. You may also choose to take along extra light footwear.

Such easily laundered items as underwear and handkerchiefs need not be included in the proportions sometimes witnessed. One always seems to be finding use for a spare woolen shirt, on the other hand.

MEDICINE KIT

Unreservedly recommended is the four-ounce first aid kit, earlier discussed, which can be used to treat everything from a cut to disentery. Using this outfit as a basis for your mutual consideration, talk the matter over with your personal M.D. so that you'll be sure to include provisions for treating any particular individual troubles, perhaps chronic, that may arise. Such a kit might well save you and your companion's life under survival conditions when no doctor is available.

SNAKEBITE KIT

If you are in poisonous snake country, you'll do well to carry at least one suction snakebite kit, inexpensively obtainable in any drugstore. Each of these contains three suction cups, lymph constrictor, surgical scalpel, and antiseptic, plus swiftly and simply understood illustrated instructions. Most physicians today feel that first aid during the first half hour after a poisonous bite is extremely important and should be carried out by the one bitten or by the most competent individual at hand.

A snakebite kit is inexpensive and compact, and could save your life in poisonous snake country.

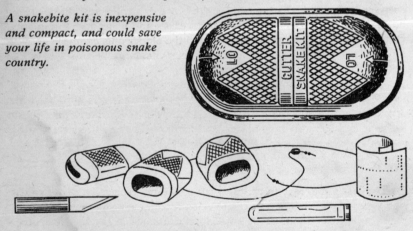

The suction cups in these neat and compact kits, each no larger than a twelve-gauge shotgun shell, can also be used for bee stings and severe insect bites which may be treated by applying suction to the affected part without any cuts. But their main application is for snakebite.

WIRE

A coil of light wire that can be used for snares may keep you eating regularly at some future date. Considerable specific data on snares appears earlier in this book.

CORD OR ROPE

A length of good new rope, perhaps three-eighths-inch manila, may come in handy a lot of different ways if you can manage the extra weight and bulk. If not, at least include a few yards of nylon cord, strong enough to bear your weight in a pinch.

COOKING EQUIPMENT

Except for a preferably large boiling utensil, which will be practically a necessity if you plan to live to any reasonable extent off the country, you can get along without a cooking outfit while surviving. As a matter of fact, you could do with something such as bark holders, for example, but at the expense of considerable time and energy. On the other hand, a large fruit juice can — with its top smoothly removed and a wire bail twisted on loosely between two nail holes punched near the rim — will serve admirably for boiling wild foods and beverages.

One of the old surplus frypans will do a lot of jobs although, actually, it is heavier than necessary. Yet the high bowl-like sides make it admirable even for stews. If you'll cover sourdough bread or a roast with the platelike lid, the whole thing can be buried in hot coals and ashes like a miniature Dutch oven. If you choose to carry one of the old surplus canteens as well, it will be just about as easy to include the cup which fits over the end of this and which can be used in numerous ways.

Handiest of all in the culinary department, of course, is one of the small nested sets that are available at sporting goods stores and through some of the large catalog-issuing firms. Even this will be far more functional if the cups and preferably the plates as well are made of stainless steel rather than of the more fragile, all-too-ardent aluminum.

SOAP

The best initial way to handle a cut or scrape, especially in the wilderness where help is not at hand, is to wash it with plenty of soap and water, then dry it well. Inasmuch as no soap is contained in the tiny four-ounce first aid kit that I discuss and recommend elsewhere, a small bar should be packed elsewhere in the survival kit.

TOILET KIT

This may be where you choose to carry your soap if the supply is to be limited. You'll also likely want a small rough towel that can be regularly washed, toothbrush, dentifrice which may be common baking soda or table salt which will have utility elsewhere, comb, and any small items you may wish such as manicure scissors and safety razor with spare blades.

WHISTLE

Some camping mothers often tie whistles around the necks of their youngsters, who are instructed to blow them if they ever find themselves in trouble. All in all, a whistle can be useful for juvenile and adult alike for attracting attention, keeping a group together, transmitting messages, and for any other uses when it will serve better than a shout.

FLASHLIGHT

Although there are several ways of making wilderness torches, a flashlight today is considered pretty much of a necessity when one is away from power. A conventional two-cell light is generally sufficient, preferably a model with smoothly rounded edges that will not be so likely to wear holes in a pocket.

A spare bulb, protected by cotton batten, can often be carried inside the spring at the end. I've always found it a sound idea, too, to keep a second spare elsewhere in the outfit, in my case softly inside a box of adhesive bandages. If you've the capacity for them, two extra, long-life batteries are also a good idea.

In any event, the batteries will last you considerably longer if you get in the habit of switching on the light only for very brief periods of time; all that will be needed, for example, when you are traveling through the woods at night. To prevent the accidental waste of power, use some tactic such as reversing the batteries, inserting paper between battery post and bulb, or even taping the switch when the flashlight is packed.

INSECT REPELLENT

Mosquitoes, biting flies, gnats, and other winged drillers become so pestiferously thick in some widespread localities at certain times of the year that they can kill you. You should, by all means, have an effective insect repellent in your survival outfit.

BINOCULARS

These are only for the more lavishly filled survival kits, but a precise light pair may be a whole lot more valuable than commonly credited; for finding landmarks, for marking the most likely routes, and assuredly for securing meat.

PAPER AND PEN

Whenever you quit a survival camp, you should leave behind for possible would-be rescuers a written record of who you are, where you've been, and in which direction you are headed.

When you are traveling without maps in strange country anywhere, a map sketched as you proceed will help to keep you straight. In other words, the survival kit should include some substantial paper and a pencil, or better still a new and dependable ballpoint pen.

WATER PURIFICATION TABLETS

The small two-ounce bottles that each hold a hundred halazone tablets take up no more room than a shotgun shell and provide good insurance against the contaminated drinking water that may be encountered anywhere, even far from the ravages of man.

Because these tiny pellets must be fresh in order to function, you'll need to renew your supply periodically, and to buy them from a reputable drugstore rather than from a surplus concern. A bottle sells for less than fifty cents and should be kept firmly closed in a dark, preferably dry place.

The similarly used iodine tablets, effective in tropical and semitropical regions where chlorine will not always do the job, can be obtained by your drugstore at two or three times this price. They are standard with the U.S. armed forces.

FISHING OUTFIT

This need not be elaborate. A few yards of good tough line, perhaps half a dozen hooks, and some of the small strips of lead that can be twisted into position as sinkers should catch enough fish to keep you eating for a long while. Later, if necessary, you will be able to make additional line and hooks on your own if necessary as we've already considered.

I keep such a tiny kit in my pocket whenever I'm in the bush. You're usually where you can cut a pole on the spot. Guides for the line? Safety pins work in a pinch, or just tie it to the end of the pole.

SURVIVAL RATIONS

For the long pull, you'll find that fat, in calories the most concentrated of foods, is the hardest to come by when you're living off the country. Butter, margarine, bacon drippings, and lard, boast more than double the calories, ounce for ounce, than such a staple as sugar, and nearly three times as much as honey. For limited survival rations for wilderness stints of unknown duration you may determine, therefore, to pack along a preponderance of edible fats with the idea of completing your diet from natural sources.

For the shorter haul, you may care to include some of the compact, tasty, and nutritious rations now especially manufactured and distributed for campers as a whole and for exploration teams and other scientific adventurers in particular.

ASSEMBLED EMERGENCY KITS

There are a number of pre-assembled emergency kits on the market, and inasmuch as they take up little room, some may care to include one or more in a larger survival kit for perhaps, in the wilderness, carrying in a pocket for possible immediate use. I've tested such kits in the Far North and found them of substantial value for anyone temporarily delayed, injured, lost, or isolated by fire, flood, storm, or other mishap.

WALLE-HAWK

The single most ingenious and functional survival tool on the market is the Walle-Hawk, so called because it can be easily carried in your wallet every day of the year and because it is as handy to the modern survivor as the tomahawk was to the primitive Indian. This was invented by Jessie

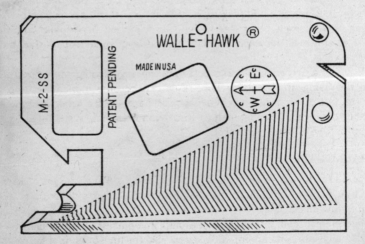

The Walle-Hawk, a pocket-sized survival tool

Morrision, the president of the Walle-Hawk Corporation, located in Burlington, Vermont, which distributes it internationally.

The Walle-Hawk can do everything from digging edible roots to skinning game and signalling for help. Suspended from a thread, string, or hair, it is also an accurate compass. It will last a lifetime.

FOAM RUBBER PADDING

It is quite easy for even an experienced woodsman to bruise the tissue of the foot. This only requires striking the arch on a ridge or bending the foot in an unnatural way. An injury of this sort can be very painful to walk on. If you have to get out afoot, a bit of foam rubber padding may make all the difference. A sheet of quarter-inch foam rubber padding about a foot square, obtainable from your drugstore or a surgical supply house, can be used to cushion fragile articles in the kit, while a section can be easily cut off to fit inside a boot to pad and support the injured foot.

SNOW KNIFE

A long-bladed snow knife or the combination snow-knife-saw — a long, saw-toothed blade with a crooked handle for more convenient handling — is essential to survival during the cold months in country above the widely varying timber line.

ARROWHEADS

Particularly if you can gain some previous experience on an archery range, it will not be a bad idea to include several steel, hunting-type arrowheads, as well as a bowstring. Then, as described previously, a hunting outfit, useful even for securing fish, can be constructed on the spot with relative ease.

Bows and arrows can make both hunting and fishing more productive than not using any weapon. Too, rifles can become inoperable, and one can run out of ammunition. When you're hard up for food, arrows even without points are often enough to stun a small animal long enough for you to get to it with a club or knife.

REPAIR OUTFIT

You'll have your own needs and ideas for this. Mine, the one I keep in my large survival kit, has changed little over the years after a lot of initial adding and discarding.

The present contents include: a small, fine pair of pointed scissors, the best I could find. Small pointed tweezers, also the finest obtainable, valuable for minor repairs and for removing especially pesky slivers and thorns. Two rolls of narrow adhesive tape, valuable for mending as well as for personal uses, particularly if in cold weather it is warmed prior to applying. A roll of dental floss.

Pliers with a fine cutting edge — that could slice through the shank of a fishhook, for example, if someone in the party is ever unfortunate enough to get one in his body — and with tightly fitting edges that could remove porcupine quills from a dog. Incidentally, such quills will pull out more easily if their tops are first cut off to ease the suction that helps hold their barbed points in place.

Two short, assorted screwdrivers with yellow plastic handles, rugged enough to be held by the pliers. A bit of nylon fishline rolled on some cardboard. Rawhide lacing. An extra coil of light snare wire to keep me in meat if the need ever arises. Recently, I've also been carrying a small, compact, very light clasp knife with two excellent cutting blades, scissors, file, screwdriver, and a can opener.

A small tube, well wrapped, of all-purpose adhesive. A small square of rubber for patching and some rubber cement. A small file for sharpening. Safety pins of several sizes, all pinned to the largest. Some copper rivets. An empty metal toothpaste tube that will serve as emergency solder, along with the pitch from an evergreen tree for flux.

I also carry a small, stoutly constructed can of gun oil and a few cleaning patches. One of these can be tied to the middle of a length of the nylon cord, when you are ready for it, and thus worked back and forth through the barrel, without the need of a cleaning rod which would be bulky even when disjointed.

Finally, I have a small sewing roll that can be shifted to my pocket when I am traveling too light for the entire repair kit. This contains strong thread, wax for further strengthening it, assorted needles, and a couple of cards that I've wound with darning wool for sock repair. There are only several buttons, as these latter can be easily improvised from leather, bone, or wood.

HUDSON'S BAY COMPANY

One of the best and lightest possible survival kits is the one long used by the three-centuries-old Hudson's Bay Company. Its contents include food in the form of tea bags, vitamin pills, pilot bread, butter, strawberry jam, Klik, condensed milk, and chocolate bars.

For multiple purposes there is a knife, and a spoon. A whistle and a double-faced mirror are included for signalling. To aid in securing food there are fishhooks and snare wire. The kit also contains candles, paper handkerchiefs, and camphor. And, of course, there are matches.

PORTABLE MEMORY

So as to get the most and the best out of any survival kit, you may choose to include a copy of this book, if only for the value as a portable memory. With such a preponderance of basics at hand for reference, it should be relatively simple in times of stress to come up with reasonable solutions to almost any problem of survival.

YOU'RE THE ONE

Survival in the final analysis is up to you personally. It will cost very little time, effort, and money to be ready. If you are not ready, it may cost your life.

Index